RESPIRATORY CARE
A CLINICAL APPROACH

Gayle A. Traver, RN, MSN
University of Arizona
Tucson, Arizona

Joyce Tremper Mitchell, RN, MS, NS
Department of Veteran Affairs Medical Center
Tucson, Arizona

Gail Flodquist-Priestley, RN, MS
University Medical Center
Tucson, Arizona

AN ASPEN PUBLICATION®
Aspen Publishers, Inc.
Gaithersburg, Maryland
1991

Library of Congress Cataloging-in-Publication Data

Traver, Gayle A.
Respiratory care : a clinical approach /
Gayle A. Traver, Joyce Tremper Mitchell, Gail Flodquist-Priestley.
p. cm.
Includes bibliographical references and index.
ISBN: 0-8342-0207-7
1. Respiratory therapy. 2. Respiratory organs—Diseases—Nursing.
I. Mitchell, Joyce Tremper. II. Flodquist-Priestley, Gail. III. Title.
[DNLM: 1. Respiration—nurses' instruction.
2. Respiratory Tract Diseases—nursing.
WY 163 T779r]
RC735.I5T173 1990
616. 2'06—dc20
DNLM/DLC
for Library of Congress
90-14524
CIP

The authors have made every effort to ensure the accuracy of the information
herein, particularly with regard to drug selection and dose. However, appropriate
information sources should be consulted, especially for new or unfamiliar drugs
or procedures. It is the responsibility of every practitioner to evaluate the
appropriateness of a particular opinion in the context of actual clinical situations
and with due consideration to new developments. Authors, editors, and the
publisher cannot be held responsible for any typographical or other errors found
in this book.

Editorial Services: Lisa Hajjar

Library of Congress Catalog Card Number: 90-14524
ISBN: 0-8342-0207-7

Printed in the United States of America

1 2 3 4 5

To our families—
their tolerance, patience, and support
were recognized and appreciated—
and
to the patients
who taught us many of the
"tricks of the trade" that we share
with our readers

Table of Contents

Preface

Care of the patient with pulmonary problems is a major concern to many care providers. Physicians, nurses, and respiratory therapists all fulfill important roles in the care of pulmonary patients. The care must also be provided in a variety of clinical settings. The patient may have a primary or secondary pulmonary diagnosis; be in an intensive care unit, general unit, nursing home, or home; and be young or old.

We have written this text to assist the clinician in the care of the pulmonary patient, from childhood through adulthood, regardless of the clinical setting. Techniques specific to neonatal care have been omitted. Our intent has been severalfold. First, we believe it is necessary to have an understanding of the physiologic basis of pulmonary problems. This understanding will facilitate communication among the various caregivers, provide a basis for comprehensive assessment, and facilitate the knowledgeable choice of alternative interventions. We have also discussed a variety of interventions specific to the patient with a pulmonary problem. Within these discussions we have included when an intervention is appropriate and how the intervention should be applied. The text should serve as a resource for students and a reference handbook for clinicians.

Throughout the text, we have selected those principles and patient care techniques that we, from our own clinical experience, see as those most commonly used and those that most frequently generate questions. We hope that readers will find this a useful text that will increase the scientific base for their care, enable them to trouble shoot more easily, and provide them with a greater range of alternative interventions.

part I

Clinical Physiology

chapter 1

Lung Defense Mechanisms

The lung's defense mechanisms fall into two general categories:

1. The nonspecific lung defense system. This system's major role is to prevent the entrance of noxious material via the lung.
2. The antigen-specific lung immunologic mechanisms. Some of these mechanisms help prevent the entrance of noxious material while many others respond to an insult or injury.

These two lung defense systems are amazingly efficient considering that, in the adult, more than 9000 liters of gas, along with foreign material such as dust and microorganisms, enter the airway every day, and yet serious lung infections or injury are relatively rare.

NONSPECIFIC DEFENSE MECHANISMS

The lung's nonspecific defenses are the basis for normal airway clearance. Understanding how these mechanisms normally protect the airway as well as the causes and effects of dysfunction provides a basis for the assessment of airway clearance.

Normal Protective Mechanisms

The following defense mechanisms help protect the lungs from noxious substances.

Mucociliary clearance. The upper and lower airway, to the level of the terminal bronchiole, is covered by a layer of mucus. Particles in the inspired air

3

tend to get trapped on this mucus; particles larger than 10 microns in size tend to impact in the upper airway, while smaller particles impact or fall out onto the mucus of the lower respiratory tract. (Particles in the range of two or less microns in size can elude the mucociliary system.) Cilia then propel the mucus, with its entrapped foreign material, toward the pharynx where it is swallowed. It is estimated that a healthy adult swallows approximately 10 cc of this transported mucus every day.

Macrophage clearance. Particles that elude the mucociliary system are deposited at the acinar level (respiratory bronchiole to alveoli) and can be engulfed by wandering alveolar macrophages. The macrophages destroy the material by phagocytosis or transport it out of the gas exchange area via the mucociliary or lymphatic systems. (Some of the macrophage functions are nonspecific while others are enhanced by specific immunologic reactions.)

Cough. A cough is initiated by stimulation of irritant receptors in the airways; these receptors respond to chemical and mechanical stimulation (eg, noxious fumes, high concentrations of dust in the air, aspiration of foreign material, and mucus accumulation). During a cough, large volumes of gas at high velocities are expelled from the lung; the high velocity allows mucus and other foreign material to be carried in the exhaled gas and thus expelled. The normal cough follows these steps:

1. stimulation of irritant receptors
2. deep inspiration
3. glottic closure
4. contraction of expiratory muscles
5. glottic opening
6. expulsion of a portion of the gas in the lung

Steps 3 to 6 are usually repeated several times. In other words, the normal cough involves several forced expiratory maneuvers following a single inspiration—not all the air inhaled is expelled with one cough.

Factors in Altered Function

A number of factors decrease the effectiveness of the nonspecific defense mechanisms.

Loss of upper airway functions. This deficit is usually due to mechanical bypass, such as tracheostomy or an endotracheal tube. In addition to the loss of upper airway filtering of the inspired air, the upper airway functions of heating and humidifying inspired air are also lost. Normally the upper airway heats inspired gas to body temperature and humidifies it to 100% relative humidity. This conditioning of the inspired gas is necessary for optimal function of the lower airway mucociliary system.

Abnormal hydration state. Both over- and under-hydration will impair mucociliary transport (eg, mucus is too tenacious to be moved by cilia; cilia are covered by a thin watery [sol] layer and do not reach the thicker mucus [gel] layer, which is normally transported).

Impaired ciliary movement. The cilia may not "beat" due to genetic defects (immotile cilia syndrome), or their action may be impaired by drugs (eg, narcotics, high inspired oxygen levels, or nicotine) or mechanical damage (eg, burns, tracheal tubes, or trauma from suctioning).

Increased mucus production. A variety of diseases, such as chronic bronchitis, asthma, infectious diseases, and bronchiectasis, can cause an increase in the amount of mucus secreted and/or a change in the characteristics of the mucus (making it thicker, for example).

Impaired cough effectiveness. Cough can be impaired by factors limiting the ability to take a deep breath (eg, pain, neuromuscular disease, parenchymal lung disease, or chest wall deformities), factors limiting the ability to do a forced expiratory maneuver (eg, neuromuscular disease, pain, or fatigue), and factors decreasing the ability of the airways to generate high flows (eg, airway obstructive diseases). Although glottic closure is a component of a normal cough, individuals who are intubated or tracheotomized and cannot perform effective glottic closure are still able to maintain effective cough. (See Chapter 10 for a discussion of interventions to improve cough effectiveness.)

Impaired macrophage function. Some of the factors known to impair general macrophage function include high inspired oxygen concentration and malnourishment.

Effects of Dysfunction

Dysfunction of the nonspecific defense mechanisms increases the risk of noxious material entering the lungs, direct lung injury, and the inability of the lungs to maintain airway clearance. The sequelae of these risks include infection, inflammation, airway obstruction, and gas exchange abnormalities.

ANTIGEN-SPECIFIC DEFENSE MECHANISMS

Knowledge of the immunologic function of the lung is rapidly expanding. For the purposes of this handbook, this section will clarify pertinent immunologic terminology and present an overview of current concepts.

Protective Immunologic Functions

The following factors are known to help protect the lungs.

Immunoglobulins. Immunoglobulins, or antibodies, can be found in secretions, in plasma, and attached to tissue. Of the five classes of immunoglobulins, three are known to be active in lung protection. Immunoglobulin A (IgA) is found in airway secretions (secretory IgA) and helps prevent bacterial colonization. Immunoglobulins G and M (IgG, IgM) protect against invading bacteria and aid phagocytosis by facilitating the attachment between the foreign organism and phagocytic cells, such as macrophages. The immunoglobulins are specific, meaning they respond, for example, to a specific organism to which the individual has been previously exposed (versus responding to any organism).

Cellular components (lymphocytes, neutrophils, macrophages). Several types of cells are active in the normal protection of the lung. Lymphocytes of both the T and B types are found in the lung. The B lymphocytes are the cells that produce antibodies; the T lymphocytes are active in cell-mediated immunity (CMI) and help B-cell antibody production. The antibodies help phagocytic cells bind to their targets while T cells produce lymphokines, which stimulate the phagocytes and encourage the accumulation of phagocytic cells in the area so that the target can be destroyed more effectively.

Neutrophils (polymorphs) and macrophages, both of which are found in the lung, are phagocytic cells. The neutrophils are active against bacteria primarily, while the macrophage is active against bacteria, fungi, viruses, inorganic material, and immune complexes. Eosinophils are also found in the lung. Although their role has not been clearly delineated, researchers think that eosinophils regulate the immediate hypersensitivity response.

Complement. Complement, which is a group of serum proteins, also plays a role in protecting the lung. The presence of complement is important in protection against bacteria and some viruses. The complement proteins, when activated, bind to the cell membrane and facilitate phagocytosis or lysis of invading bacteria and virus-infected cells.

Hypersensitivity Reactions of the Lung

A hypersensitivity reaction occurs when immune responses cause significant host damage. The mechanisms involved in the hypersensitivity reactions are similar to those involved in lung protection, but they are excessive (usually due to an intense inflammatory response or inability to destroy foreign material) so that host tissue damage occurs. There are four main types of hypersensitivity responses. (See Figure 1-1.)

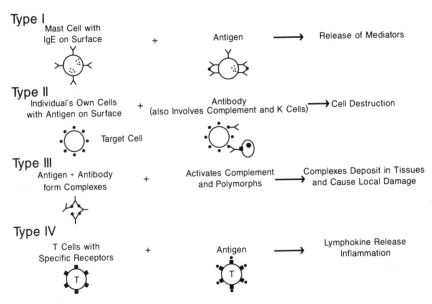

Figure 1-1 Hypersensitivity reactions. The four major hypersensitivity reactions are depicted.

Type I

The type I response is also referred to as immediate hypersensitivity or ana-phylactic response. The reaction involves specific IgE, an immunoglobulin pro-duced in response to a specific allergen. In the lung, most of the IgE is bound to mast cells in the airway. Once the susceptible individual has been sensitized to an allergen and has produced the specific IgE, subsequent exposure to the allergen initiates an antigen-antibody response that releases mediators from the mast cell. The mediators cause bronchospasm, inflammation, and mucus hy-persecretion. The Type I response occurs within minutes of exposure and is responsible for most allergic asthma and the "wheal and flare" response to skin testing. The Type I reaction may also involve a delayed phase and prolonged inflammation of the airway.

Type II

Type II hypersensitivity, also referred to as an antibody-dependent cytotoxic reaction, involves a reaction between antibodies (IgG and IgM) and antigens on cell surfaces or tissue antigens. The reaction activates complement and involves K cells (a type of lymphocyte that is cytotoxic). A Type II reaction damages the cells and surrounding tissue. A transfusion reaction is a classic example of a Type II response. Goodpasture's Syndrome is a pulmonary disease caused by a

Type II reaction. (The basement membrane of the kidney and lung are involved; nephritis and pulmonary hemorrhage result.)

Type III

Type III hypersensitivity reactions involve immune complex formation. Although antigen-antibody (IgG and IgM) reactions normally produce immune complexes, they are usually removed by phagocytes and do not cause host damage. In the hypersensitivity reaction, which may also involve complement, the complexes cannot be removed and are deposited in tissues. The result is inflammation and increased vascular permeability; in addition, enzymes are released from phagocytic cells, creating more tissue damage. An example of a pulmonary disease resulting from a Type III response is Farmer's Lung, an extrinsic allergic alveolitis. (An antigen from moldy hay initiates the formation of immune complexes, which are deposited in alveoli.)

Type IV

The Type IV response is a hypersensitivity reaction of cell-mediated immunity (CMI). The response, which involves T lymphocytes, not antibodies, results in the release of lymphokines or direct cytotoxicity or both. The reaction develops over 24 to 48 hours (antigen-antibody reactions occur much more rapidly). The predominant cells involved are lymphocytes and macrophages. The classic example of a Type IV reaction is the delayed skin test response (eg, skin testing for tuberculosis) which demonstrates induration at 48 hours after an intradermal injection of antigen. This response is used as a marker of the individual's prior contact with the antigen and his or her ability to mount an immunologic response. Clinically, the Type IV reaction is responsible for the granuloma formation seen in tuberculosis, sarcoidosis, and a variety of fungal infections. The granulomatous Type IV reaction develops over a period of weeks.

Factors That Lead to Decreased Immunologic Functions

Several factors act to lessen normal immune functions.

Age. Both antibody response and CMI appear to decrease with age.
Immunodeficiency states. Immunodeficiency states can be congenital or acquired and may affect one or more of the following aspects of normal immune function: antibody response, CMI, phagocytosis, or complement. The resulting disease and symptomatology will depend on which aspects are involved and the extent of the deficiency. Some examples affecting the pulmonary systems are: hypogammaglobulinemia resulting in recurrent infections and bronchiectasis,

disseminated fungal disease (eg, coccidioidomycosis), sarcoid due to decreased CMI, selective IgA deficiency resulting in recurrent pulmonary infection, and acquired immunodeficiency syndrome (AIDS).

Pharmacologic immunosuppression. Cytotoxic drugs, irradiation, and corticosteroids suppress humoral and cellular immune responses. These agents are often used therapeutically to decrease the immune response, but they may also cause morbidity. For example, a patient with pulmonary fibrosis due to Farmer's Lung may be treated with corticosteroids to decrease the immune response. If the patient's tuberculin skin test is positive, tuberculosis could be reactivated due to a depressed CMI response; and isoniazid would be prescribed for prophylaxis.

Clinical Tests of Immunologic Function

There are a variety of tests of immune function available. The following are the most common diagnostic tests for patients with pulmonary disease:

1. *Levels of a particular immunoglobulin class in serum* (eg, IgE levels in asthma or IgG levels in hypogammaglobulinemia).

2. *Immunodiffusion precipitin tests* are used to diagnose such diseases as coccidioidomycosis and aspergillosis. (Antigen is added to patient serum; if the patient has antibodies to that antigen, a reaction occurs.)

3. *Complement fixation* is a test used to detect and quantify the presence of specific antibodies for such diseases as coccidioidomycosis and aspergillosis. This test involves antibodies (usually IgG) that react with antigen and complement; the test is done using serial dilutions to help quantify the amount of antibody present. (The dilutions progress as follows: undilute, 1:2, 1:4, 1:16, 1:32, 1:64, 1:128, and so forth.) The more dilute the serum when a positive reaction occurs, the more antibodies are present. High titers mean that the patient's immune system has not controlled the infection.

4. *Radioallergosorbent test (RAST)* is used to identify specific IgE; for example IgE produced against the allergen for ragweed.

5. *Immunofluorescent stains of lung tissue* are special stains used to identify immune complex deposition in such diseases as Farmer's Lung.

6. *Delayed skin tests* are used to test the individual's ability to develop a CMI response to a specific antigen. In a positive response, induration develops 48 to 72 hours after intradermal injection of the antigen. The classic example is the tuberculin skin test; a positive reaction means that the individual has had prior exposure to the antigen, not necessarily active disease. If one cannot produce a positive response to a variety of common antigens, the individual is considered anergic.

7. *Prick skin tests* are used to detect immediate hypersensitivity; a positive wheal and flare reaction will occur within 20 minutes of the skin test application if the individual is allergic to that antigen (a drop of antigen is placed on skin, and then that area of skin is gently pricked with a needle). Those individuals who demonstrate positive prick skin tests are said to be allergic/atopic.

8. *Bronchoalveolar lavage (BAL)* is a procedure used to assess the cellular components and complement in the lung. In the procedure, the lung is washed with saline and the retrieved saline analyzed for cells and proteins. The BAL is usually done via a fiberoptic bronchoscope. The bronchoscope is wedged into a midsize bronchus and saline instilled; the usual procedure uses 50 mL aliquots to a total of 200–300 mL. Analysis of the retrieved fluid, which also includes cultures, can be used to aid in the diagnosis and management of some lung diseases.

SUGGESTED READING

Brain JD. Lung macrophages: How many kinds are there? What do they do? *Am Rev Respir Dis.* 1988;137:507–509.

Bullock BL, Rosendahl PP. *Pathophysiology: Adaptations and Alterations in Function.* Boston: Scott, Foresman and Company; 1988: unit 5, Immunology, and unit 9, Respiration.

Graziano FM, Bell CL. The normal immune response and what can go wrong. *Med Clin No Amer.* 1985;69:439–452.

Harman EM. Immunologic lung disease. *Med Clin No Amer.* 1985;69:705–714.

Irwin RS, Rosen MJ, Braman SS. Cough—a comprehensive review. *Arch Intern Med.* 1977;137:1186–1191.

Kemp D. Development of the immune system. *Crit Care Quart.* 1986;9:1–6.

Langlois PF, Qawryl MS, Zeller J, Lint T. Accentuated complement activation in patient plasma during the adult respiratory distress syndrome: a potential mechanism for pulmonary inflammation. *Heart Lung.* 1989;18:71–84.

Murray JF. *The Normal Lung.* Philadelphia: W B Saunders Company; 1986.

Reynolds HY. Bronchoalveolar lavage. *Am Rev Respir Dis.* 1987;135:250–263.

Roitt I, Brostoff J, Male D. *Immunology.* St. Louis: CV Mosby Co.; 1985.

Sleigh M, Blake JR, Nadau L. The propulsion of mucus by cilia. *Am Rev Respir Dis.* 1988;137:726–741.

Smith SL. Physiology of the immune system. *Crit Care Quart.* 1986;9:7–13.

chapter 2

Pulmonary Mechanics

Assessment of the mechanical ability of the ventilatory apparatus to move air in and out of the lung is referred to as the study of pulmonary mechanics, which is the evaluation of the forces and resistances to producing gas flow and volume change. This chapter discusses the physiologic basis and clinical assessment of the factors that affect lung mechanics.

NORMAL BREATHING

In normal breathing, contraction of the inspiratory muscles enlarges the thorax and decreases intrathoracic pressure. This action creates a pressure gradient between the mouth and the alveoli so that air flows into the lung. The inspiratory muscle force is not, however, the only determinant of that inhaled breath. One must also consider the resistance against which the muscles must work, ie, rigidity of the chest wall, stiffness of the lung, and the caliber of the airways.

To exhale, in normal relaxed breathing, no muscle force is required. Rather, the inspiratory muscles relax, and the recoil of the lung produces a pressure gradient that causes air to flow out of the lung (see Appendix 2-A, Glossary). The recoil produces the pressure change, but the caliber of the airway also affects gas flow out of the lung. Thus normal, relaxed breathing involves a variety of mechanical factors. The following sections examine these factors in more detail, discussing both normal and abnormal function.

The Respiratory Muscles

The following section outlines the muscles used during both quiet breathing and periods of increased ventilation (see Figure 2-1). Note that during mechan-

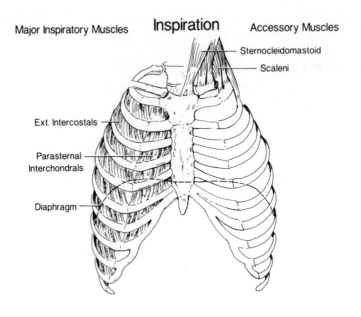

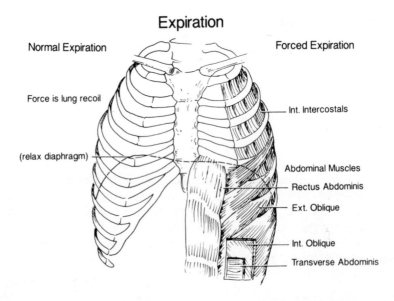

Figure 2-1 The respiratory muscles. The major muscles used during both quiet breathing and periods of increased ventilation are shown.

ical ventilation, the pressure gradient generated by the ventilator, rather than the inspiratory muscle contraction, becomes the inspiratory force.

1. *The diaphragm.* The diaphragm is the major inspiratory muscle. With contraction, the diaphragm descends and the rib cage moves up and out. It is important to recognize that diaphragmatic action expands the rib cage; during quiet breathing, the majority of rib cage movement is attributed to the diaphragm, not intercostal contraction. (In neonates the rib cage is pulled in by the negative pressure generated by diaphragmatic contraction. As the neonate matures and costochondral junctions become more stable, the rib cage moves up and out.)

2. *Rib cage muscles.*

- *Parasternal interchondrals* are muscles located between the ribs and the sternum; they act to elevate the rib cage and sternum, the so-called bucket-handle motion of the rib cage. These muscles are probably active during normal inspiration.
- *Internal and external intercostals* are muscles no longer considered to have a major ventilatory role during normal quiet breathing. (Their role in posture, twisting, etc usually takes precedence.) Under certain conditions such as a weak or inefficient diaphragm, however, the intercostals become the major inspiratory muscles. In the past, one group, the external intercostals, was considered inspiratory and the other, the internal intercostals, expiratory. Researchers now hypothesize that both groups may serve an inspiratory function, especially in an individual with hyperinflated lungs.
- *Scalenes* are muscles that act to elevate the first and second ribs and thus account for the "pump handle" motion of the rib cage; these muscles are usually cited as accessory inspiratory muscles, but may also have a role in normal breathing.
- *Sternocleidomastoids,* like the intercostals, are muscles used primarily for posture; their role in ventilation is as accessory muscles.

3. *Abdominal muscles.* These muscle groups are not used for normal quiet breathing, but they do serve as expiratory muscles when expiration is forced. Their contraction increases abdominal pressure and produces an upward displacement of the diaphragm. Note that normal abdominal tone is needed for efficient diaphragmatic action.

Resistances to Ventilation

The respiratory muscles must provide the force necessary to overcome airway resistance, expand the chest wall, and overcome the natural tendency of the lung to recoil.

Airway resistance depends on the caliber of the airway. Normally, intrathoracic airways are narrower during expiration than during inspiration. (When the lung is expanded, so are the airways.) This normal variation is accentuated in disease states and explains why wheezing is more evident on expiration than inspiration. Secretions, bronchospasm, edema, and endotracheal tubes can all further reduce airway caliber, thus increasing resistance and the work needed to overcome that resistance.

The chest wall, in the normal tidal volume range, usually wants to expand. Taking deep breaths, however, requires extra force to accomplish additional expansion of the chest wall. In addition, various disease states can make the chest wall stiffer and less easily distended; in these situations, extra force is required to expand the chest wall.

Finally, inspiratory muscle forces must overcome the normal tendency of the lung to *recoil,* or become smaller. The stiffer the lung, the higher the recoil and the more work the respiratory muscles must perform.

OBSERVING THE VENTILATORY PATTERN

During *normal, relaxed breathing,* the ventilatory pattern varies with position. An upright individual exhibits greater chest movement than abdominal movement. To maintain the upright posture, there must be greater tension of the abdomen and therefore there is greater chest wall motion with diaphragmatic contraction. In the supine individual, the predominant movement should be an outward bulging of the abdominal wall during inspiration. When the individual is in the supine position, not as much abdominal tone is required to maintain the position and abdominal motion can be observed. Expiration in normal breathing is passive, so no muscle contraction should be detected.

Abnormalities of the ventilatory pattern can be detected by simple inspection. The addition of palpation (to detect muscle contraction) can further specify abnormalities. A variety of examples of such observations and their interpretations follows.

1. *Limited chest movement* in the upright position. This finding is due to conditions that make the chest wall stiffer than normal, eg, chest wall pain as a result of pleuritis or thoracic surgery and bony changes as seen in ankylosing spondylitis.

2. *Limited abdominal movement* in the supine position. This finding is due to weak diaphragmatic contraction, increased abdominal tone, or splinting and is commonly observed as a result of distention, pain, and obesity.

3. *Abnormal recruitment of rib cage muscles* (involves contraction of the accessory muscles and palpable or observable contraction of the scalenes and parasternal interchondrals). These muscles are involved in the predominant

movement of the upper rib cage with inspiration, and their use results in the symptom known as labored breathing. This pattern is due to diaphragmatic weakness or the variety of conditions that can cause an increase in the work of breathing (increased airway obstruction, increased stiffness of the lung or chest wall, inefficient diaphragm as seen in hyperinflation, and increased ventilatory drive). This pattern is often associated with the tripod posture (torso flexed forward, leaning on the elbows) which facilitates the action of the rib cage muscles.

4. *Active muscle contraction on expiration.* Active expiration is seen normally with cough maneuvers and during periods of dramatically increased minute ventilation, eg, heavy exercise. If observed during normal quiet breathing, such muscle contraction is abnormal and denotes such conditions as lung hyperinflation or increased airway resistance. To detect abdominal muscle contraction on expiration, palpate the abdominal wall and observe for flank movement. In some patients, contraction of the abdominal muscles is observed as an inward movement of the flanks and an outward movement of the abdominal wall.

5. *Paradox* (the observation that the rib cage and/or abdomen moves in the opposite direction of that expected). Paradox is usually observed on inspiration.

- *Inspiratory abdominal paradox* is characterized by the inward movement of the abdominal wall with inspiration. The observation of this pattern may be due to a variety of factors, including diaphragmatic fatigue or paralysis, severe hyperinflation as seen in severe chronic obstructive pulmonary disease, or inspiration following expiration using abdominal muscle contraction. (In some individuals, contraction of the expiratory muscles on expiration causes the abdomen to move outward and the flanks inward; thus, on inspiration the abdomen appears to move inward. The presence of this abnormality can be clarified by palpating the abdominal muscles during inspiration and expiration to detect the time of contraction.)
- *Rib cage paradox* means that the rib cage moves in and down during inspiration. This observation is seen with paralysis, weakness, and/or instability of the rib cage; in the case of a flail chest, the paradoxical motion is limited to the area of the chest involved in the flail. In the presence of severe hyperinflation, as seen in far advanced obstructive lung disease, the flattened position of the diaphragm causes the lower ribs to move in and down with inspiration.

6. *Respiratory alternans.* In this pattern, there is alternation between rib cage and abdominal motion with inspiration. On some breaths, motion is limited to the rib cage, while on other breaths, motion is limited to the abdomen. This pattern is thought to represent respiratory muscle fatigue.

LABORATORY MEASURES OF VENTILATORY MECHANICS

In the pulmonary function laboratory, a variety of tests are used to assess lung mechanics. The terminology used to describe these measures of lung function is presented in Appendix 2-A. When results are reported, the patient's values are usually given in absolute numbers and as percent predicted. Because "normal" values vary with the size, age, and sex of the individual, the percent predicted allows one to determine the degree of abnormality. (Due to individual variability, an individual is considered normal if the percent predicted is 100 ± 20%.)

The most common laboratory measure of mechanics is *spirometry*, which provides basic measures of the amount of air a person can move in and out of the lung (volume) and how fast that air can be moved (flow). Spirometry, when done in the laboratory setting, often uses sophisticated equipment and protocols. Repeated measures are done to ensure reproducibility and maximal effort. In addition, the maximal voluntary ventilation (MVV) is usually measured, and the protocol may include studies before and after administration of an inhaled bronchodilator. Spirometry may also be done at the bedside or in the office setting; in these situations, less sophisticated equipment may be used and the procedure is often referred to as screening spirometry.

When spirometry is done, the patient is asked to perform some specific maneuvers while breathing through a mouthpiece. The maneuvers require the person to breathe with maximal effort while inhaling and exhaling. Due to the effort required, spirometry is often very fatiguing to patients. In very young children, spirometry is not possible because the child cannot do the required maximal maneuvers upon request. In these age groups, if the child can follow simple instructions, measurement of peak flow may be possible even when full spirometry is not. (Only flow, not volume , is measured.)

The basic data obtained in spirometry are the forced vital capacity (FVC), the forced expiratory volume in 1 second (FEV_1), and the FEV_1/FVC ratio. Other data that may be reported include the following: IVC, FEF_{25-75}, $FEF_{200-1200}$, $\dot{V}max_{75}$, $\dot{V}max_{50}$, $\dot{V}max_{25}$, and MVV. (For definitions of these measurements, see Appendix 2-A.) From these data certain conclusions may be made about the person's lung function. The major differentiation is whether the individual has an obstructive or restrictive defect or normal function. As seen in Figure 2-2, spirometry plots volume against time; when flow is plotted against volume, the maximal expiratory flow volume curve (MEFV) is obtained. Most pulmonary function laboratory spirometers present the data obtained during an FVC maneuver as both time/volume and flow/volume output.

An *obstructive defect* is characterized by flows that are reduced out of proportion to any reduction in volume. In other words, the FEV_1 and FEV_1/FVC ratio are reduced (the FVC may be reduced, but not to the same extent as the FEV_1). The other flow values (measures of FEF and $\dot{V}max$) are also reduced. Clinically,

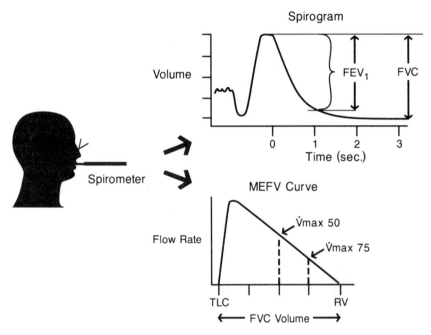

Figure 2-2 Measurement of forced vital capacity. During pulmonary function tests, both a spirogram and maximal expiratory flow volume curve (MEFV) are usually obtained. The tracings as well as basic data derived from each are shown.

it means that the patient has some obstruction, or narrowing, of the airways and that the major problem is in exhalation. Examples of diseases that produce an obstructive defect are emphysema, asthma, and the presence of a foreign body or mass in a large airway.

A *restrictive defect* is characterized by limited volume excursion. The FVC and FEV_1 are reduced but the FEV_1/FVC ratio is normal (flow is not limited because of an airway problem but because there was never enough air in the lung). Clinically, patients who have such a defect have a major problem inhaling; exhaling is not a problem. The restriction may be due to chest wall problems (weak muscles or a deformed chest) or to a stiff lung (due to pulmonary fibrosis or adult respiratory distress syndrome).

Knowledge of the patient's spirometry results enhances patient assessment, helps explain abnormal ventilatory patterns, helps evaluate response to therapy, and aids in planning interventions (especially when dealing with airway clearance and dyspnea).

Other lung function studies may also be done. One study, *lung volumes*, provides information about the patient's total lung capacity (TLC) and residual volume (RV). These data are used to further discriminate between obstructive and restrictive defects. In obstructive defects, the RV is usually increased; the TLC may or may not be increased. In restrictive defects, the TLC and RV are usually both reduced.

Other studies may be done to assess the elastic properties of the lung. These studies look at the relationship between pressure and volume change in the lung, the pressure-volume (PV) curve. In "stiff" lungs (ones that are difficult to inflate) *lung recoil* is increased and *compliance* is decreased; lung volumes would demonstrate a decreased TLC, RV, and VC. Examples of diseases that produce stiff lungs are interstitial fibrosis, heart failure, and adult respiratory distress syndrome. In "floppy" lungs (ones that are more easily inflated than normal), recoil is decreased and compliance is increased; lung volumes would demonstrate an increased TLC and RV. An example is emphysema.

Interpreting Pulmonary Function Tests

When interpreting the data from pulmonary function studies, it is important to remember that the volume and flow measures are interrelated.

If volume is significantly decreased, then flow will often be decreased simply because there is less air to be moved, regardless of the fact that the air can be moved rapidly.

If flow is markedly reduced (as in severe obstructive disease), the lung will contain more gas than normal at end expiration (due to increased functional residual capacity [FRC]); therefore, there is less room for inhalation and volume will also be reduced. Note that in obstructive disease, expiratory time may not be sufficient and/or airways will completely close before sufficient gas is exhaled.

If lung recoil is decreased, flow will also be decreased; lung recoil is one of the driving pressures to produce flow, so with less driving pressure, flow will be reduced.

Relationships between Pulmonary Function Tests and Clinical Observations

1. The FEV_1 value is often used as a guide for when to expect shortness of breath; it is only a guide because many factors affect when and to what extent a person perceives breathlessness; the level of physiologic impairment is not the only factor. General guidelines are:

- FEV$_1$ 1500 mL or less—breathlessness with exercise.
- FEV$_1$ less than 750 mL—breathlessness with activities of daily living.
- FEV$_1$ 500 mL or less—breathlessness at rest.

Thus a patient with an FEV$_1$ of 700 mL may not appear short of breath at rest, but with any increase in activity, he or she will be short of breath.

2. Patients with a prolonged expiratory phase on chest auscultation are likely to have an obstructive ventilatory defect.
3. Patients with an obstructive defect are more likely to use a forced expiratory pattern.
4. Patients with an obstructive defect are more likely to be hyperinflated. Hyperinflation may lead to the use of the rib cage muscles on inspiration because the diaphragm is in a low and inefficient position.
5. Patients with a restrictive defect are likely to use the rib cage muscles on inspiration; because the lung is stiff, more force must be applied to obtain the volume change.
6. Patients who use the rib cage muscles are likely to assume the tripod posture to increase efficiency of the accessory muscles.
7. Patients who have a prolonged exhalation or forced expiratory pattern are likely to rock forward while exhaling to increase abdominal pressure.
8. The more severe the patient's ventilatory defect, as assessed by lung function testing, the more likely pattern changes compatible with respiratory muscle fatigue will be observed.

SUGGESTED READING

Banzett RB, Topulos GP, Leith DE, et al. Bracing arms increases the capacity of sustained hyperpnea. *Am Rev Respir Dis.* 1988;138:106–109.

Bullock BL, Rosendahl PP. *Pathophysiology: Adaptations and Alterations in Function.* Boston: Scott, Foresman and Company; 1988.

Clausen JL. Clinical interpretation of pulmonary function tests. *Resp Care.* 1989;34:638–650.

Derenne J-P, Bernard F, Pariente R. Acute respiratory failure in chronic obstructive pulmonary disease. *Am Rev Respir Dis.* 1988;138:1006–1033.

DeTroyer A, Kelly S, Zin WA. Mechanical action of the intercostal muscles on the ribs. *Science.* 1983;220:87–88.

Grassino A, Macklem PT. Respiratory muscle fatigue and ventilatory failure. *Annu Rev Med.* 1984;35:625–647.

Hopp LJ, Williams M. Ineffective breathing pattern related to decreased lung expansion. *Nurs Clin North Am.* 1987; 22:193–206.

Javaheri S, Blum J, Kazemi H. Patterns of breathing and carbon dioxide retention in chronic obstructive pulmonary disease. *Am J Med.* 1981;71:228–234.

Keister LD, ed. *Comprehensive Respiratory Nursing.* Philadelphia: WB Saunders Company; 1989.

Lareau S, Larson JL. Ineffective breathing pattern related to airflow limitation. *Nurs Clin North Am*. 1987;22:179–191.

Larson JL, Kim MJ. Ineffective breathing pattern related to malnutrition. *Nurs Clin North Am*. 1987;22:225–247.

Larson JL, Kim MJ. Ineffective breathing pattern related to muscle fatigue. *Nurs Clin North Am*. 1987;22:207–223.

Macklem PT. Respiratory muscle dysfunction. *Hosp Practice*. March 15, 1986;83–96.

Murray JF: *The Normal Lung*. Philadelphia: W B Saunders Company; 1986.

Petty TL. ABCs of simple pulmonary function assessment. *Nurse Practitioner*. 1986;11:50–60.

Snapper JR. Lung mechanics in pulmonary edema. *Clinics in Chest Medicine*. 1985; 6:393–412.

Tobin MJ, Guenther SM, Perez W, et al. Konno-Mead analysis of ribcage-abdominal motion during successful and unsuccessful trials of weaning from mechanical ventilation. *Am Rev Respir Dis*. 1987;136:1320–1328.

Traver GA. *Respiratory Nursing: the Science and the Art*. New York: John Wiley and Sons; 1982.

Glossary

Lung Volumes and Capacities

Total Lung Capacity (TLC): The total amount of gas in the lung after a maximal inspiration (VC + RV).

Residual Volume (RV): The volume of gas left in the lung after a maximal exhalation.

Vital Capacity (VC): The maximal amount of gas that can be exhaled after a maximal inspiration. The vital capacity can be measured during inspiration or expiration. If designated as an inspired vital capacity (IVC), the maximal amount of gas that could be inhaled beginning at residual volume was measured. If designated as a forced vital capacity (FVC), the amount of gas exhaled doing a forced (rapid) maximal exhalation was measured.

Functional Residual Capacity (FRC): The volume of gas left in the lungs after a normal exhalation; it is also referred to as the resting lung volume. Hyperinflation refers to increased FRC.

Tidal Volume (VT): The volume of gas expired or inspired with each breath during normal breathing.

Flows

Forced Expiratory Volume in One Second (FEV₁): The volume of gas exhaled during the first second of an FVC maneuver. Because FEV_1 is a measurement of volume per unit of time, it is actually a flow rate.

FEV₁/FVC Ratio (FEV₁/FVC × 100): The percentage of the total FVC exhaled during the first second of the FVC maneuver. For example, if FEV_1 = 2400 mL and the FVC is 3000 mL, then the ratio is 80%. The normal ratio is 80% in young adults; in older adults, a ratio of 70% is considered normal by many.

Peak Expiratory Flow Rate (PEFR): The greatest flow that can be obtained during a forced expiratory maneuver begun at TLC.

Forced Expiratory Flow between 25% and 75% of the FVC (FEF$_{25-75}$): Previously called the MMF (maximum mid-expiratory flow rate), this value expresses the mean expiratory flow rate during the middle of the FVC. (The first 25% of the FVC is ignored, and flow is measured over the following 50%.)

Forced Expiratory Flow between 200 mL and 1200 mL of the FVC (FEF$_{200-1200}$): This measurement (and the FEF$_{25-75}$) is intended to avoid the effort dependent portions of the spirogram. The first 200 mL of the FVC is ignored, and flow measured over the next 1000 mL.

Maximal Flow (V̇max): This measurement is usually expressed as flow at a specific lung volume and is the greatest flow attained at that volume during a forced expiratory maneuver. For example, V̇max$_{50}$ is the flow attained when 50% of the FVC has been exhaled. V̇max is usually measured at 25%, 50%, and 75% of the exhaled FVC. (Some reports use the terminology FEF at specific volumes instead of V̇max.)

Measures of Elastic Properties

Lung Elastic Recoil (Pst$_L$): This measure expresses the tendency of the lung to return to its resting volume. In any one individual, the specific recoil pressure varies with the lung volume at which the measurement is made—the more the lung is inflated, the greater the pressure tending to make it return to its resting volume.

Lung Compliance (C$_L$): This measure of lung distensibility refers to the amount of volume change per unit of pressure change. The measurement is usually made in the tidal volume range. If the pleural pressure changes by 4 cm of water pressure for a tidal volume of 500 mL, then the C$_L$ is 125 mL/cm H$_2$O. A lung with high recoil usually has low compliance; a lung with low recoil usually has high compliance.

chapter 3

Pulmonary Circulation

The lung is supplied by two circulation systems, the pulmonary and the systemic. Most of the lung receives its blood nutrient supply from the bronchial vessels, which are part of the systemic circulation. The major role of the pulmonary circulation is gas exchange. It also supplies nutrients to the terminal lung units (respiratory bronchioles and alveoli). The two circulations are not completely separate; there are connections between them. (Blood from the bronchial circulation flows into the vessels of the pulmonary system.) This chapter will concentrate on the physiology and functions of the pulmonary circulation.

HEMODYNAMICS OF THE PULMONARY CIRCULATION

The pulmonary circulation receives the entire cardiac output, which in an adult is approximately 5 liters per minute. The following are some of the unique characteristics of the pulmonary circulation.

- It is a *low pressure–high flow* system. See Table 3-1 for a comparison of pulmonary and systemic pressures.
- It is a *distensible* system. If cardiac output is increased to three or four times normal, there is only a small increase in pulmonary vascular resistance. (Vessels are distended and additional vessels are recruited.) The ability to recruit vessels and increase flow through those already perfused provides a means of increasing the available gas exchange surface during exercise.
- The *pulmonary arteries* carry unoxygenated blood from the right ventricle to the lung; *pulmonary veins* carry arterialized or oxygenated blood back to the left side of the heart.
- The *distribution of blood flow* through the lung is gravity dependent; in an upright individual, less blood goes to the apex of the lung than to the base. The

Table 3-1 Comparison of Pulmonary and Systemic Pressures

	Pulmonary Pressures	Systemic Pressures
atrial pressure (mm Hg)	5	10
ventricular pressure (mm Hg)	25/0	120/0
arterial pressure (mm Hg)	25/8	120/80
mean arterial pressure (mm Hg)	10–15	90–100
vascular resistance (dynes)	144	800–1200

distribution of blood flow is influenced by the pulmonary arterial pressure, pulmonary venous pressure and alveolar pressure.

In an upright individual, the capillaries at the lung bases (the dependent area) are relatively distended and flow is unimpeded. In this area (called zone III), the pressures on the arterial side of the pulmonary circulation are greater than both the alveolar pressure and the pulmonary venous pressure, and the venous pressures exceed alveolar pressure. Higher up, in the mid-lung zones (zone II), pressures on the arterial side exceed alveolar pressure, but alveolar pressure exceeds the venous pressures. Thus, flow is slightly impeded by the alveolar pressure; capillaries are no longer distended at the alveolar level. Flow gradually decreases from the bottom to the top of this zone.

In a normal individual, zone II extends to the lung apex and blood flow is limited but present at the very top of the lung. Very tall individuals and those with lung pathology have the potential for a zone I, in which flow is nonexistent because alveolar pressures exceed the arterial pressure (see Figure 3-1).

This distribution of perfusion depends on gravity. Therefore, if the individual is in a side-lying position, the gradient will be between the right and left lungs (dependent and nondependent) versus the base-to-apical gradient in an upright individual. In a healthy individual, the distribution of ventilation roughly parallels the distribution of perfusion so that gas and blood are relatively well matched, regardless of position. This matching of ventilation and perfusion is necessary for effective gas exchange (see Chapter 4).

• *Increases in pulmonary artery pressure* or in left atrial pressure will normally result in a passive decrease in pulmonary vascular resistance. (In a normal individual, the pulmonary capillaries are easily distended.)

• *Alveolar hypoxia* results in an increase in pulmonary vascular resistance. In a basically healthy individual, this mechanism is protective. For example, if the individual develops a small area of pneumonia, the involved alveoli become hypoxic because ventilation is decreased in the involved area. The blood vessels to the area thus constrict. Because both ventilation and perfusion to the area are

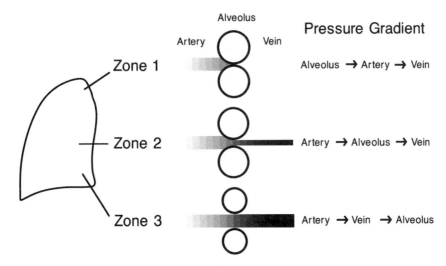

Figure 3-1 The lung zones. The changes in blood flow from the bottom to the top of the upright lung are depicted. The right side of the figure represents the pressure gradient from high to lower pressure for each of the three lung zones; for example in zone III, arterial pressure exceeds venous pressure which exceeds alveolar pressure.

decreased, the gas exchange abnormality is less than would be observed if perfusion continued at normal levels. (Chapter 4 discusses ventilation perfusion abnormalities and their effect on gas exchange.)

• *Elevated hematocrit* (greater than 60%) will increase pulmonary vascular resistance due to the increased viscosity of the blood being circulated.

CLINICAL IMPLICATIONS OF HEMODYNAMICS

Some selected examples of clinical situations in which knowledge of pulmonary hemodynamics is utilized are discussed.

• The *source of bleeding* when hemoptysis occurs may be either the bronchial or pulmonary circulation. When the source of bleeding is from an artery in the airway, the blood is usually from the systemic circulation and is usually bright red in color; in such situations, the patient is more prone to massive bleeding because the blood is coming from a high pressure system. When the source of blood is from the pulmonary circulation, as when a pulmonary embolus occurs, the blood is usually darker in color (because the pulmonary artery carries unoxygenated blood) and is under less pressure.

• *Samples of mixed venous blood* are obtained from the pulmonary artery.

• Patients who have had a lung surgically removed do not develop *pulmonary hypertension* (assuming that the remaining lung tissue is relatively normal), even though large portions of the pulmonary circulation are removed.

• In disease, *the distribution of perfusion* may have profound effects on gas exchange. As is discussed more fully in Chapter 5 in the section on ventilation perfusion mismatching, increased perfusion of an area relative to ventilation can result in hypoxemia. If a patient with unilateral pneumonia is positioned with the involved lung dependent, blood flow would increase to that lung but ventilation could not be increased (because alveoli are filled with exudate). The result would be worsening of the patient's gas-exchange abnormality.

If, however, the same patient was positioned with the uninvolved lung dependent, then both perfusion and ventilation, and consequently gas exchange, would be improved. Thus, as the clinical maxim states, "To maximize gas exchange, position the patient with the good lung down."

Another common clinical problem related to the distribution of pulmonary perfusion is the placement of a flow-directed pulmonary artery catheter. The catheter must be placed in a lung zone where flow is not impeded by alveolar pressure. If the tip of the catheter is positioned in the upper lung zones, pulmonary capillary wedge pressures will reflect alveolar pressure, not left atrial pressures. (Monitoring with a flow-directed pulmonary catheter is discussed in Chapter 16.)

• The lack of the normal hypoxic vasoconstrictive response may contribute to *abnormal gas exchange* in certain clinical settings. For reasons that are not completely clear, patients with gram-negative pneumonias are less able to generate the protective vasoconstrictive response and therefore demonstrate a more severe degree of hypoxemia in response to pneumonia (because perfusion of the involved area continues).

• When patients have generalized pulmonary disease, which causes alveolar hypoxia throughout the lung, the hypoxic vasoconstrictive response can result in *pulmonary hypertension* and consequently *cor pulmonale*. (All vessels become constricted or at least unable to distend in response to increases in cardiac output.)

• Although the *hemopoietic response* to hypoxemia is usually protective, when the hematocrit becomes excessively elevated it contributes to the development of pulmonary hypertension. This part of the hypertension is due to the increased viscosity of the blood and to the increased intravascular fluid load that usually accompanies the polycythemia. The treatment of choice, to relieve the load on the right ventricle, is oxygen therapy. When the hematocrit is at levels of 60% or greater, phlebotomy is also used to remove both red blood cells and fluid.

FUNCTIONS OF THE PULMONARY CIRCULATION

The major function of the pulmonary circulation is its role in gas exchange. There are, however, other roles that are also extremely important for normal body function. A summary of the functions of the pulmonary circulation follows.

1. Its primary role is in *gas exchange*. This function is discussed in detail in Chapter 5.

2. It *filters the venous drainage* from the entire body. Small emboli, such as small aggregates of red blood cells and fibrin, tissue fragments, and fat particles, are filtered from the circulation so that they will not pass into the systemic arterial system where they could obstruct blood flow.

3. It *provides nutrition* to the terminal respiratory unit. This role includes supplying the oxygen and metabolites needed for the production of surfactant.

4. It serves as *a reservoir of blood* for the left ventricle. Even with the normal small changes in the output of the right ventricle, left ventricular output remains constant because of the reservoir role of the pulmonary circulation.

5. It also has *a metabolic role* in modifying pharmacologic substances (eg, it converts angiotensin I into angiotensin II; removes norepinephrine; and synthesizes, releases, and inactivates some of the prostaglandins). Although the loss of these metabolic functions is perhaps most evident during heart-lung bypass, the role of the various metabolic functions of the lung is an area of intensive research because these functions may well play an important role in the pathogenesis of a variety of diseases.

FLUID DYNAMICS IN THE LUNG

Although the lung is considered to be a dry organ, there is normally a fluid flux from the pulmonary capillaries into the interstitium of the lung. This fluid is readily removed by the lymphatic drainage system. When excessive fluid accumulates (the amount of fluid flux exceeds the capabilities of the lymphatic drainage system), pulmonary edema results.

Fluid flux in the lung (and the rest of the body) is determined by the relationship between hydrostatic and oncotic pressure gradients (see Figure 3-2). In the lung, hydrostatic pressures in the microvasculature are approximately 10 mm Hg, while hydrostatic pressure in the interstitium is -3 to -5 mm Hg (the pressures are negative because of the influence of negative pleural pressure). Thus, the net hydrostatic pressure (approximately 14 mm Hg) tends to drive fluid out of the vessel and into the interstitium. At the same time, oncotic pressure is higher in the vessel versus the interstitium; thus there is a net oncotic force (approximately 6 mm Hg) driving fluid back into the vessel. Since the sum of

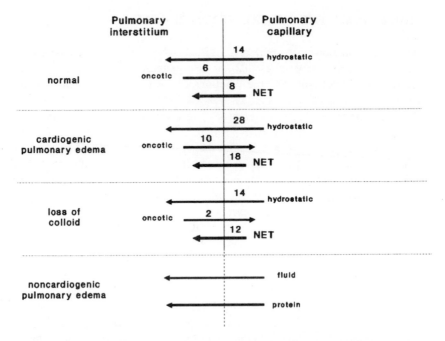

Figure 3-2 Fluid flux in the lung. The normal hydrostatic and oncotic pressures favoring fluid movement and the direction of the movement are shown in the top panel. The net force refers to the sum of the oncotic and hydrostatic forces. The lower panels provide examples of the changes that occur in various disease states.

these two forces favors fluid movement out of the microvasculature into the interstitium, the resulting fluid flux (approximately 10 to 20 mL/h) must be removed.

When clinical pulmonary edema develops it is due to changes in these basic forces. Left ventricular failure leads to an increase in hydrostatic pressure and greater movement of fluid into the interstitium. The flux is usually greater in the bases of the lung where blood flow is highest due to the effect of gravity. As more fluid enters the interstitium, the colloid there becomes diluted. The result is an oncotic gradient that increases fluid movement back into the vessel.

Noncardiogenic factors may also cause pulmonary edema. One example is the adult respiratory distress syndrome (ARDS). In this syndrome, a variety of conditions appear to affect the cellular junctions of the capillary endothelium. Although the exact mechanism is unclear, the pulmonary capillaries develop leaks. As a result, not only can fluid move unencumbered into the interstitium, but so can colloid. The result is that both the hydrostatic and oncotic pressure gradients favor fluid flux out of the vessel. (The protection afforded by the dilution of interstitial colloid, as seen in patients with cardiogenic pulmonary edema, is not present.)

Another noncardiogenic mechanism that can lead to pulmonary edema is the loss of intravascular colloid (eg, low serum albumin). In such circumstances, the oncotic gradient, which would counteract the hydrostatic pressure gradient, is reduced, thus allowing greater fluid flux out of the vessel.

An understanding of these principles of fluid and solute movement will help care providers better use the data from hemodynamic monitoring and enable them to identify patients in whom pulmonary edema should be anticipated.

SUGGESTED READING

Bullock BL, Rosendahl PP. *Pathophysiology: Adaptations and Alterations in Function.* Boston: Scott, Foresman and Company; 1988.

Burrows B, Knudson RJ, Quan SF, Kettel LJ. *Respiratory Disorders—A Pathophysiologic Approach.* Chicago: Year Book Medical Publishers, Inc.; 1983.

Dantzker DR. Diagnosis of secondary pulmonary hypertension: invasive techniques. *Heart Lung.* 1986;15:423–429.

Gil J. The normal lung circulation. *Chest.* 1988;93:80S–82S.

Huerwitz AN, Bergofsky EH. Pathogenetic mechanisms in chronic pulmonary hypertension. *Heart Lung.* 1986;15:327–335.

Matthay MA. Pathophysiology of pulmonary edema. *Clinics in Chest Medicine.* 1985;6:301–314.

Murray JF. *The Normal Lung.* Philadelphia: WB Saunders Company; 1986.

Snapper JR. Lung mechanics in pulmonary edema. *Clinics in Chest Medicine.* 1985;6:393–412.

Taylor AE, Rehder K, Hyatt RE, Parker JC. *Clinical Respiratory Physiology.* Philadelphia: WB Saunders Company; 1989.

Traver GA. *Respiratory Nursing: the Science and the Art.* New York: John Wiley and Sons; 1982.

chapter 4

Ventilatory Control

The specific mechanisms by which the rate, depth, and rhythmicity of breathing are controlled are complicated. Exactly how these mechanisms regulate ventilation under many circumstances is unclear. This chapter will define the terminology used to describe those factors of the ventilatory control system that are most closely related to the clinical assessment of the patient. The factors described include both the controllers of ventilation as well as the sensory input to those controllers. Figure 4-1 is a diagram of the basic factors.

Breathing is usually an unconscious act that involves the rhythmic contraction and relaxation of the respiratory muscles. A variety of conditions can vary the rate and depth of breathing. These conditions range from the normal variations that go with speech, emotional stimuli, exercise, and sleep to variations caused by abnormal factors, such as lung and heart disease. When one considers the variety of factors that can affect the respiratory pattern, it becomes evident that there must be a variety of stimuli that affect ventilatory control and that there must be some way to integrate these stimuli ultimately to produce the ventilatory pattern observed (see Figure 4-1).

CENTRAL NERVOUS SYSTEM CONTROLLERS

Central nervous system control of ventilation involves: (1) the brainstem, which regulates automatic or unconscious ventilation, (2) the cerebral cortex, which regulates voluntary breathing, and (3) the spinal cord, where input from both the brainstem and cortex are integrated along with information from peripheral receptors. It should be remembered that the final output also depends on the ability of the effector system (for example, respiratory muscles, airways) to respond to the ventilatory drive.

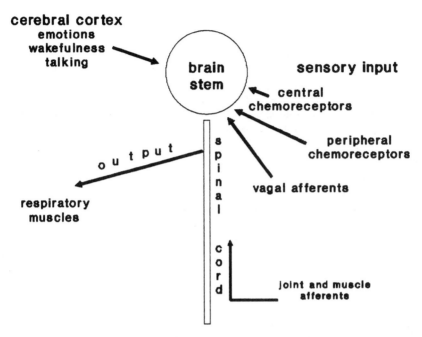

Figure 4-1 Ventilatory control. The major components involved in ventilatory control are depicted. For further discussion see the text.

Brainstem Controllers

The central respiratory centers are located in the pons and the medulla. The respiratory area of the medulla is thought to be the primary center for spontaneous, automatic breathing; the medulla also receives stimuli from the vagus and processes them to produce a respiratory response. The pontine areas are believed to smooth the transition between inspiration and expiration. Thus, it is in the brainstem that incoming stimuli are received, processed, and integrated, and a response is effected.

Cerebral Cortex

The variations in ventilatory pattern that occur with voluntary activities and with emotion are derived from the cerebral cortex. In fact, wakefulness itself influences the ventilatory pattern via the cerebral cortex. Some normal activities that override the automatic control of ventilation are talking, swallowing, and laughing.

Spinal Cord

The spinal cord carries the neural output of the respiratory centers of the brainstem and cerebrum. This output is integrated with local proprioceptive data before the final respiratory muscle activity is determined. It is interesting to note that voluntary and automatic output travels in different spinal tracts. Thus, patients with specific neurologic lesions may lose voluntary respiratory control but not lose automatic control, or vice versa.

SENSORY INPUT

Input to the controllers of ventilation comes from a variety of sources. The most important recognized stimuli come from chemical receptors and various vagal receptors in the lungs and airways.

Central Chemoreceptors

These receptors are located in the medulla and respond to chemical changes in the interstitial fluid surrounding the medulla. This fluid is in equilibrium with cerebrospinal fluid rather than arterial blood. Because of the blood-brain barrier, acute changes in the chemical composition of the arterial blood are not necessarily reflected directly in the cerebrospinal fluid. (Carbon dioxide diffuses across the blood-brain barrier easily, while hydrogen ion and bicarbonate do not.) The major stimulus to the central chemoreceptors is a fall in pH, usually due to a rise in arterial PCO_2 (carbon dioxide diffuses into the cerebrospinal fluid and hydrogen ion is formed). Hypoxemia is not a stimulator of the central chemoreceptors and may even depress ventilation.

Peripheral Chemoreceptors

The major peripheral chemoreceptors in humans are located in the carotid bodies. Chemostimulation of the aortic body in humans has little ventilatory effect. The carotid body is stimulated by (1) a fall in PaO_2, (2) an increase in $PaCO_2$, or (3) a fall in pH. Each of these stimuli causes an increase in ventilation. (Note that a fall in oxygen content will not stimulate the carotid bodies as long as the PaO_2 is adequate; an example is anemia.) The response to hypoxemia is greatest when the PaO_2 is in the range of 30 to 60 mm Hg. With severe hypoxemia (PaO_2 below 30 mm Hg), the peripheral chemoreceptor response becomes blunted. If, at the same time, the PCO_2 and/or pH is changing in a direction that would also stimulate ventilation, the net effect is greater than would be expected from the sum of the individual responses. In addition to the chemical changes that stimulate the carotid body, decreases in systemic blood pressure or vasoconstriction of the vessels supplying the carotid body may also stimulate the carotid bodies.

Vagal Receptors

There are several types of vagal receptors. The major ones that have known clinical effects are the irritant receptors and the J receptors. The *irritant receptors,* located in the airways, may be stimulated by rapid inflation or deflation of the lung, mechanical stimulation, inhalation of noxious gases, pneumothorax, or hyperpnea. The effect on the ventilatory pattern is to produce rapid, shallow breathing; in addition, bronchoconstriction, cough, and mucus hypersecretion may occur.

The *juxtapulmonary capillary receptors (J receptors)* are probably located near the alveolar capillary membrane and respond to interstitial congestion from such causes as pulmonary edema and pneumonia. The effect of stimulation is to produce rapid shallow breathing.

CLINICAL APPLICATIONS

Knowledge of ventilatory control has clinical significance in three general areas. These are: (1) in syndromes related to altered ventilatory control, (2) in specific types of abnormal ventilatory patterns that are related to altered ventilatory control, and (3) in the use of concepts of ventilatory control to assess patients with a variety of disease conditions.

Syndromes Related to Altered Ventilatory Control

Sleep apnea is a syndrome that is closely associated with altered ventilatory control. Normally, when an individual inhales, the pharyngeal muscles develop tone in order to maintain upper airway patency. In some individuals, this tone is not maintained when the wakefulness drive is absent (during sleep). People who are obese and have large amounts of subcutaneous fat in the neck area are especially at risk. Consequently, the upper airway becomes obstructed during sleep and the patient exhibits obstructive sleep apnea with episodes of potentially severe hypoxemia.

Even in normal individuals, periods of apnea occur during sleep, especially during rapid eye movement (REM) sleep. In some people, these episodes are more frequent and of longer duration than normal, even without upper airway obstruction. Such individuals have central sleep apnea (impaired central ventilatory drive during sleep).

The sequelae of sleep apnea can be serious. Patients complain of daytime somnolence, which may be so severe that the patient will even fall asleep while driving. In extreme cases, the patient becomes chronically hypoxemic and hypercapnic with resulting pulmonary hypertension and right ventricular hypertrophy.

The sleep apnea syndromes are more common in males and in the obese. One should suspect the diagnosis of sleep apnea when a patient, or more often the bed partner, describes severe, loud snoring (frequently the bed partner must sleep in another room); wild, thrashing movements of the limbs during sleep; and periods of apnea. Excessive daytime somnolence is also a clue that should be further investigated. Treatment of the sleep apnea syndrome will vary with the mechanisms implicated. Modalities used include respiratory stimulants, nasal continuous positive airway pressure (CPAP) to maintain upper airway patency during sleep, oxygen to treat or prevent hypoxemia, weight loss for the obese, tracheostomy to bypass the upper airway obstruction, and oropharyngeal surgery to enlarge the caliber of the upper airway.

Chronic carbon dioxide retention may be the result of a primary defect in ventilatory control or may be due to abnormalities of the effector system. When the carbon dioxide tension (PCO_2) of the cerebrospinal fluid is elevated for extended periods, the amount of buffer in the cerebrospinal fluid also increases. The result is that additional increases in carbon dioxide levels will cause less of a pH change and therefore less stimulation of ventilation.

Because individuals who demonstrate chronic carbon dioxide retention are no longer as sensitive to changes in PCO_2, hypoxemia becomes a major factor in their usual ventilatory drive. In these individuals a high arterial PO_2 can abolish the hypoxemic drive and, because there is little hypercapnic drive, ventilation becomes severely depressed. The arterial PCO_2 rises acutely and a state of altered consciousness may result. (In the past this situation was referred to as CO_2 narcosis.) In many patients with chronic CO_2 retention, this response to oxygen is only seen during an acute illness; it does not occur when the patient is stable.

When providing supplemental oxygen therapy to individuals with chronic carbon dioxide retention, the caregiver should be concerned about the level of arterial oxygen tension obtained, not the actual liter flow of oxygen. Just as too much oxygen is dangerous, so is too little oxygen! The aim of oxygen therapy should be to raise the arterial oxygen tension to a level of approximately 60 mm Hg. Accomplishing that goal may require only 1 liter per minute (or less), or it may require flows of 5 L/min or higher. At the same time, the arterial carbon dioxide tension must be monitored. Small increases in the arterial carbon dioxide tension are not uncommon subsequent to oxygen therapy, but an acute, large increase should be avoided. The clinical symptomatology of decreased ventilatory drive accompanied by a large rise in carbon dioxide and acidemia includes confusion, lethargy, somnolence, and asterixis. (See Chapter 5 for further discussion of the effects of hypercapnia.)

In addition, concern about oxygen administration should not be limited to patients with chronic obstructive pulmonary disease (COPD), nor should it be generalized to all patients with COPD. Oxygen administration has the potential to decrease ventilation in patients who have chronic carbon dioxide retention regardless of their diagnosis, and not all patients with COPD have chronic carbon dioxide retention. Limiting the amount of supplemental oxygen a patient receives simply because of the patient's diagnosis is dangerous. Oxygen is administered to correct hypoxemia. Its effect on both arterial oxygen and arterial carbon dioxide tension must be monitored by blood-gas analysis.

Specific Abnormal Ventilatory Patterns

Some of the abnormal ventilatory patterns that are due to altered ventilatory control have specific names. Those most commonly encountered are:

Cheyne-Stokes respiration is one form of periodic breathing. The pattern observed is one of waxing and waning of the respiratory rate and depth. Rate and depth gradually increase and then decrease, followed by a period of apnea. Following the apnea, the rate and depth again gradually increase. Cheyne-Stokes respirations are observed in a variety of clinical situations. The pattern may occur normally in the elderly during sleep, but it may also occur in patients with cardiovascular and neurologic problems.

Other types of *periodic breathing* also occur, such as periods of hyperpnea alternating with apnea. When the defining characteristics of Cheyne-Stokes are not met, the character of the periodic breathing should be described.

Kussmaul's respiration is the name given to the hyperpneic pattern of increased rate and depth that is seen in cases of metabolic acidemia (eg, diabetic ketoacidosis). The acidemia stimulates the ventilatory drive through the effect of increased hydrogen ion concentration on chemoreceptors.

Assessing the Impact of Ventilatory Control in Disease States

Changes in ventilatory drive can be a consequence of many different disease abnormalities. For example, cardiovascular disease can increase ventilatory drive (ie, hypotension stimulates peripheral chemoreceptors; pulmonary edema due to left heart failure stimulates J receptors). Similarly, some pulmonary diseases are also more likely than others to stimulate receptors that produce an increased ventilatory drive (ie, asthma stimulates irritant receptors; interstitial fibrosis stimulates J receptors). In many of these disease states, the tachypnea and hyperpnea have in the past too frequently been related to anxiety. Although anxiety is often an important factor, the effect of the other sensors must also be considered in assessing the patient and planning interventions. An approach that has the goal of slowing a patient's respiration by offering support and comfort to decrease anxiety may be ineffective if a potent physiologic stimulator of ventilatory drive is the cause.

SUGGESTED READING

Bullock, BL, Rosendahl PP. *Pathophysiology: Adaptations and Alterations in Function.* Boston: Scott, Foresman and Company; 1988.

Burrows B, Knudson RJ, Quan SF, Kettel LJ. *Respiratory Disorders - a Pathophysiologic Approach.* Chicago: Year Book Medical Publishers, Inc.; 1983.

Murray JF. *The Normal Lung.* Philadelphia: W B Saunders Company; 1986.

Saunders NA, Sullivan CE, eds. *Sleep and Breathing.* New York: Marcel Dekker, Inc.; 1984.

Taylor AE, Rehder K, Hyatt RE, Parker JC. *Clinical Respiratory Physiology.* Philadelphia: WB Saunders Company; 1989.

Traver GA. *Respiratory Nursing: The Science and the Art.* New York: John Wiley and Sons, 1982.

chapter 5

Gas Exchange and Transport

The major function of the lungs is to exchange respiratory gases (oxygen and carbon dioxide) between the environment and the blood. To accomplish this exchange, several conditions must be met.

1. *Adequate alveolar ventilation.* Alveolar ventilation refers to the volume of gas that reaches perfused alveoli. It is equal to the minute volume ($\dot{V}e$) minus the dead space ventilation ($\dot{V}d$), and in an adult, it is approximately five liters per minute. (See Appendix 5-A for definitions of terms.)

2. *Adequate pulmonary blood flow.* Pulmonary perfusion ($\dot{Q}$), the blood flow through the pulmonary circulation, is approximately five liters per minute in an adult (the same as cardiac output).

3. *Adequate diffusion of gases across the alveolar capillary membrane.* Diffusion is not usually a limiting factor in gas exchange. For example, in one-third of the time the red blood cell is in contact with the alveolus, and complete equilibration of gases between the alveolus and capillary has taken place; thus, there must be an extreme decrease in diffusion before diffusion limits gas exchange.

4. *Matching of gas and blood in the lung.* This relationship is referred to as the ventilation perfusion ratio, or $\dot{V}/\dot{Q}$. Normally, blood and gas are relatively well matched; the average $\dot{V}/\dot{Q}$ is 0.8 for the entire lung. The amount of blood and gas that goes to different areas of the lung, however, varies. As a general rule, the more dependent areas of the lung receive a greater proportion of the ventilation and a greater proportion of the perfusion. (For example, when an individual is standing, more blood and gas go to the bases of the lung as compared to the apices.)

At the same time, however, the gradients for perfusion and ventilation are not completely equal. The result is that although more blood and more gas go to the dependent areas, there is proportionately more blood than gas in these areas. Therefore, alveolar capillary units in the dependent areas have a lower $\dot{V}/\dot{Q}$ (less

37

ventilation than perfusion) than do the nondependent areas, which have a higher $\dot{V}/\dot{Q}$ (less perfusion than ventilation).

Although this small amount of variation in $\dot{V}/\dot{Q}$ is normal, more extreme mismatching is not. Areas that have less ventilation than perfusion are referred to as low $\dot{V}/\dot{Q}$ areas; the extreme example of low $\dot{V}/\dot{Q}$—absence of ventilation with continued perfusion—is called *shunt*. Areas that have more ventilation than perfusion are referred to as high $\dot{V}/\dot{Q}$ areas; the extreme of high $\dot{V}/\dot{Q}$—absence of perfusion with continued ventilation—is called *dead space*.

In addition to the requirements for gas exchange, one must also consider the requirements for gas transport (oxygen must be delivered from the lungs to the tissues and carbon dioxide must be transported from the tissues to the lungs). Two major factors are the amount of hemoglobin present and the systemic circulation.

Table 5-1 presents normal gas tensions at sea level. The basic terminology and notation system used in the discussion of gas exchange and transport should be reviewed. This information can be found in Appendixes 5-A and 5-B.

EXCHANGE AND TRANSPORT OF CARBON DIOXIDE

The partial pressure (P) of carbon dioxide in the arterial blood ($PaCO_2$) is dependent upon the relationship between the amount of carbon dioxide the body produces and alveolar ventilation. The normal $PaCO_2$ is 40 mm Hg, with a range of 38 to 42 mm Hg. Although physiology texts cite the normal range as 35 to 45 mm Hg, clinicians often prefer the narrower range of 38 to 42 mm Hg; patients who demonstrate a $PaCO_2$ at the lower or upper limits of the wider range (35 to 37 mm Hg or 43 to 45 mm Hg) do not have a definite abnormality of CO_2 exchange, but need to be observed carefully to be sure one does not develop. To maintain the $PaCO_2$ within this narrow range means that alveolar ventilation must change whenever the body's production of carbon dioxide changes. If carbon dioxide production increases, so must alveolar ventilation, and conversely, when carbon dioxide production is decreased, alveolar ventilation will fall. Based on this relationship, the $PaCO_2$ is the value used to determine if the individual's

Table 5-1 Normal Gas Tensions (mm Hg)

	Room Air	Alveolar Gas	Arterial Blood	Mixed Venous Blood
PO_2	159	100	95	40
PCO_2	0	40	40	46

level of ventilation is adequate or not. If the person's alveolar ventilation is inadequate, the $PaCO_2$ will be elevated; this situation is referred to as *hypoventilation*. If the person is ventilating in excess of the level needed to remove carbon dioxide, the $PaCO_2$ will be low; this situation is defined as *hyperventilation*. (Note that the terms hypo- and hyperventilation do not refer to the respiratory rate but to the adequacy of alveolar ventilation as defined by the $PaCO_2$.)

Causes of Hyperventilation (Hypocapnia)

Hyperventilation, defined as hypocapnia, may be caused by:

1. *Voluntary hyperventilation.* This mechanism may be seen in response to the emotions of anxiety and fear.

2. *Hypoxemia with PaO_2 less than 60 mm Hg.* This response is seen in people living at high elevations, and those with congenital heart disease and primary pulmonary disorders. (Note that hypoxemia does not become a significant stimulus until the PaO_2 falls below 60 mm Hg.)

3. *Metabolic acidemia.* Hyperventilation is the normal respiratory compensatory response to metabolic acidemia.

4. *Increased vagal input to the respiratory centers.* This stimulation is thought to be a major factor in the hyperventilation that accompanies asthma and pulmonary fibrosis.

5. *Hypotension.* Several mechanisms are involved with this response, such as decreased perfusion of chemoreceptors and accumulation of lactate.

6. *Head injuries.* The hyperventilation response is not observed in all cases of head injury, but when it is present it can be dramatic.

7. *Iatrogenic causes.* A common example is the mechanically ventilated patient who hyperventilates due to the excess ventilation delivered by the ventilator.

Effects of Hypocapnia

The effects of hypocapnia, or hyperventilation, are:

1. *Cerebral vasoconstriction.* It is the reason hyperventilation may be used to treat increased intercranial pressure.
2. *Decreased ventilatory drive.*
3. *Nerve hyperexcitability.* This is the probable cause of tetany seen in cases of severe hypocapnia.
4. *Alkalemia.* Further discussion of the relationship between $PaCO_2$ and pH can be found in the section on acid base relationships below.

Causes of Hypoventilation (Hypercapnia)

The causes of hypoventilation, or hypercapnia, are:

1. *Decreased ventilatory drive* (as seen in some cases of drug overdose). The decreased drive will result in a decreased alveolar ventilation.

2. *Decreased ability to respond to the ventilatory drive* (as may be seen in cases of severe airway obstruction and flail chest). Although the drive may be normal, the ventilatory apparatus cannot move an adequate amount of gas to maintain alveolar ventilation.

3. *Increased proportion of dead space ventilation.* If a greater part of every tidal breath is wasted ventilation (movement of air in and out of the dead space), then alveolar ventilation will decrease. For example, if minute volume remains the same but respiratory rate increases (so that tidal volume decreases), then the proportion of gas available for effective alveolar ventilation is decreased. The increase in dead space may be due to an increase in anatomic dead space (as occurs with an increase in respiratory rate) or an increase in alveolar dead space (as occurs with pulmonary emboli). Note that in an individual with a basically good lung, minute volume increases as the dead space increases and therefore alveolar ventilation is maintained or increased.

4. *Increased production of carbon dioxide.* As the production of carbon dioxide increases (with infection or exercise, for example), the alveolar ventilation must increase if $PaCO_2$ is to be maintained. If, however, the individual is unable to increase effective alveolar ventilation, then the $PaCO_2$ will increase.

Effects of Hypercapnia

The effects of hypercapnia, or hypoventilation, are listed below. Many of the clinical symptoms are related to the hypoxemia and acidemia that accompany acute hypercapnia and are not observed in chronic hypoventilation where the pH is normalized and the hypoxemia treated.

1. *Decrease in the arterial oxygen tension (PaO₂).* As the $PaCO_2$ rises, the PaO_2 must fall; this relationship is discussed more fully in the section on causes of hypoxemia.

2. *Increase in hydrogen ion concentration* (or decrease in pH). This relationship is discussed more fully in the section on acid-base relationships.

3. *Depletion of body potassium.* As hydrogen ion concentration increases, the hydrogen ion diffuses into the cells and potassium exits. Increased renal excretion of potassium ensues. Thus, even though serum potassium may be normal or elevated, total body potassium is depleted. (Note that this effect is more directly linked to the change in hydrogen ion concentration than it is to $PaCO_2$.)

4. *Aggravation of the pulmonary hypertension resulting from hypoxemia.* The vaoconstrictive effect on the pulmonary vasculature is related to the pH rather than to the $PaCO_2$. In addition, a change in pH alone will not cause pulmonary hypertension, but when the acidemia occurs concurrently with hypoxemia, the resulting increase in pulmonary artery pressure is greater than would occur with hypoxemia alone.

5. *Increased renal retention of sodium and water.* The exact mechanisms are not clear, but fluid retention occurs as a result of an elevated $PaCO_2$.

6. *Central nervous system effects.* The effects, which include morning headache, asterixis, lethargy, confusion, combative behavior, and somnolence, are more likely related to the hypoxemia and acidemia that accompany hypercapnia than to the hypercapnia per se. The more severe central nervous system effects have been called CO_2 narcosis. Clinically they occur after an acute rise in $PaCO_2$ and a fall in pH and are characterized by a change in the level of consciousness, ranging from difficulty to arouse to inability to arouse.

Carbon Dioxide Transport

The majority of carbon dioxide is transported in the plasma as bicarbonate ion. There is also a small amount of dissolved carbon dioxide present in the plasma (the $PaCO_2$ measures the tension of the dissolved carbon dioxide). In addition, some carbon dioxide is carried on proteins (by the formation of carbamino compounds), mainly in combination with hemoglobin.

Bicarbonate is formed by the hydration of carbon dioxide. (Hydration also forms hydrogen ion.) See Figure 5-1 for the reversible reaction. This reaction occurs more readily in red blood cells than in plasma. The bicarbonate formed then diffuses into the plasma.

Carbamino transport is not limited to transport via chemical combination with hemoglobin, but the amount carried in combination with other proteins is small. In itself, the amount of carbon dioxide carried in chemical combination with hemoglobin is quite small, but the mechanism is important in that hemoglobin is capable of carrying more carbon dioxide in venous versus arterial blood (the Haldane effect). Of the total increase in CO_2 content between the arterial and venous blood, one-third of the increase is carried by the carbamino mechanism. Thus the increase in PCO_2 is less than would be expected from the total increase in CO_2 content, and at the same time the reduced hemoglobin has a greater

$$CO_2 + H_2O \longleftrightarrow H_2CO_3 \longleftrightarrow H^+ + HCO_3^-$$

Figure 5-1 Hydration of CO_2.

buffering effect. (For more information on the Haldane effect refer to the reading list at the end of this chapter.)

Relationship of $PaCO_2$ to Acid-Base Balance

Acid-base balance is necessary for optimal function. The optimal range of arterial pH (the negative log of hydrogen ion concentration) is 7.36 to 7.44; an equivalent range for hydrogen ion concentration is 44 to 36 nEq. In other words, as the hydrogen ion concentration increases, the pH falls; as hydrogen ion concentration decreases, pH rises. Values for pH that are below 7.36 indicate acidemia; values for pH that are above 7.44 indicate alkalemia.

The carbon dioxide/bicarbonate system is used to evaluate acid-base balance. The equation for the hydration of carbon dioxide (Figure 5-1) shows that both bicarbonate and hydrogen ion are produced. Because carbonic acid is a weak acid, it does not completely dissociate to hydrogen ion and bicarbonate. At any one time, CO_2, H_2CO_3, $[H^+]$, and $[HCO_3{}^-]$ can be detected. The more CO_2 that is present, the greater the amount of $[H^+]$ that will be produced. Similarly, if excessive amounts of CO_2 are eliminated, the equation will shift to the left, leaving less $[H^+]$. The pH is the result of the ratio (rather than absolute value) of bicarbonate to carbonic acid (carbonic acid is derived by multiplying the PCO_2 × .03). The ratio is normally 20:1. Thus, as the PCO_2 increases, pH falls, and as PCO_2 decreases, pH increases.

An abnormal pH, either acidemic or alkalemic, can be due to a respiratory or metabolic cause. (See Figure 5-2 for simple acid-base disorders.)

1. In metabolic acidemia the primary change can be due to addition of a nonvolatile acid (eg, lactic acidosis or ketoacidosis) or loss of bicarbonate (eg, diarrhea).

2. In respiratory acidemia, the primary change is the addition of carbon dioxide (hypoventilation).

3. Metabolic alkalemia is due to loss of nonvolatile acids (eg, vomiting) or addition of alkali (eg, increased alkali content of bath in hemodialysis).

4. Respiratory alkalemia is due to loss of carbon dioxide (hyperventilation).

When analyzing acid-base problems, use of electrolytes may help to differentiate the specific cause of the acid-base disturbance. One use of electrolytes is in measuring the anion gap, the difference between serum sodium and the sum of serum chloride and bicarbonate. Normally this difference is 8 to 12 mEq. An increase in the anion gap denotes an increase in accumulated organic acids, such as ketones or lactate, rather than an accumulation of hydrochloric acid. Examples of metabolic acidosis related to an elevated anion gap include renal failure, ketoacidosis (diabetes mellitus, starvation), lactic acidosis (decreased cardiac output), and salicylate overdose. Examples of metabolic acidosis associated

pH	P_{CO_2}	HCO_3	Pattern
↓	↑	⇑	respiratory acidemia
↓	⇓	↓	metabolic acidemia
↑	↓	⇓	respiratory alkalemia
↑	N – ⇑	↑	metabolic alkalemia

Figure 5-2 Basic acid-base patterns. The arrows designate the direction of change. For PCO_2 and HCO_3, the large, filled arrows designate the primary change; the *smaller, open arrows* designate the secondary or compensatory changes; *N* refers to no change.

with a normal anion gap include renal tubular acidosis, diarrhea, and early stages of renal failure.

Serum potassium is also a helpful indicator. Both hypo- and hyperkalemia may be seen in metabolic acidosis; when present, however, the changes in potassium can help differentiate the cause of the acidosis. Similarly, in patients with acute CO_2 retention (respiratory acidosis) the serum potassium may rise, but in patients with chronic CO_2 retention the potassium may fall. (For more information on the use of the electrolytes in interpreting acid-base disturbances, refer to the references at the end of the chapter.)

EXCHANGE AND TRANSPORT OF OXYGEN

The partial pressure of oxygen in arterial blood (PaO_2) is dependent upon the inspired oxygen fraction (FIO_2), alveolar ventilation, diffusion, and $\dot{V}/\dot{Q}$ relationships. The PO_2 in inspired air is approximately 159 mm Hg; however, at the level of the cell mitochondria that use the oxygen, the PO_2 is only 4 to 22 mm Hg. This decrease in PO_2 depends not only on the factors affecting the arterial PO_2 but also on the amount of hemoglobin, systemic circulation, and cellular utilization of oxygen. The steps that account for the normal fall in oxygen tension from the inspired air to the tissue level are referred to as the oxygen cascade. (See Figure 5-3.) Understanding the mechanisms by which the step-by-step fall in oxygen tension occurs explains not only normal function but also helps the clinician understand the pathophysiologic mechanisms that cause an abnormal oxygen tension.

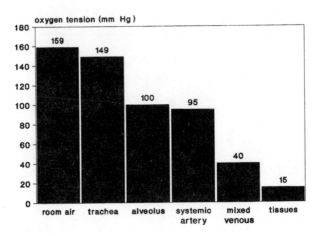

Figure 5-3 Oxygen cascade.

Oxygen Cascade

Each step of the oxygen cascade describes a normal decrease in oxygen tension. The change from one level to the next can be calculated.

1. *Inspired partial pressure of oxygen (PIO$_2$)*. The PIO$_2$ is dependent on the fraction of oxygen in the inspired gas and on barometric pressure. In air, the FIO$_2$ is approximately 21%. At sea level, where the atmospheric pressure is 760 mm Hg, the PIO$_2$ is 159.6 mm Hg (760 × 0.21). At a higher elevation, the FIO$_2$ would remain the same, but the barometric pressure would fall; thus the PIO$_2$ would also fall. For example, at an elevation of 2600 ft, the barometric pressure would be approximately 700 mm Hg and the inspired PO$_2$ would be 147 mm Hg. If, on the other hand, an individual received supplemental oxygen, the FIO$_2$ would change. So, at sea level, if a person was breathing 40% oxygen, the PIO$_2$ would be 304 mm Hg (760 mm Hg × 0.4).

2. *Dilution by water vapor (humidity)*. Since water vapor is a gas, it also exerts a partial pressure, and gas in the trachea is fully saturated with water vapor. Since the sum of the partial pressures must equal the total pressure, the addition of another gas must have a dilutional effect on the PO$_2$. It is known that the partial pressure of 100% relative humidity at body temperature is 47 mm Hg. The corrected oxygen tension is

(barometric pressure - 47mm Hg) × FIO$_2$

Applying this calculation to room air at sea level, the corrected PIO$_2$ in the trachea is 149.7 mm. Hg:

(760 mm Hg - 47 mm Hg) × 0.21

3. *Alveolar oxygen tension (PAO$_2$)*. The change in oxygen tension from the airway to the alveolus is determined by the level of alveolar ventilation and the

respiratory exchange ratio. The arterial PCO_2, which is assumed to equal the alveolar PCO_2, is used as the measure of alveolar ventilation; the respiratory exchange ratio is assumed to be 0.8. The alveolar oxygen tension can then be calculated using the alveolar gas equation:

$$PAO_2 = PIO_2 - [PaCO_2/0.8]$$

At sea level, if an individual breathes room air with an arterial PCO_2 of 40 mm Hg, the PAO_2 would be 100 mm Hg (150 mm Hg $-$ [40/0.8]). It is evident that whenever the $PaCO_2$ rises the PAO_2 must fall; conversely, whenever the $PaCO_2$ falls, the PAO_2 must rise.

4. *Alveolar arterial difference for oxygen (A-a DO_2).* Although there is usually complete equilibration of the oxygen tension between any one alveolus and its capillary, there is a fall in oxygen tension between the calculated ideal alveolar oxygen and the arterial PO_2, which is obtained from blood in a systemic artery. The normal A-a difference (ideal alveolar oxygen minus the arterial PO_2) is usually 15 mm Hg or less but may rise to the 30s in healthy elderly adults breathing room air. Thus the normal arterial PO_2 in the young healthy adult at sea level is approximately 90 to 95 mm Hg.

Several factors influence the difference between the alveolar and arterial oxygen tensions. First, there is normally some venous admixture—the addition of unoxygenated blood to the oxygenated blood leaving the lung. The sources of this unoxygenated blood are the venous drainage of the heart and anastomoses between the bronchial and pulmonary circulations. The second factor is the fall in oxygen tension related to the varying $\dot{V}/\dot{Q}$ relationships in the normal lung. (In disease states, this factor becomes the major cause of hypoxemia.)

5. *Fall in oxygen tension between the arterial and mixed venous blood.* By the time blood reaches the pulmonary artery (the source of mixed venous blood), the PO_2 has fallen to 40 mm Hg. This level is determined by the arterial PO_2, the oxygen-carrying capacity of hemoglobin, cardiac output, and the oxygen consumption of the body.

6. *Intracellular oxygen tension.* The actual oxygen tension within cells varies, but it is estimated to be between 4 and 23 mm Hg.

The oxygen cascade provides the basis for understanding the changes in PO_2 that occur between the atmosphere and the tissues. The first four steps of the cascade are the determinants of whether or not the individual will be hypoxemic (have a decreased arterial PO_2). To avoid tissue hypoxia, however, the caregiver must also evaluate the system of oxygen transport, namely, hemoglobin-carrying capacity and circulation and oxygen utilization or consumption.

Oxygen Transport

Oxygen is transported in the blood in two forms—dissolved and in chemical combination with hemoglobin. In the normal adult who breathes room air, the arterial oxygen content (CaO_2) is approximately 20 cc per 100 cc blood or 20 vol%. Of this amount, approximately 0.3 cc (0.003 cc per mm Hg PO_2) is carried in the dissolved form while the remaining 19.7 cc is carried in chemical combination with hemoglobin, as oxyhemoglobin. Since the majority of the oxygen carried in the blood is carried on hemoglobin, the percentage of hemoglobin saturation becomes extremely important.

The relationship of hemoglobin saturation to the PO_2 is depicted by the oxyhemoglobin dissociation curve. (See Figure 5-4.) The relationship, which is sigmoid shaped rather than linear, is one that offers protection from normal changes in PaO_2. For example, if a person goes to an elevation above sea level, the PaO_2 may fall from 95 mm Hg to 60 mm Hg, yet the oxyhemoglobin saturation (SO_2) will only fall from 97% to 93%. The middle portion of the curve is nearly linear, and it also serves a physiologic function. As blood delivers oxygen to the tissues, the PO_2 falls. Now hemoglobin has less affinity for oxygen, releases it, and makes it available to the tissues. Although the oxygen content is dependent on the amount of oxygen carried on the hemoglobin, the level of oxyhemoglobin saturation is dependent on the PO_2. In the lung, oxygen first diffuses into the plasma; as the oxygen tension increases, oxygen binds to hemoglobin, thus allowing more oxygen to diffuse into the plasma. At the tissue level, as the dissolved oxygen diffuses into the tissue, oxygen tension falls and hemoglobin releases more oxygen. Thus, there is a relationship between the oxygen tension and oxyhemoglobin saturation; one cannot have a low PO_2 and a high saturation.

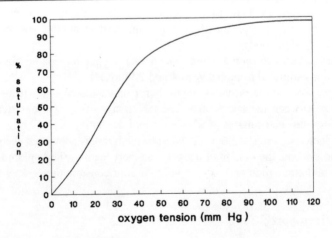

Figure 5-4 Oxyhemoglobin dissociation curve.

To determine how much oxygen the blood is carrying, the following calculations can be done:

1. Determine the amount of oxygen carried in the dissolved form: Multiply the PO_2 times 0.003.

2. Determine the amount of oxygen carried on hemoglobin:

- Calculate the oxygen capacity. It is known that, when fully saturated, one gram of hemoglobin can carry approximately 1.34 cc of oxygen/100 cc blood. Therefore, the oxygen capacity is: gms Hgb $\times$ 1.34.
- Calculate how much oxygen the hemoglobin is actually carrying by multiplying the oxygen capacity by the percentage of saturation. As an example, a person has a hemoglobin of 15 gms with a saturation of 97%. The amount of oxygen being carried on hemoglobin is 19.5 vol%. (1.34 $\times$ 15 gms = 20.1; 20.1 $\times$ 0.97 = 19.5) This example also demonstrates that the measured saturation is the saturation of the hemoglobin present. If the person were anemic and had a hemoglobin of 10 gms with a saturation of 97%, the amount of oxygen being carried on the hemoglobin would be 13 vol%. Thus, even though the PO_2 and SO_2 are normal, if the person has a low hemoglobin, the oxygen content of the blood will be low.

3. Sum the amount of oxygen carried in the dissolved form and that carried in chemical combination with hemoglobin to obtain the total oxygen content.

It becomes obvious that once the hemoglobin is fully saturated, additional increases in the PO_2 have virtually no effect on oxygen content. For example, at a hemoglobin level of 15 gms, if the PO_2 is increased from 95 to 300 mm Hg, total oxygen content (oxygen in the dissolved form plus that combined with hemoglobin) will increase only from 19.8 to 20.8 vol%. Exhibit 5-1 provides several examples of calculating oxygen content.

Certain conditions cause a shift in the position or shape of the oxyhemoglobin dissociation curve. Many of these conditions serve a normal physiologic function. For example, a fall in pH or an increase in temperature will shift the curve to the right; at the same PO_2, the level of saturation will be lower than anticipated. This shift is helpful in normal oxygen delivery because blood in the area of working muscles will release oxygen from the hemoglobin more readily than usual, thus supplying more oxygen faster to that working muscle. Other conditions that affect the oxyhemoglobin dissociation curve are outlined in Table 5-2.

Another aspect of oxygen transport that must always be considered is the systemic circulation. Even if the oxygen content is adequate, if it is not transported to the metabolizing tissues, tissue hypoxia will result. A decreased car-

Exhibit 5-1 Examples: Calculating Oxygen Content

PaO_2 95 mm Hg SaO_2 97%   Hgb 15 gms
dissolved oxygen: 95 × 0.003 = 0.285
oxygen capacity: 15 × 1.34 = 20.1
oxygen carried on hemoglobin: 20.1 × 0.97 = 19.5

arterial oxygen content: 0.285 + 19.5 = 19.8 vol%

PaO_2 60 mm Hg SaO_2 90%   Hgb 15 gms
dissolved oxygen: 60 × 0.003 = 0.18
oxygen capacity: 15 × 1.34 = 20.1
oxygen carried on hemoglobin: 20.1 × 0.90 = 18.09

arterial oxygen content: 0.18 + 18.09 = 18.27 vol%

PaO_2 40 mm Hg SaO_2 75%   Hgb 15 gms
dissolved oxygen: 40 × 0.003 = 0.12
oxygen capacity: 15 × 1.34 = 20.1
oxygen carried on hemoglobin: 20.1 × 0.75 = 15.08

arterial oxygen content: 0.12 + 15.08 = 15.2 vol%

PaO_2 60 mm Hg SaO_2 90%   Hgb 11 gms
dissolved oxygen: 60 × 0.003 = 0.18
oxygen capacity: 11 × 1.34 = 14.74
oxygen carried on hemoglobin: 14.74 × 0.90 = 13.27

arterial oxygen content: 0.18 + 13.27 = 13.45 vol%

PaO_2 200 mm Hg SaO_2 99%   Hgb 15 gms
dissolved oxygen: 200 × 0.003 = 0.6
oxygen capacity: 15 × 1.34 = 20.1
oxygen carried on hemoglobin: 20.1 × 0.99 = 19.9

arterial oxygen content: 0.6 + 19.9 = 20.5 vol%

Note the effect of lowering PaO_2 below 60 mm Hg; raising the PaO_2 above 100 mm Hg; low hemoglobin

---

diac output can also result in a lower than normal mixed venous PO_2. Because less blood is being circulated, more oxygen is extracted from the blood available. Methods of calculating oxygen transport in the clinical setting are discussed in Chapter 16.

These principles of normal oxygen exchange and transport are basic to evaluating abnormalities in oxygenation. The following sections review the basic causes and effects of abnormal oxygen exchange.

Table 5-2 Oxyhemoglobin Affinity

*Decreased Affinity**	*Increased Affinity***
acidemia	alkalemia
elevated carbon dioxide tension	low carbon dioxide tension
elevated temperature	decreased temperature
increased 2,3-DPG	decreased 2,3-DPG
chronic hypoxemia	stored blood
anemia	hypophosphatemia
sickle hemoglobin	fetal hemoglobin

* saturation lower than expected for Pao_2
** saturation higher than expected for Pao_2

Causes of Hyperoxia

Hyperoxia is an abnormality that is usually iatrogenic. It is the result of administering an FIO_2 that is too high. In some cases of extreme voluntary hyperventilation, however, the PaO_2 may be as high as 120 mm Hg.

Effects of Hyperoxia

The effects of hyperoxia are of two types. Some are related to the attainment of an above normal arterial oxygen tension while others are related to an excessively high inspired oxygen concentration (FIO_2 greater then 0.5).

1. Atelectasis may occur in areas of low $\dot{V}/\dot{Q}$ after breathing 100% oxygen. Normally alveoli are held open by the inert gas nitrogen. When all the gas in the alveolus is oxygen, the volume of the alveolus decreases as the oxygen is absorbed into the circulation.

2. Depression of the ventilatory drive may occur in individuals who depend on a hypoxic ventilatory drive.

3. Retrolental fibroplasia in the neonate that results in blindness.

4. Ciliary activity in the airway is decreased.

5. Thickening of the alveolar-capillary membrane (usually referred to as oxygen toxicity) occurs. Note that the occurrence of oxygen toxicity depends on the inspired oxygen tension, the duration of exposure, and individual susceptibility; as a general guide, administration of 50% oxygen for periods of 48 to 72 hours is considered the safe upper limit used to avoid toxicity.

Causes of Hypoxemia

Hypoxemia refers to a decreased arterial oxygen tension. The causes of hypoxemia are:

1. *Decreased inspired oxygen.* Going to a higher elevation will result in a decreased arterial oxygen tension.

2. *Decreased alveolar ventilation (hypercapnia).* Any increase in arterial PCO_2 will cause a proportional decrease in PO_2. For example, if an individual's $PaCO_2$ rises from 40 to 60 mm Hg, the PaO_2 will fall from 90 mm Hg to approximately 65 mm Hg.

3. *Impaired diffusion.* Impaired oxygenation due to changes in the alveolar capillary membrane is not usually seen when an individual is at rest, but may be seen at exercise when cardiac output increases.

4. *Decreased ventilation to perfusion matching.* This is the most common cause of hypoxemia and is the result of a variety of disorders, eg, pulmonary edema, pneumonia, asthma, emphysema, and interstitial fibrosis. In these situations, the PaO_2 is lower than would be anticipated based on the inspired oxygen level and the $PaCO_2$.

The concept of ventilation perfusion mismatching is a difficult one to understand and requires further clarification. When a patient is described as having a low $\dot{V}/\dot{Q}$ problem, what is meant is that there are areas of decreased ventilation, not that all areas of the lung are uniformly underventilated. The "good" areas can compensate for the low $\dot{V}/\dot{Q}$ areas for carbon dioxide but not for oxygen.

The explanation for this phenomenon can be found in the differences in the way the two gases are transported. The PCO_2, in the physiologic range, has an almost linear relationship to CO_2 content. Therefore, the good areas of the lung can hyperventilate, thus lowering the PCO_2 and CO_2 content of the capillary blood. When the blood from these areas is mixed with blood from the low $\dot{V}/\dot{Q}$ areas (blood with an elevated PCO_2 and CO_2 content), the resulting average PCO_2 and CO_2 content is normal or low. (Only when the $\dot{V}/\dot{Q}$ abnormality is so widespread that there is a total mean decrease in alveolar ventilation for the entire lung will the PCO_2 rise.) An equivalent mechanism cannot occur for oxygen. The good areas of the lung hyperventilate and the PO_2 rises. Oxygen content is not, however, significantly increased as the hemoglobin is normally almost completely saturated; it cannot be supersaturated. Thus the blood from the good areas does not carry extra oxygen and cannot compensate for the blood coming from the low $\dot{V}/\dot{Q}$ areas with a low PO_2. The result is a low arterial PO_2.

Within the general mechanism of low $\dot{V}/\dot{Q}$, two subcategories can be identified. One is shunt, which is a complete absence of ventilation and continued perfusion. When shunt is present, the patient's arterial oxygen will demonstrate little response to oxygen therapy. Because the involved areas have a complete lack of ventilation, the blood from those areas continues to have a low oxygen tension. Increasing the PO_2 of the good areas of the lung will do little to increase the oxygen content (hemoglobin is already saturated); therefore, the arterial PO_2 remains low.

If, however, there are areas of low $\dot{V}/\dot{Q}$ that still have some ventilation, providing supplemental oxygen will improve the arterial oxygenation. Even if ventilation to the involved areas is low, increasing the inspired oxygen can, over time, increase the alveolar oxygen tension. Thus, blood leaving these areas will have an increased PO_2 and oxygen content (increasing the PO_2 from 40 mm Hg to 50 mm Hg will increase the content from 15 to 17 vol%). When this blood is mixed with that from the good areas of the lung, the result is an increase in the arterial PO_2. In summary, when the hypoxemia is due to shunt (as in atelectasis) the patient's response to oxygen therapy is minimal, while in cases of decreased but continued ventilation (as in emphysema) relatively small increases in the inspired oxygen can dramatically increase the arterial PO_2. (See Figures 5-5 and 5-6.)

Causes of Hypoxia

Hypoxia refers to a lack of oxygen at the cellular level that is sufficient to result in anaerobic metabolism. Anaerobic metabolism causes decreased function of the involved tissue and organ, and the accumulation of lactate.

1. *Hypoxemia.* Hypoxemia must be relatively severe to result in tissue hypoxia. In the clinical situation, efforts are made to keep the PaO_2 at 60 mm Hg or higher in the acutely ill individual; in the chronically ill individual, an arterial PO_2 in the 50s is usually sufficient to prevent hypoxia. If a healthy person were made hypoxemic, the PO_2 would probably fall to 30 mm Hg or lower before cerebral anoxia occurred. (The alveolar oxygen tension of climbers on the summit of Mt. Everest without supplemental oxygen has been measured at 28 mm Hg.)

2. *Decreased total or functioning amount of hemoglobin.* Reduced carrying capacity of the blood means that reduced amounts of oxygen are delivered to the tissues even if the PaO_2 appears adequate. The extent to which the anemia will cause hypoxia will depend on the ability to evoke compensatory mechanisms, such as cerebral vasodilatation and increased cardiac output.

3. *Decreased cardiac output.* Even with an adequate PaO_2 and adequate amount of hemoglobin, sufficient oxygen may not be delivered to the tissues if cardiac output is severely impaired. Regional tissue hypoxia may occur with regional impairment of circulation.

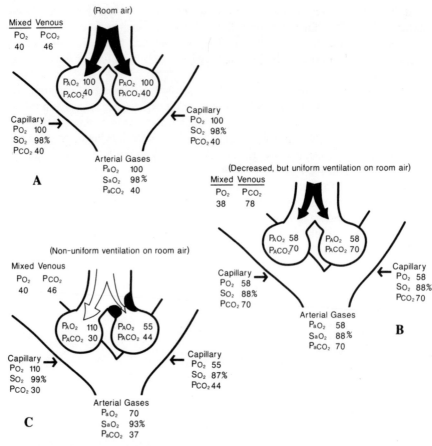

Figure 5-5 The effects of hypoventilation and low $\dot{V}/\dot{Q}$ abnormalities are schematically compared to gas exchange in the "ideal" lung. For each panel, the mixed venous gas tensions, alveolar gas tensions, capillary tensions and arterial tensions are given. In the ideal lung (**A**), adequate and equal amounts of ventilation and perfusion go to each lung unit. The result is that alveolar, capillary and arterial gases are in equilibrium. With hypoventilation (**B**), equal but abnormally low amounts of ventilation are delivered to each lung unit; perfusion remains normal. The result is that the $PaCO_2$ is elevated and the PaO_2 is proportionately decreased. In the low $\dot{V}/\dot{Q}$ abnormality (**C**), the perfusion is normal but ventilation is nonuniformly reduced; although the amount of carbon dioxide in the blood leaving the good lung unit can be lowered, the oxygen content cannot be significantly increased (effect of hemoglobin); thus, when capillary blood from the two units is mixed, the PaO_2 is lower than normal while the $PaCO_2$ is in the normal range.

Effects of Hypoxemia

The effects of hypoxemia are:

1. *Hyperventilation.* This response becomes evident with a PaO_2 below 60 mm Hg, but it does not become marked until the PaO_2 falls below 50 mm Hg.

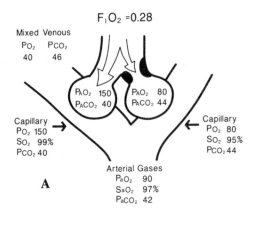

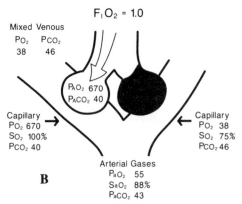

Figure 5-6 Effects of oxygen therapy in low $\dot{V}/\dot{Q}$ abnormalities. In **A**, 28% oxygen is delivered in a situation of low $\dot{V}/\dot{Q}$ matching. Because the affected lung unit does not have a complete absence of ventilation, over time the alveolar PO_2 can be raised (although not to normal levels). The result is improvement of arterial oxygenation. **B** depicts the administration of 100% oxygen in the situation of complete shunt. In this two-unit example, no matter how much oxygen is administered, half of the blood is never oxygenated. (Because the shunt unit is never ventilated, oxygen cannot be delivered to that capillary.) Thus, there is little response to oxygen therapy in complete shunt.

Some patients are unable to increase alveolar ventilation due to their pulmonary disease.

2. *Increased cardiac output.* The initial cardiac response is tachycardia. The increase in cardiac output will maintain oxygen delivery. If the hypoxemia is severe, however, cardiac ischemia will develop and result in decreased cardiac function.

3. *Increased pulmonary artery pressure.* Initially the increase in pulmonary artery pressure will result in improved pulmonary blood flow. When there are

sustained PaO_2 levels below 50 mm Hg, however, there is also an increase in pulmonary vascular resistance, which can lead to right ventricular hypertrophy (cor pulmonale) and right heart failure. (If acidemia accompanies the hypoxemia, the increase in pulmonary artery pressure and resistance is greater than would be observed with hypoxemia alone.)

4. *Erythrocytosis.* With chronic hypoxemia, red blood cell production increases and the hematocrit increases.

5. *Shift in the oxyhemoglobin curve to the right* (for the same PaO_2, the percent saturation is less). This mechanism improves tissue delivery of oxygen.

6. *Anaerobic metabolism.* If the hypoxemia is severe (PaO_2 in 40s or less), anaerobic metabolism increases with a subsequent rise in lactate and a resulting metabolic acidemia.

7. *Decreased cerebral function.* Clinical findings will vary but range from decreased concentration and poor memory to confusion and loss of consciousness.

8. *Cyanosis.* Cyanosis is the blue tinge caused by the change in color of reduced hemoglobin. Experts generally agree that the presence of cyanosis indicates 5 gm of reduced hemoglobin, which usually means that the PaO_2 is less than 50 mm Hg. It must be remembered that hemoglobin level and peripheral circulation will also affect the amount of reduced hemoglobin. The best sites for observing cyanosis are the tongue, lips, and oral mucosa. A blue tinge of the nailbeds or ears is notoriously inadequate as a valid indicator of hypoxemia.

SUGGESTED READING

Buckingham AK. Arterial blood gases made simple. *Nurs Life*. 1985;56:48–51.

Bullock BL, Rosendahl PP. *Pathophysiology: Adaptations and Alterations in Function.* Boston: Scott, Foresman and Company; 1988.

Cohen JJ, Kassirer JP. *Acid-Base.* Boston: Little, Brown and Company; 1982.

Harper RW. *A Guide to Respiratory Care.* Philadelphia: J B Lippincott; 1981.

Kersten LD, ed. *Comprehensive Respiratory Nursing.* Philadelphia: W B Saunders Company; 1989.

Light RW, Mahutte CK, Brown SE. Etiology of carbon dioxide retention at rest and during exercise in chronic airflow obstruction. *Chest*. 1988;94:61–62.

Martin L. Abbreviating the alveolar gas equation: an argument of simplicity. *Resp Care.* 1986;31:40–44.

Murray JF. *The Normal Lung.* Philadelphia: W B Saunders Company; 1986.

Norton LC, Conforti CG. The effects of body position on oxygenation. *Heart Lung.* 1985;15:45–52.

Perutz MF. Hemoglobin structure and respiratory transport. *Scientific American*. December 1978:92–123.

Pfister SM, Bullas JB. Arterial blood gas evaluation: Metabolic acidemia. *Crit Care Nurse.* 1989;9:71–72.

Pfister SM, Bullas JB. Interpreting arterial blood gas values. *Crit Care Nurse.* 1986;6: 9–14.

Reischman RR. Impaired gas exchange related to intrapulmonary shunting. *Crit Care Nurse.* 1988;8:35–49.

Reischman RR: Review of Ventilation and Perfusion Physiology. *Crit Care Nurse.* 1988;8:24–28.

Shapiro BA, Harrison RA, Cane RD, et al. *Clinical Application of Blood Gases.* Chicago: Year Book Medical Publishers; 1989.

Traver GA. *Respiratory Nursing: the Science and the Art.* New York: John Wiley and Sons; 1982.

Terminology

Alveolar Ventilation ($\dot{V}A$): The volume of gas reaching perfused alveoli per minute; the part of ventilation which is effective in gas exchange. The alveolar ventilation is equal to the minute volume minus the dead space ventilation.

Dead Space (VD): That part of the tidal volume that does not come in contact with perfused alveoli. Dead space can be further subdivided into that volume of gas in the conducting airways (anatomic dead space) and that volume of gas that reaches non-perfused alveoli (alveolar dead space). Alveolar dead space results in a high ventilation-perfusion ratio.

Gas Content (C): Gas content refers to the total amount of the specific gas carried in blood. It is expressed in vol% (cc of the gas per 100 cc blood). The source of the blood and specific gas are noted as subscripts, eg, CaO_2 is the oxygen content of the arterial blood.

Minute Volume (($\dot{V}e$): The volume of gas exhaled per minute; it is equal to the tidal volume times the respiratory rate.

Partial Pressure (P): The partial pressure or tension of a gas (Px) is equal to the barometric pressure multiplied by the fractional concentration of the gas (Fx). At sea level, with a barometric pressure of 760 mm Hg and a room air concentration of oxygen of approximately 21%, the partial pressure of the inspired oxygen (PIO_2) is 159.6 mm Hg ($760 \times 0.21 = 159.6$).

Shunt ($\dot{Q}S$): The part of total blood flow that does not come in contact with a ventilated alveolus. Shunt causes a low ventilation-perfusion ratio.

Ventilation-Perfusion Ratio ($\dot{V}/\dot{Q}$): Expresses the relationship between alveolar ventilation and blood flow. In low $\dot{V}/\dot{Q}$, ventilation is decreased in relation to perfusion. In high $\dot{V}/\dot{Q}$, perfusion is decreased in relation to ventilation.

Notation System

General Symbols:

P_{gas} — partial pressure of a gas
F_{gas} — fractional concentration (or percent) of a gas
SO_2 — percent oxyhemoglobin saturation
C_{gas} — content of a gas
V — gas volume
$\dot{V}$ — volume per unit time
$\dot{Q}$ — blood flow

Qualifying Symbols:

I — inspired		E — expired	
A — alveolar		a — arterial	
C — capillary		v̄ — mixed venous	

Examples of Gas Pressures:

FIO_2 — fraction of oxygen in inspired air
PIO_2 — partial pressure (or tension) of oxygen in the inspired gas
PAO_2 — partial pressure of oxygen in the alveolar gas
PaO_2 — partial pressure of oxygen in the arterial blood
$P\bar{v}O_2$ — partial pressure of oxygen in the mixed venous blood
PCO_2 — partial pressure of oxygen in the capillary blood
$PACO_2$ — partial pressure of carbon dioxide in the alveolar gas
$PaCO_2$ — partial pressure of carbon dioxide in the arterial blood
$P\bar{v}CO_2$ — partial pressure of carbon dioxide in the mixed venous blood

Examples of Saturation and Gas Content:

SaO_2 — oxyhemoglobin saturation of the arterial blood
$S\bar{v}O_2$ — oxyhemoglobin saturation of the mixed venous blood

CaO_2 — oxygen content of the arterial blood
$C\bar{v}O_2$ — oxygen content of the mixed venous blood
$C(a-\bar{v})O_2$ — arterial-mixed venous oxygen content difference

Other Examples:

$\dot{V}O_2$ — oxygen consumption per minute
$\dot{V}CO_2$ — carbon dioxide production per minute
R   — respiratory exchange quotient; the ratio of carbon dioxide production to oxygen consumption
$\dot{Q}T$ — cardiac output
$\dot{Q}S$ — shunt flow
$\dot{Q}S/\dot{Q}T$ — shunt fraction

chapter 6

Clinical Application: Interpretation of Blood Gas and Acid-Base Data

The patient with gas exchange and related acid-base abnormalities presents many challenges to the clinician. Of obvious importance is the analysis and interpretation of blood gas and acid-base data. This chapter will present a systematic approach to interpreting acid-base and blood-gas data. Although the process may seem lengthy at first, it will quickly be put to use automatically and easily. Using a step-by-step approach provides interpretations that include information about interrelationships. These interrelationships facilitate the assessment, planning, and evaluation of care.

At the end of the chapter a variety of examples are given so that readers may test their ability to interpret acid-base and blood-gas data. In addition, each example includes a discussion of the clinical implications, including indications for further assessment and the planning of interventions.

DETERMINING THE ACID-BASE STATUS

Basic interpretation of the acid-base data is done by first determining if there is an abnormal pH and if a respiratory mechanism is responsible for the abnormal pH. If a respiratory mechanism is not present, then, by exclusion, the problem is metabolic. To accomplish the process, ask the following questions:

1. Is the pH acidemic or alkalemic?
2. Is the mechanism respiratory?

- If the pH is acidemic, is the PCO_2 elevated? If yes, the disorder is respiratory acidemia. If no, the disorder is metabolic acidemia.
- If the pH is alkalemic, is the PCO_2 low? If yes, the disorder is respiratory alkalemia. If no, the disorder is metabolic alkalemia.

Once the basic acid-base disorder has been determined, then evaluate the normal compensatory mechanisms. The compensatory mechanisms attempt to bring the ratio of carbon dioxide to bicarbonate back to the normal range; thus, the pH will also return toward the normal range. In cases where a mechanism that could produce an altered pH is present, the term acidosis or alkalosis is used, even if the pH is in the normal range. In other words, the suffix "osis" refers to the mechanism while the suffix "emia" refers to an abnormal arterial pH. Examples may further clarify this terminology:

1. A patient has a $PaCO_2$ of 60 mm Hg and a pH 7.24. These data demonstrate respiratory acidosis and respiratory acidemia. There is a mechanism that leads to a decreased pH (elevated PCO_2), and there is an abnormally low pH as a result (respiratory acidemia).

2. A patient has a $PaCO_2$ of 60 mm Hg and a pH 7.37. These data demonstrate a respiratory acidosis but not acidemia. There is a mechanism present (elevated $PaCO_2$) that could lead to a decreased pH (acidosis), but the pH is in the normal range so there is no acidemia.

In the second example, the body's normal compensatory processes have returned the pH to more normal levels; the kidney has retained bicarbonate in order to reestablish the 20:1 ratio. When interpreting any acid-base disorder, the clinician must evaluate these compensatory processes so that additional problems of acid-base balance are not obscured (see Table 6-1).

Table 6-1 Helpful Hints for Calculating and Predicting Acid-Base Changes

Acidosis
> *Respiratory*
> > acute   —pH falls by 0.08 for every 10 mm Hg increase in $PaCO_2$
> > —HCO_3 increased 1 mEq for every 10 mm Hg increase in $PaCO_2$ (HCO_3 should be in 23 to 32 range)
> > chronic—pH down by 0.03 for every 10 mm Hg increase in $PaCO_2$
> > —HCO_3 increased 3.5 mEq for every 10 mm Hg increase in $PaCO_2$
>
> *Metabolic*
> > expect hypocapnea (in steady state, $PaCO_2$ is approximately equal to the last two digits of the pH)

Alkalosis
> *Respiratory*
> > acute   —pH rises by 0.08 for every 10 mm Hg fall in $PaCO_2$
> > —HCO_3 will decrease approximately 2 mEq for every 10 mm Hg increase in $PaCO_2$
> > chronic—pH is increased by 0.017 for every 10 mm Hg in $PaCO_2$
>
> *Metabolic*
> > may see a rise in $PaCO_2$ if pH higher than 7.5; $PaCO_2$ should not be below normal or higher than 55 mm Hg

A brief discussion of the anticipated basic and compensatory findings for each of the simple acid-base disorders follows:

1. *Respiratory acidosis.* As the PCO_2 rises, the pH falls. This relationship means that for every acute rise in PCO_2 of 10 mm Hg, the pH will fall by 0.08. For example, if the $PaCO_2$ acutely rises from 40 to 55 mm Hg, the pH will fall from 7.4 to 7.28 ($0.08 \times 1.5 = 0.12$; $7.4 - 0.12 = 7.28$). Concurrent with the rise in PCO_2, there is also a small increase in bicarbonate (when carbon dioxide is put into solution, the end products include hydrogen ion and bicarbonate). In uncomplicated acute respiratory acidemia, the bicarbonate should not be above 32 mEq or below 23 mEq. (Acutely, the bicarbonate will increase 1 mEq for every 10 mm Hg increase in PCO_2.) Bicarbonate values that are too high or too low could indicate a complicating metabolic alkalosis or metabolic acidosis.

After 6 to 12 hours of respiratory acidosis, the kidney retains and synthesizes bicarbonate in order to correct the pH. As the bicarbonate is retained, chloride is excreted; this "chloride shift" is the cause of the hypochloremia seen in the patients with chronic respiratory acidosis. In chronic respiratory acidosis, the bicarbonate increases by approximately 3.5 mEq for every 10 mm Hg rise in PCO_2; with the increased levels of bicarbonate, the pH change is now approximately 0.03 for every 10mm Hg increase in PCO_2. For example, if the person has a chronically elevated $PaCO_2$ in the range of 60 mm Hg, a pH of 7.34 would be expected ($0.03 \times 2 = 0.06$; $7.4 - 0.06 = 7.34$). If the pH is not in the expected range, one should suspect an additional acid-base disorder. Compensation does not produce a normal pH.

2. *Metabolic acidosis.* As the pH falls, the respiratory center is stimulated, ventilatory drive increases, and the $PaCO_2$ falls. This response is immediate (although the maximal respiratory response may require 12 to 24 hours) so that the clinician should *always* see hypocapnia in conjunction with metabolic acidosis. When the full respiratory response to metabolic acidosis has occurred (after 12 to 24 hours), the $PaCO_2$ will usually be approximately equal to the last two digits of the pH. (For example, if the pH is 7.28, one would expect the $PaCO_2$ to be about 28 mm Hg.) As the $PaCO_2$ falls, the ratio of bicarbonate to CO_2 returns to more normal levels, as does the pH. (For example, using the preceding data, if the patient did not have respiratory compensation, the pH would be in the range of 7.20 rather than 7.28.) If the patient does not hyperventilate, the clinician should suspect an additional respiratory problem. Also, do not attempt to correct the hyperventilation because that would make the acidemia more severe; the hyperventilation is a normal, helpful compensatory response.

3. *Respiratory alkalosis.* As the $PaCO_2$ falls, the pH rises. In acute respiratory alkalosis, the pH rises 0.08 for every 10 mm Hg drop in PCO_2. For example, if the $PaCO_2$ acutely falls from 40 to 30 mm Hg, the pH should rise from 7.4 to 7.48 ($0.08 \times 1 = 0.08$; $7.4 + 0.08 = 7.48$). Concurrently, the bicarbonate will decrease approximately 2 mEq for every 10 mm Hg fall in PCO_2.

In chronic respiratory alkalosis, renal mechanisms act to conserve acid. Although renal mechanisms tend to move the pH toward normal levels, up to two weeks are required before the pH is normal. The guideline for predicting compensation of a chronic respiratory alkalosis is a 0.017 change in pH for every 10 mm Hg decrease in PCO_2. For example, if the patient has been chronically hyperventilating to a $PaCO_2$ of 30 mm Hg, a pH of 7.42 would be expected ($0.017 \times 1 = 0.017; 7.4 + 0.017 = 7.417$).

4. *Metabolic alkalosis.* In metabolic alkalosis, the elevated bicarbonate leads to an elevated pH. Although the logical compensatory mechanism for this disorder is retention of carbon dioxide, such a situation is not frequently seen. There are so many other factors affecting ventilatory drive that ventilation is frequently maintained even in the presence of metabolic alkalosis. A simplified guide is that a metabolic alkalosis along with $PaCO_2$ below normal or a $PaCO_2$ above 55 mm Hg indicates a superimposed respiratory disorder.

INTERPRETATION OF BLOOD GASES

This section concentrates on the interpretation of PaO_2 and $PaCO_2$, with emphasis on determining the adequacy of ventilation and the physiologic mechanisms of an abnormal PaO_2. A number of steps are involved.

1. Determine the adequacy of total alveolar ventilation.

- If the $PaCO_2$ is in the normal range (38 to 42 mm Hg), total alveolar ventilation is adequate.
- If the $PaCO_2$ is greater than 45 mm Hg, the patient is hypoventilating. If the pH is in the normal range, the hypoventilation is probably chronic, although there may be a concurrent problem of metabolic alkalosis. (The guidelines for normal compensation, which were discussed in the preceding section, will facilitate the interpretation.) If the pH is acidemic, the decrease in ventilation is probably acute. The rules for estimating a pH change for any given change in $PaCO_2$ will help in determining if there is also metabolic acidemia; mixed, chronic, and acute respiratory acidosis; or other problems present.
- If the $PaCO_2$ is less than 35 mm Hg, the patient is hyperventilating. If the pH is in the normal range, the hyperventilation is probably chronic; if the pH is alkalemic, the hyperventilation is probably acute. Again, the guidelines for compensation and expected pH change must be applied so that a mixed acid-base disorder is not missed. Further assessment of the blood gases may help determine the cause of the hyperventilation. For example, hyperventilation is the expected response to metabolic acidemia and to hypoxemia; if hyperventilation is not seen

in these situations, then the patient has relative hypoventilation. (If a patient does not hyperventilate in response to a PaO_2 less than 50 mm Hg or to metabolic acidemia, then the clinician should be concerned that the patient is unable to respond to the increased drive to breathe appropriately.)

2. Determine if there is a problem of oxygen exchange. This determination requires knowledge of the normal PaO_2 that would be expected if the patient had normal gas exchange. For example, if the person was at an elevation of 3000 ft, the normal PaO_2 would be 80 mm Hg, not 95 mm Hg. Similarly, the effect of supplemental oxygen must be considered. If an individual with normal lungs breathed gas with an FIO_2 of 0.4 at sea level, then the expected PaO_2 would be approximately 230 mm Hg (barometric pressure, 760 mm Hg × FIO_2).

- Determine if PaO_2 is in the expected range for the PIO_2.
- If the PaO_2 is not in the expected range, determine if the difference is due to the level of alveolar ventilation.
  a. A PaO_2 that is higher than expected (after considering the effect of supplemental oxygen), may be due to hyperventilation. For example, if an individual with normal lungs was breathing room air at sea level and was hyperventilating to a $PaCO_2$ of 25 mm Hg, one would expect the PaO_2 to be approximately 105 mm Hg)
  b. If the PaO_2 is lower than expected, can the decrease be accounted for by hypoventilation? For example, if a patient is breathing room air at sea level but has a $PaCO_2$ of 60 mm Hg, then the expected PaO_2 is 70 mm Hg (see discussion of ideal alveolar PO_2 in Chapter 5). If the decrease in the PaO_2 is even greater than can be expected from hypoventilation or if hypoventilation is not present, then there must be an additional mechanism for the decrease in PaO_2.
  c. If the above steps have not accounted for the patient's level of hypoxemia, then the patient must have a ventilation perfusion mismatch, specifically a problem of low $\dot{V}/\dot{Q}$. (1) If the problem is low $\dot{V}/\dot{Q}$ without generalized hypoventilation, the PaO_2 will be lower than expected and the $PaCO_2$ will be normal or low. (2) If the problem is both hypoventilation and low $\dot{V}/\dot{Q}$, the $PaCO_2$ will be elevated and the PaO_2 will be lower than anticipated from the alveolar gas equation.
  Although more sophisticated tests are available, in the usual clinical setting the differentiation between general low $\dot{V}/\dot{Q}$ and shunt is made by the response to oxygen therapy. If high levels of inspired oxygen (FIO_2 greater than 0.5) do not raise the PaO_2 to an acceptable

level (PaO$_2$ in the 60s), then the patient probably has large areas of shunt.

In summary, the caregiver must always:

1. *Determine acid-base status* (Figure 6-1). Examine the pH, the relationship between pH and PCO$_2$, and the effects of other variables as needed (HCO$_3^-$, anion gap, electrolytes).

2. *Determine the adequacy of ventilation* (Figure 6-2). Examine the PaCO$_2$; consider potential causes of increased ventilatory drive and their influence on expected PaCO$_2$.

3. *Determine if PaO$_2$ is abnormal.* (Don't forget elevation effect.) (Figure 6-3). Examine the relationship between PO$_2$ and PaCO$_2$ to determine the physiologic mechanism for an abnormal PaO$_2$.

CLINICAL EXAMPLES

This section presents several clinical examples. For each, the blood gases and acid-base status are interpreted and clinical implications are stated. (For blood-gas interpretation, assume all values obtained at sea level and that the hemoglobin level is normal.)

Patient A: PaO$_2$ 60 mm Hg   PaCO$_2$ 50 mm Hg
pH 7.38   status: breathing room air

Interpretation: Patient is hypoxemic, hypercapnic, and has a normal pH. The PaO$_2$ is lower than expected breathing room air at sea level. Since the patient is also hypercapnic, at least part of the decrease in PaO$_2$ can be accounted for by the rise in PaCO$_2$; if the hypoventilation was the only reason for the PaO$_2$ to be low, the PaO$_2$ would be approximately 80 to 85 mm Hg. (Ideal alveolar oxygen is 90 mm Hg: 760−47 × 0.21 −[PaCO$_2$/0.8]. A short cut estimation is that,

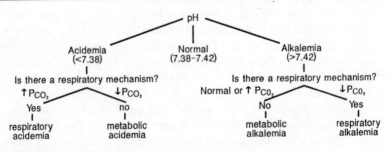

Figure 6-1 Evaluate acid-base status (pH-PCO$_2$ relationship).

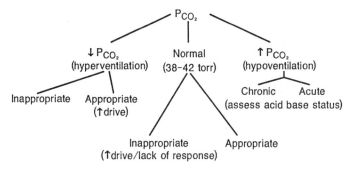

Figure 6-2 Determine the adequacy of alveolar ventilation.

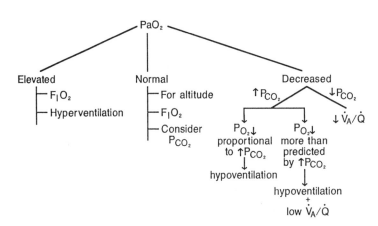

Figure 6-3 Evaluate oxygen exchange.

with no change in inspired oxygen, a 10 mm Hg rise in $PaCO_2$ will cause a 10 to 12 mm Hg fall in oxygen [as the $PaCO_2$ increases by 10 mm Hg, the PaO_2 would be expected to fall from 95 to 85 mm Hg]). Since the PaO_2 is even lower than expected from the rise in $PaCO_2$, the patient must have a second mechanism contributing to the hypoxemia, that of low $\dot{V}/\dot{Q}$. Finally, because the pH is in the normal range, one can assume that the hypoventilation is chronic. An elevated bicarbonate level and lower than normal serum chloride would be expected. In summary, these blood-gas results show respiratory acidosis, chronic hypoventilation with a compensated pH, and hypoxemia due to hypoventilation and a low $\dot{V}/\dot{Q}$.

Clinical implications: Although the PaO_2 is low, it is at an adequate level. Therefore, given that there are no symptoms of tissue hypoxia (polycythemia, heart failure, pulmonary hypertension), the patient would not require supplemental oxygen. The $PaCO_2$ is elevated but is well compensated. Therefore, no acute intervention to lower the $PaCO_2$ is required. If the patient has no acute respiratory symptoms (eg, acute bronchitis), these gases probably demonstrate the usual status of a patient with a primary or secondary chronic respiratory problem, such as COPD or kyphoscoliosis. Reviewing serial blood gases and clinical status will allow the clinician to confirm or reject that interpretation.

Patient B:	PaO_2 80 mm Hg	$PaCO_2$ 38 mm Hg
	pH 7.42	status: breathing 2 L/min
		oxygen by cannula

Interpretation: The patient's $PaCO_2$ and pH are normal; therefore, ventilation is adequate and there is no acid-base disturbance. The patient's PaO_2 is lower than would be expected since the patient is on supplemental oxygen. (The specific FIO_2 is not known, but the PaO_2 is definitely lower than it should be for someone breathing an FIO_2 greater than 0.21.) Because hypoventilation is not present, the mechanism for the lower than expected PaO_2 is a low $\dot{V}/\dot{Q}$.

Clinical implications: The caregiver needs to determine the specific cause of the low $\dot{V}/\dot{Q}$ abnormality—is it from retained secretions, bronchospasm, atelectasis, or something else. Interventions can then be aimed at the specific problem. Evaluation of those interventions should include their effect on PaO_2.

| **Patient C:** | PaO_2 43 mm Hg | $PaCO_2$ 40 mm Hg |
| | pH 7.33 | status: breathing room air |

Interpretation: The patient's pH is acidemic, but the $PaCO_2$ is normal. Therefore, the clinician would conclude that the patient has metabolic acidemia. In light of the low PaO_2, which could result in anaerobic metabolism, also check electrolytes for an anion gap due to an accumulation of lactate. The patient is hypoxemic and the $PaCO_2$ normal. Therefore, none of the hypoxemia can be accounted for by hypoventilation and must be due to a low $\dot{V}/\dot{Q}$. Although the $PaCO_2$ is normal, the patient would be expected to hyperventilate in response to such a low PaO_2 as well as the low pH. Therefore, the patient has a relative hypoventilation, and further assessment of the patient's ventilatory drive and ability to respond to that drive needs to be made.

Clinical implications: The first priority for this patient is to provide supplemental oxygen because the PaO_2 is extremely low. At the same time, the patient's relative hypoventilation is a warning sign to carefully monitor the individual's ability to maintain or increase alveolar ventilation (a change in respiratory rate and/or depth, increasing fatigue, or lethargy). Interventions that would decrease ventilatory drive should be avoided (sedation, for example). The pH should rise after oxygen therapy if the patient has a component of metabolic acidosis due to anaerobic metabolism.

In addition, the clinician should be aware of why the patient cannot respond appropriately to the increased drive, eg, due to pain, malnutrition, or obstruction. Some of the mechanisms may be amenable to interventions. Others will influence the selection of interventions so that the patient's decreased response is not further aggravated.

Continuing care would involve identification of the basis for the low $\dot{V}/\dot{Q}$ abnormality, such as retained secretions, pulmonary edema, bronchospasm, or atelectasis. The patient's response to oxygen therapy would help determine if there is a shunt mechanism present. (A poor response to oxygen therapy would indicate shunt, while a good response would indicate decreased but not absent ventilation.)

Patient D:	PaO_2 65 mm Hg	$PaCO_2$ 65 mm Hg
	pH 7.2	status: breathing room air

Interpretation: The patient is acidemic and his $PaCO_2$ is elevated; therefore the patient has respiratory acidemia. Also, the pH has fallen by 0.2 units with a rise in $PaCO_2$ of 25 mm Hg (40 to 65 mm Hg); thus, this is a problem of acute respiratory acidemia (for every 10 mm Hg rise in $PaCO_2$, the pH has fallen by 0.08 units). The patient is also hypoxemic. The fall in PaO_2 can be accounted for by the rise in $PaCO_2$. ($PaCO_2$ has risen by 25 mm Hg and the PaO_2 has fallen by 30 mm Hg. Use the alveolar gas equation or estimate by using this rule: there is a 12 mm Hg fall in PaO_2 for every 10 mm Hg rise in $PaCO_2$.) Thus, the primary defect in this patient is hypoventilation; the changes in PaO_2 and pH are subsequent to the rise in $PaCO_2$.

Clinical implications: The primary intervention for this patient would be to avoid further hypoventilation and to increase ventilation. If the patient was unresponsive (ie, due to a drug overdose), mechanical ventilation would probably be instituted. As therapy progresses, the pH and PaO_2 would be expected to rise to normal levels as the $PaCO_2$ falls to normal levels.

Patient E:	PaO_2 105 mm Hg	$PaCO_2$ 28 mm Hg
	pH 7.3	status: breathing room air

Interpretation: The pH is acidemic with a lower than normal $PaCO_2$. Therefore, the patient has a metabolic acidemia. The patient is hyperventilating, but when interpreted in light of the acidemia, the level of hyperventilation is appropriate. The PaO_2 is higher than normal but can be accounted for by hyperventilation of a normal lung.

Clinical implications: The primary aim is to diagnose the cause and correct the metabolic acidemia. Concurrently, the clinician would observe the patient to be sure that the hyperventilation is maintained, eg, the patient is not tiring. The clinician would not attempt to decrease the patient's rate or depth of respirations.

Patient F:	PaO$_2$ 58 mm Hg	PaCO$_2$ 28 mm Hg
	pH 7.5	status: breathing 2 L/min
		oxygen by cannula

Interpretation: The patient is alkalemic and the PaCO$_2$ is low; the rise in pH can be accounted for by the decrease in PaCO$_2$; therefore the patient has a respiratory alkalemia. The hyperventilation is probably a response to the patient's underlying pulmonary condition and hypoxemia. The PaO$_2$ is low; since hypoventilation cannot be a cause, the patient's hypoxemia is due to a low $\dot{V}/\dot{Q}$.

Clinical implications: The cause of the low $\dot{V}/\dot{Q}$ abnormality needs to be identified and appropriate interventions applied. In the meantime, the patient would probably profit from an increase in the FIO$_2$; although the PaO$_2$ is in an acceptable range, the patient has to hyperventilate to maintain it—potentially contributing to fatigue and dyspnea. (If the patient were not hyperventilating, the PaO$_2$ would probably be in the 40s.) Increasing the FIO$_2$ may allow the patient to maintain an equivalent PaO$_2$ without as much hyperventilation. For example, a response to 3 L/min of oxygen may be a PaO$_2$ of 60 mm Hg with a PaCO$_2$ of 38 mm Hg; this response would be desirable. Although the PaO$_2$ is relatively unchanged (looking at the individual numbers), the patient is no longer required to hyperventilate so there has been an effective increase in PaO$_2$. As the PaCO$_2$ returns to normal levels, the pH will correct.

Patient G:	PaO$_2$ 93 mm Hg	PaCO$_2$ 40 mm Hg
	pH 7.53	status: breathing room air

Interpretation: The pH is alkalemic with a normal PaCO$_2$; therefore the patient has metabolic alkalemia. Ventilation is adequate and the PaO$_2$ is normal.

Clinical implications: The patient does not have a gas exchange problem. Further assessment would include ruling out factors that would cause metabolic alkalemia (eg, gastric suction, hypokalemia from diuretics, or steroids).

Patient H:	PaO$_2$ 60 mm Hg	PaCO$_2$ 66 mm Hg
	pH 7.28	status: breathing 2 L/min
		oxygen by cannula

Interpretation: The patient is hypoxemic, hypoventilating, and acidemic. The relationship between the PaCO$_2$ and the pH demonstrates that the patient has a problem of chronic and acute respiratory acidosis. If the patient had acutely experienced a rise in PaCO$_2$ from 40 to 66 mm Hg, the pH would be expected to be approximately 7.24; if the patient had only chronic hypoventilation, a pH in the 7.35 range would be expected. Therefore, from the data presented, one would expect that the patient had had chronic CO$_2$ retention and now had an exacerbation that produced superimposed acute CO_2 retention. Previous blood-gas data would allow confirmation of this interpretation; checking for the absence of an anion gap would also allow the clinician to rule out a superimposed metabolic acidemia.

The patient is on supplemental oxygen; therefore, the decrease in PaO_2 is due to both hypoventilation and low $\dot{V}/\dot{Q}$.

Clinical implications: The patient is adequately oxygenated at the present time, with supplemental oxygen, and it is important that that level be maintained. The adverse effects of acidemia are much greater if accompanied by hypoxemia. The patient must be closely observed for any signs of worsening of the hypoventilation (which would further decrease the pH and worsen the hypoxemia), any interventions that could potentially increase the $PaCO_2$ should be avoided (sedation, increasing CO_2 production by exercise), and efforts should be made to increase ventilation. To accomplish increased ventilation, it is important to decrease the workload against which the respiratory apparatus is functioning; eg, bronchodilators will decrease airway resistance. At the same time, it must be remembered that the goal of therapy is to return the $PaCO_2$ to the patient's usual level, not to 40 mm Hg.

The previous examples have looked at a single set of blood-gas and acid-base data. It is important to follow changes over time. The example below analyzes the changes between two sets of data in the same patient.

Time A:	PaO_2 60 mm Hg	$PaCO_2$ 55 mm Hg
	pH 7.3	status: breathing 30% oxygen
Time B:	PaO_2 63 mm Hg	$PaCO_2$ 45 mm Hg
	pH 7.38	status: breathing 30% oxygen

Interpretation: Between time A and time B, the level of alveolar ventilation has improved, as demonstrated by the fall in $PaCO_2$. Related to the change in $PaCO_2$, the pH has risen appropriately to the normal range. The PaO_2 has also risen between time A and time B, but the change is not of the magnitude expected from the change in $PaCO_2$. (With no change in the FIO_2, the PaO_2 would be expected to increase by approximately 10 mm Hg, but it only increased by 3 mm Hg.) An interpretation can be made that the $\dot{V}/\dot{Q}$ abnormality is worse or at least not better. The improvement in alveolar ventilation was due to increased ventilation to those areas already ventilated; the increase was not due to improved ventilation of those areas not previously ventilated.

Clinical implications: At time B, the goal is no longer to improve overall ventilation, but rather to improve the distribution of the ventilation. For example, if this was a patient with airway clearance problems, the intervention would be to increase efforts aimed at airway clearance, such as cough or suctioning, as appropriate to the situation.

SUGGESTED READING

Gong H, Tashkin DP, Lee EY, Simmons MS. Hypoxia—altitude simulation test. *Am Rev Respir Dis*. 1984;130:980–986.

Harper RW. *A Guide to Respiratory Care*. Philadelphia: J B Lippincott; 1981.

Mountain RD, Sahn SA. Clinical features and outcome in patients with acute asthma presenting with hypercapnia. *Am Rev Respir Dis*. 1988;138:535–547.

Narins RG, Emmett M. Simple and mixed acid-base disorders: a practical approach. *Medicine*. 1980;59:161–187.

Shapiro BA, Harrison RA, Cane RD, et al. *Clinical Application of Blood Gases*. Chicago: Year Book Medical Publishers; 1989.

Traver GA. *Respiratory Nursing: the Science and the Art*. New York: John Wiley and Sons; 1982.

Traver GA, Flodquist-Priestley G. Management problems in unilateral lung disease with emphasis on differential lung ventilation. *Critical Care Nurse*. 1986;6:40–50.

chapter 7

Clinical Application: The Patient with Dyspnea

Dyspnea, or breathlessness, is a complicated symptom. There are a variety of factors that may precipitate dyspnea. In addition to the stimuli, the caregiver must consider the patient's perception of the dyspnea (Do the stimuli evoke a response?) and the actual behavioral response to the dyspnea. Only when all of these factors are considered in a comprehensive assessment can an optimal plan of care be developed.

ASSESSMENT OF DYSPNEA

The assessment of dyspnea requires a systematic approach to identify potential contributing factors. These factors include stimuli that precipitate dyspnea, the perception of dyspnea, and the response to dyspnea. The steps to be used in assessing dyspnea are discussed in this section. Each step includes the rationale and sources of data for the assessment.

1. *Determine potential factors contributing to the sensation of dyspnea.* Physiologically, the development of dyspnea is related to a respiratory effort that approaches the maximal potential output of the ventilatory apparatus. Therefore, dyspnea is usually related to a combination of impaired ventilatory function and an increased ventilatory drive.

- Investigate factors that denote impaired ventilatory function. Pulmonary function studies provide objective data regarding the level and type of physiologic impairment. (See Chapter 1 and the discussion of ventilatory monitoring in Chapter 15.) Observation of the ventilatory pattern (Chapter 1), chest auscultation, and chest x-rays are all additional sources of data and in many situations are the primary sources of information. It is important that the type of ventilatory impairment be determined as well as the presence of impairment. (Obstructive and restrictive ventilatory problems require different types of interventions.) It is also necessary to know the degree of physiologic impairment. At mild levels of impairment, dyspnea would not be expected to occur, while at the more severe levels, it would. The individual's perceptions may, however, produce dyspnea at lower than expected levels of impairment; while in other individuals, dyspnea may not be a complaint, even at more severe levels of impairment.

- Investigate factors that could increase ventilatory drive. These factors were discussed in Chapter 4. Some of the more common factors include acidemia, interstitial processes (stimulation of J receptors), and hypoxemia. Cerebral factors, such as anxiety, may also be present. When assessing the role of increased ventilatory drive, the clinician should remember that intermittent dyspnea may be due to periods of increased drive, eg, exercise, which demands increased work.

2. *Assess the individual's perception of the dyspnea.* This process involves an evaluation of the degree of impaired ventilatory function and changes in ventilatory drive as well as the interrelationships between function and drive. Some individuals will have severely impaired function and may not perceive dyspnea unless drive is also increased. Other persons may perceive dyspnea at lower levels of physiologic impairment. These differences in the perception of dyspnea are difficult to measure objectively and are usually based on the clinician's evaluation of the physiologic dysfunction and the patient's behavioral response. There are tools, such as the modified Borg scale (See Figure 7-1), which help to assess perception on a more objective level.

3. *Assess the individual's behavioral response.* Direct observation of the patient during episodes of dyspnea is extremely helpful. Look for changes in the ventilatory pattern (refer to Chapter 2), general muscle tenseness, attention level, and extraneous muscle movement. The clinician should also ask the patient how he or she feels when short of breath, including concurrent symptoms. For example, does the patient have periods of incontinence (only with dyspnea?), does he feel his heart racing, does he have sensations of numbness or tingling, does he have a sense of doom?

Such reports of the sensation of breathlessness as well as accompanying sensations can help the clinician to discriminate between physiologic and behavioral responses. For example, tingling and numbness are often related to hyperventilation; incontinence is frequently related to anxiety and excessive abdominal muscle contraction. It also is important to remember that many patients have a relatively "calm" response to dyspnea, "I just slow down till I catch my breath and then I'm OK." Effective behavioral responses as well as those that increase patient distress should be identified.

	0	nothing at all
	0.5	very, very, slight (just noticeable)
	1	very slight
	2	slight
	3	moderate
	4	somewhat severe
	5	severe
	6	
	7	very severe
	8	
	9	very, very, severe (almost maximal)
	10	maximal

Figure 7-1 Borg scale. The modified Borg scale is used to obtain a measure of the patient's perception of dyspnea. For example, after walking, the patient is requested to mark the scale at the point that best represents how he or she judges his or her dyspnea at that time.

In addition to determining what the patient's response is to dyspnea, the clinician must also delineate those activities or times when the patient is breathless. For example, is the patient always short of breath? Only with moderate exercise? With any addition of physical activity (personal hygiene, dressing)? If all answers do not appear consistent, then further assessment is necessary to identify, if possible, the commonalties between episodes. For example, all may involve upper limb exercise; dyspnea is only present when the additional factor of emotional stress is added to the activity. Remember, however, that patients with chronic lung disease will have ups and downs in their disease; there are times when they will perceive more dyspnea, and no cause can be identified.

PLANNING INTERVENTIONS

The first step in planning interventions is to analyze the information gathered in the assessment. Some aspects of dyspnea may be amenable to physiologic intervention, others may require a change in the patient's behavioral response, while still others cannot be modified. It is important that these three levels of intervention be defined. It is not to the patient's benefit when interventions are aimed solely at the behavioral response if pharmacologic intervention could have a positive impact.

1. In many instances, the stimuli resulting from impaired function or increased drive can be modified by pharmacologic interventions. In others, the stimuli can be eliminated or modified by other interventions.

The obstructive diseases are probably the most amenable to pharmacologic intervention. The reversible component of the disease is treated to maximize the physiologic function. If hypoxemia is severe enough to increase ventilatory drive, oxygen therapy can help. Many of the restrictive diseases, such as pulmonary interstitial fibrosis, are less amenable to treatment. In some cases, pharmacologic therapy can at least arrest the progression of the disease. Frequently, however, the restrictive ventilatory defect and the increased drive related to J receptor stimulation remain. For those individuals with restrictive disease and hypoxemia, oxygen therapy can relieve the hypoxic aspect of increased ventilatory drive. For those patients with breathlessness related to impaired cardiac function, some relief can be obtained by diuresis and improved cardiac function.

Although it is a physician's function to prescribe these pharmacologic interventions, it is the role of the nurse or therapist to facilitate their appropriate use. In the acute-care setting, it is usually the nurse who ensures that the medications are administered and it is also the nurse who monitors the patient's response to medication. If the medication is given to reduce airway obstruction, the nurse should make the appropriate observations to determine the effectiveness of the drug as well as any side effects. Similarly, the nurse should evaluate the effects of drugs to reduce the sources of increased drive.

In the chronic setting, the evaluation of the pharmacologic effects must include assessment of patient compliance. The patient must understand why the drug is prescribed, how it should be taken, and what effects should be expected. Frequently, the drug schedule must be modified according to the patient's lifestyle and activities known to increase dyspnea.

Another area where significant positive interventions can be instituted is the situation in which decreased ventilatory function and increased ventilatory drive are due to retained airway secretions. Effective airway care measures (see Chapter 10) can decrease the degree of obstructive abnormality and may also decrease the ventilatory drive related to stimulation of vagal receptors.

Lastly, the clinician can modify some aspects of the stimuli resulting from increased ventilatory drive by planning, or helping the patient to plan, a rest and activity schedule. For example, walks or other forms of exercise should be planned for times when the ventilatory function is optimal, eg, when the patient with obstructive disease is receiving maximal benefit from inhaled bronchodilators. If mornings are a time of increased shortness of breath, bathing and dressing should be spaced over several hours, with rest periods interspersed.

2. Interventions to affect directly the patient's perception of dyspnea are usually not possible. An exception is when codeine is prescribed to reduce the perception of increased ventilatory drive. Such a pharmacologic intervention may be used for patients with severe interstitial fibrosis or for patients with interstitial disease due to cancer (in the latter situation, the codeine or other medications are concurrently used to treat pain). It is important to monitor the patient's response. The goal in most situations is to decrease the sensation of dyspnea without significantly decreasing ventilatory drive and subsequently decreasing alveolar ventilation.

3. A variety of different interventions can be used to modify the patient's behavioral response to dyspnea (assuming that the assessment has demonstrated that such intervention is required). When the patient's response is appropriate, efforts should be made to reinforce and maintain the appropriate behavior.

A simple but often forgotten intervention is to explain to the patient why he is dyspneic. For example, many patients experience increased dyspnea with upper limb exercise. They may not understand why such activity (eg, shaving) makes them so short of breath. An explanation that exercise with the arms actually requires a lot of work and that it also inhibits their ability to use their accessory muscles will frequently help to allay their fears and anxiety. Although neither the stimulus nor the perception of dyspnea is abolished, the patient's response may be more controlled. It is easier to deal with the known versus the unknown. In addition, in the specific example given, additional interventions may be used to modify the intensity of stimuli evoked by the activity (eg, brace the elbows while shaving, or sit while shaving).

Teaching a controlled breathing pattern is also very helpful, especially for patients with an obstructive ventilatory defect. This intervention serves several purposes. For the patient with obstructive disease, a slow respiratory rate, with prolonged expiration, will allow the patient to exhale as much as he inhales. Therefore, the lung will not become further hyperinflated, thus impairing diaphragmatic function. (If the patient with obstructive disease does not allow sufficient time to exhale, he traps air and increases his functional residual capacity [FRC]; the diaphragm is then in a lower position and less efficient on inspiration.) The purpose of controlled breathing is therefore to maintain diaphragmatic effectiveness. At the same time, this intervention allows the patient a sense of control over his symptomatology and may modify his behavioral response to the dyspnea.

When instructing a patient in the use of controlled breathing, never force the patient to *always* breathe below the FRC that is functionally effective for that specific patient. In other words, the controlled pattern is to be used during times of stress or increased dyspnea—times when the respiratory rate is frequently increased and the expiratory time decreased. To imply to the patient that he must always be aware of his breathing pattern may impose a greater sense of dyspnea.

It is important to recognize that the controlled breathing pattern described is not effective or beneficial for all patients. For example, for patients with a restrictive defect, it is more effective to take shallower breaths at a more rapid rate; slow, deep breathing with a prolonged expiratory phase will increase rather than decrease dyspnea. When the use of the controlled breathing pattern causes increased dyspnea or increased patient fatigue, it has probably been taught incorrectly or has been instituted in an inappropriate patient. (See Chapter 9 for specific methods of teaching.)

Desensitization is a technique used to reduce the panic or fear response to dyspnea. The conceptual reasoning for this intervention is as follows. If a patient is exposed to periods of increased breathlessness under controlled conditions, he or she can learn to control the response. The stressors (eg, amount of exercise) are then gradually increased. Because the patient has gained the ability to control his response to lesser amounts of stress, he is now less likely to respond with the fear or panic syndrome as the stressor is increased. Many investigators have attributed the benefit of exercise training to the desensitization effect rather than direct physiologic effects. A variety of others types of interventions have also been used to decrease the panic/fear response. These include counseling, relaxation therapy, and biofeedback.

Patient education is an integral part of all the interventions cited. For many, the effect of patient education is to allow the patient to deal with the known versus the unknown and make intelligent choices between the intervention options available.

Finally, it is important that the patient who has positive, effective behavioral responses not be ignored. Responses that are effective must continually be supported and reinforced. In addition, it must be remembered that further decreases in physiologic function may result in increased perception of dyspnea, with which the patient may no longer be able to cope.

SUGGESTED READING

Anora NS, Rochester DF. Respiratory muscle strength and maximal voluntary ventilation in undernourished patients. *Am Rev Respir Dis.* 1982;126:5–8.

Burki NK. Dyspnea. *Clinics in Chest Medicine.* 1980;1:47–55.

Fishman AP, Altose M, Cherniack N. Respiratory sensation and dyspnea. *J Appl Physiol.* 1985;58:1051–1054.

Gift AG, Plaut M, Jacox A. Psychologic and physiologic factors related to dyspnea in subjects with chronic obstructive pulmonary disease. *Heart & Lung.* 1986;15:595–601.

Janson-Bjerklie S, Carrieri VK, Hudes M. The sensations of pulmonary dyspnea. *Nurs Res.* 1986;35:154–159.

Lush MT, Janson-Bjerklie S, Carrieri VK, et al. Dyspnea in the ventilator-assisted patient. *Heart & Lung.* 1988;17:528–535.

Mahler DA, Wells CK. Evaluation of clinical methods for rating dyspnea. *Chest.* 1988;93:580–586.

Rice KL. Treatment of dyspnea with psychotropic agents. *Chest.* 1986;90:789–790.

Wartak J, Sproule BJ, King EG. Dyspnea differential: Why the breathing difficulty? *J Resp Dis.* 1988;9:113–125.

Wolkove N, Dajczmon E, Colacone A, Kreisman H. The relationship between pulmonary function and dyspnea in obstructive lung disease. *Chest.* 1989;96:1247–1251.

part *II*

Techniques of
Respiratory Care

79

chapter 8

Humidification and Aerosol Therapy

Humidification and aerosol therapy are ways to increase moisture in the inspired air and deliver pharmacologically active substances to the airway. Humidification therapy, bland (water) aerosols, and aerosols of medications will be discussed.

HUMIDIFICATION THERAPY

Humidification, the addition of water vapor to an inhaled gas, is used in both inpatient and home settings. Humidification is primarily used to achieve or maintain a normal level of humidity in the inhaled gas. Since compressed gases are completely dry (0% humidity), the addition of humidity creates an atmosphere closer to normal inhaled air. Humidification is also used to replace upper airway function when the upper airway is bypassed (by an artificial airway or laryngectomy, for example). The addition of water vapor to the inspired gas, by reducing water extraction from the respiratory mucosa, will maintain normal mucociliary function and increase comfort (ie, prevent drying and irritation of the upper airway and larynx). Several different techniques are used to deliver humidification therapy.

Simple Unheated Humidifiers

Unheated humidifiers are used when only a modest increase in the relative humidity of the therapeutic gas is required. Although the level of humidification attained will vary, it is generally assumed that the usual level is 20% relative humidity or less. (When mixed with entrained room air, the relative humidity of the total gas flow to the patient is usually higher.) Use of unheated humidifiers is usually limited to those patients with an intact upper airway. The purpose is to augment upper airway function when dry gas is administered so that increased water extraction from the lower airways is avoided. Two types of this equipment are bubble and room humidifiers.

Bubble Humidifier

The bubble humidifier is the most commonly used device for simple humidification of supplemental oxygen therapy. The gas is directed below the surface of the water, usually passing through a diffuser to break up the gas into smaller bubbles, and then allowed to bubble back to the surface. The humidified gas is conducted to the patient via small bore tubing. The actual increase in humidification, especially when the gas source is at low flow rates, is questionable. Thus the cost-effectiveness of the bubble humidifier at flow rates less than 3 to 4 L/min is controversial. Many patients tolerate nasal oxygen at flows of 2 L/min without a bubble humidifier, with no upper airway side effects. However, some patients who receive chronic supplemental oxygen at home feel more comfortable and have fewer problems with nasal dryness, cracking, and bleeding when they routinely use a bubble humidifier. To evaluate the need for humidification of nasal oxygen, the clinician needs to consider the environment (patients in very dry climates may indeed need more humidification), the patient's subjective reports of comfort or discomfort, and the presence of nasal symptoms.

Bubble humidifiers are available as disposable, prefilled units that greatly decrease the risk of bacterial contamination and the time necessary for cleaning, disinfecting, or sterilization. In the home setting, nondisposable, refillable units are more common (due to cost); the nondisposable units should be cleaned and disinfected weekly.

Room Humidifier

Room humidifiers incorporate a reservoir of water that is exposed to a centrifugally spinning disk; large water droplets are produced, which are emitted into the immediate vicinity as a fog. Room humidifiers put only very small amounts of humidity into the room and are therefore basically used to increase upper airway comfort. Some individuals with permanent tracheostomies and adequate airway clearance use a room humidifier at night. In these individuals, the lower airway appears to have compensated for the loss of upper airway function and only small increases in humidity levels promote comfort. When a room humidifier is recommended for patients with permanent tracheostomies, the clinician must make sure that airway clearance does not become a problem and that the patient knows how to detect a change in clearance. The patient should also be instructed to place the room humidifier near the bed at night and to direct the fog to the area of his head and neck.

A major problem with the use of room humidifiers stems from improper cleaning of the reservoir and apparatus. Room humidifiers have been implicated as "reservoirs" for pathogens that then can be inhaled, causing pulmonary infections. Proper cleaning of room humidifiers requires that the reservoir be emptied and washed with hot soapy water every day. In addition, the reservoir should be disinfected (using a commercial disinfectant or acetic acid) once a week.

Heated Humidifiers

Heating a gas increases its ability to carry water vapor; therefore, the addition of heat greatly increases a humidifier's efficiency and ability to provide humidification. In patients whose upper airway has been bypassed, the upper airway function of humidification is lost. An attempt is made to attain 100% relative humidity of the inspired gas at body temperature. (Note that the inspired gas may be air or an oxygen-enriched mixture.) The goal of humidification therapy is to prevent water loss from the lower airways, which can lead to thick inspissated secretions, decreased mucociliary clearance, and increased risk of infection. (Although heated humidification or bland aerosol therapy is used in the inpatient setting, patients with permanent tracheostomy often do not continue to use these therapies in the home setting.)

A major problem associated with heated humidifiers is condensation and "rain out" in the tubing between the humidifier and the patient. Heated humidifiers are always used with wide bore tubing (versus narrow) and a water trap is often added, but condensation remains a problem. The fluid accumulation must be removed from the tubing at regular intervals. The fluid can interfere with gas delivery and may also become colonized with the patient's bacterial organisms. Always dispose of fluid from the tubing; do not drain it back into the reservoir of the humidifier. Another potential problem of heated humidifiers is the overheating of inspired gas, which can increase the patient's temperature or cause burns of the patient's airways.

An example of a heated humidifier is the cascade humidifier, which is commonly used with mechanical ventilators but can also be used in other settings. The cascade uses a tower and grid through which the gas travels, producing a hot water froth, thus humidifying the gas. Most cascade humidifiers on ventilators now employ a temperature feedback probe to regulate the temperature of the delivered gas.

Heat Moisture Exchanger

The newest type of humidification device is the heat moisture exchanger (HME) or the hygroscopic condenser humidifier. The HME can be used with an endotracheal tube, tracheostomy tube, or over a laryngectomy stoma. These humidifiers are commonly referred to as "artificial noses" because their function mimics that of the upper airway. Their principle of operation is that the exhaled heat and moisture are collected and subsequently used to warm and humidify inhaled gas.

One potential problem with the use of HMEs is decreased efficiency as tidal volumes, flow rates, or inspired concentrations of oxygen increase. In addition, these humidifiers can cause an increase in airway resistance, thus increasing the patient's work of breathing. The increase in airway resistance is related to the device itself and the potential complication of secretions partially obstructing the device. The potential for bacterial growth in the warm, moist environment of the HME is also a concern. As a result of these actual or potential problems, the heat moisture exchangers are not currently recommended for long-term use in ventilated patients who are not adequately hydrated, who are not normothermic, or who require therapeutic humidity for retained secretions.

Heat moisture exchangers could be useful in home settings, especially for non-ventilated patients. These devices facilitate patient activity because they are simple to use and negate the need for a cumbersome humidification or aerosol source. Alert, ambulatory patients recognize an increase in resistance whenever the HME becomes partially obstructed and can then apply a new HME; most patients use several HMEs per day.

BLAND AEROSOL THERAPY

A bland aerosol is a stable suspension of water or saline particles in a gas. Bland aerosol therapy is used to reduce irritation of the upper airway and to decrease the viscosity of mucus in airways, thereby facilitating clearance by cough or suctioning. The size of particle produced by an aerosol generator (also called a nebulizer) determines its point of deposition in the airway. To reach small airways, the particles must not exceed 0.5 to 2 microns in size; particles 2 to 5 microns in size deposit in bronchi and bronchioles; particles 6 to 10 microns in size deposit in upper airway structures. The mean size of particles generated by most nebulizers is 5 microns. Deposition in lower airways further depends on the pattern of inhalation, nasal versus oral, with the oral route yielding a higher rate. Estimates of overall deposition of therapeutic bland aerosols in lower airways is approximately 20%.

Many believe that systemic hydration is more effective than bland aerosol in decreasing viscosity of sputum and increasing mucociliary clearance. Most clinicians encourage patients with chronic airway obstruction and excessive secretions to drink 1 1/2 to 2 quarts of water daily.

Types of Aerosol Generators

The most commonly used type of aerosol device is the gas-powered jet nebulizer. Another type that is less frequently used is the ultrasonic nebulizer.

Jet Nebulizers

Jet nebulizers use a high-pressure gas source to break apart water droplets into small particles that are stable in suspension. In the hospital setting, large volume jet nebulizers are used to deliver bland aerosols. The bland aerosol may be administered periodically (usually in an attempt to improve airway clearance) or continuously (to replace upper airway function in intubated or tracheotomized patients, to decrease upper airway irritation postextubation, or as a means to improve airway clearance).

Jet nebulizers operate by using a mainstream method of nebulization; they have a high output. Their output can be increased by adding a heating element to the unit. The gas source used to drive the nebulizer may be air- or oxygen-enriched. Most large volume nebulizers employ a venturi device. The venturi allows a specific amount of air entrainment when the device is attached to an oxygen source, thus allowing delivery of oxygen concentrations of less than 100%. Use of the venturi also increases gas flow through the nebulizer and thus increases its output. (For this reason, nebulizers powered by compressed air often have the venturi set at less than 100% in order to increase total flow and output.) For specific oxygen concentrations not allowed by the venturi apparatus on the nebulizer, the unit is attached to an oxygen blender. (The blender receives gas from both an oxygen and air source; the two gases are then blended to provide the specific concentration desired.) For all large volume nebulizers, flows of the source gas must be set at 10 L/min or higher to provide adequate aerosol output, and if supplemental oxygen is being delivered, to ensure that additional air is not entrained at the mask. Another means of providing supplemental oxygen during periodic aerosol treatments is to maintain normal oxygen delivery by nasal cannula, and use air as the gas source for the nebulizer.

Ultrasonic Nebulizers

Ultrasonic nebulizers use high frequency vibrations to break up droplets of water or saline into very small particles in a nebulizer cup. The particles are suspended in a gas supplied by a blower and then delivered to the patient. The ultrasonic nebulizer devices are able to produce an aerosol with a higher water content and a more consistent particle size than the jet nebulizers. There are, however, several drawbacks to ultrasonic therapy. First, in acutely ill patients, there is the danger of fluid overload. Additionally, if administered to patients with reactive airways disease, ultrasonic therapy can precipitate acute broncho-spasm.

Sputum Induction

Aerosols may be used to induce cough and sputum production in order to collect a specimen for diagnostic purposes. Jet or ultrasonic nebulizers may be used for this procedure. Ultrasonic nebulizers produce a smaller particle size and therefore are often more effective in cough and sputum induction than are jet nebulizers. Hypertonic saline (9%) is often used for sputum induction, especially if water or normal saline nebulization has not been successful. Hypertonic saline nebulizations should be avoided in individuals with hyperreactive airways because the irritating effect of the hypertonic solution is especially likely to initiate an acute bronchoconstrictive episode.

Patient Education

The therapeutic effect of aerosols can be enhanced by modifying the patient's respiratory pattern. Mouth breathing rather than nose breathing should be encouraged to decrease the filtering effect of the nasopharynx. In addition, a slow inspiratory flow rate will decrease the amount of filtering of the aerosol particles by the upper airway. Instructing the patient to breathe slowly and deeply through his or her mouth can enhance lower airway deposition of the aerosol. (A word of caution is necessary. Many patients cannot tolerate slow, deep breathing for extended periods; they may hyperventilate or increase the work of breathing with resulting dyspnea. In such situations, simply encourage the patient to take a slow, deep breath periodically and include an inspiratory hold.) But even when the respiratory pattern is altered, aerosol particles are likely to be prevented from reaching the lower airways due to the efficient defense mechanisms in the airways (see Chapter 1). Unfortunately, therapeutic aerosol particles are not differentiated from harmful particles by airway defenses.

When bland aerosol therapy is used, even if the water particles do reach the lower airways, thinner secretions may not result; mucus does not mix with topically applied water. The aerosol may, however, contribute to increased cough effectiveness. Therefore, it is important to encourage the patient to incorporate cough maneuvers during and after bland aerosol treatment. (Refer to Chapter 10, Chest Physiotherapy.) Whenever bland aerosol therapy is used, it is important to evaluate the patient's therapeutic response and the incidence of side effects. Some patients will benefit from such therapy, some will show no change, while others may be worse.

PHARMACOLOGIC AEROSOLS

Aerosol therapy is used to deliver a variety of medications to the lower airway. Small particles of the medication are suspended in the inspired gas and inhaled. The site of particle deposition varies with particle size. Many of the medications delivered by aerosol can also be delivered by oral and parenteral routes. The aerosol route is preferred because the medication can be delivered directly to the intended site (the airway); total dose and systemic effects can therefore be reduced or eliminated. A discussion of the various approaches and devices used to deliver aerosolized medications follows.

Small Volume Jet Nebulizer

Small volume jet nebulizers (see Figure 8-1) have a small reservoir to which the medication and diluent are added. A compressed gas source, utilizing a sidestream method of nebulization, generates the aerosol in the small reservoir and then adds it to the inspiratory flow delivered to the patient. (An alternative gas source that is used by some patients in the home setting is the hand-bulb nebulizer; the gas source is generated by squeezing the bulb.) The small volume nebulizers are commonly used for aerosolized bronchodilator therapy in both acute-care and home settings. They are also used to deliver other types of medication in special situations. Examples are antibiotics to treat airway infections in some cystic fibrosis patients and aerosolized pentamidine to treat Pneumocystis carini in the immunosuppressed patients.

The source gas used to drive the nebulizer may be oxygen or air. Flow rates of approximately 6 L/min are usually required to generate adequate aerosol. The

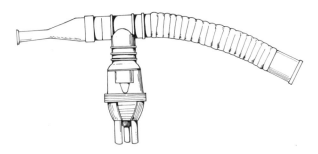

Figure 8-1 Small volume jet nebulizer. This small volume nebulizer is used to deliver aerosolized medications. Note the reservoir tubing added to prevent excessive loss of medication.

length of treatment will vary with the flow rates used and the volume of liquid in the nebulizer cup. The nebulizer may receive flow only during inspiration (flow can be controlled by a Y thumb control in the tubing connecting the nebulizer to the gas source) or may receive flow during both inspiration and expiration. Although the latter approach simplifies the administration of treatments, a proportion of the medication is lost during the expiratory phase. This loss may be somewhat reduced by placing a reservoir on the expiratory side of the unit. (See Figure 8-1.)

The actual dose of medication delivered to the lower airway by the aerosolized method is unknown; it is believed that a large amount of the aerosol never reaches the lower respiratory tract because the aerosol particles are relatively large and therefore subject to the normal lung defenses (see Chapter 1). Mouth breathing and slow inspiratory flow rate will probably improve deposition of particles.

Patients who are intubated can receive aerosolized pharmacologic therapy through an in-line placement of the nebulizer attached to the endotracheal or tracheal tube via a Brigg's adapter or tracheostomy mask. For patients who are also receiving mechanical positive pressure ventilation, the nebulizer is placed in the inspiratory side of the ventilator circuitry as close to the patient's airway as possible. This placement is believed to decrease interference with the delivery of medication due to "rain out" in the ventilator circuit tubing, and it provides medication with all breaths, not just those that are mechanically delivered. When the small volume nebulizer is added to the ventilator circuitry it is powered by an added gas source. The nebulizer cup supplied with the ventilator circuitry and the nebulizer control on some ventilators are seldom used.

For home therapy, the small volume nebulizer is usually driven by a small electric compressor that attains pressures of 20 to 40 pounds per square inch; a specific flow rate is not set, the compressor is simply turned on. Machines are available that operate on AC power or battery; some have adapters that allow the unit to be powered by being plugged into the cigarette lighter in an automobile. Very few patients require the continuous availability of jet nebulized bronchodilator therapy; a metered dose inhaler is usually sufficient. However, these portable units are convenient for patients who routinely use such therapy while they are traveling or on vacation. If the home patient also requires continuous oxygen therapy, oxygen is usually delivered by nasal cannula while the patient uses the nebulizer.

Delivery of aerosolized medications in the home setting requires some special considerations. Patients must be instructed to ensure that the medication (and diluent, if ordered) is properly measured and placed in the nebulizer cup. In addition to education about the use of the specific aerosol equipment, it is essential that patients and their families receive instructions regarding infection control. Various methods of cleaning and disinfecting the small volume nebulizer can be used. Patients should be instructed to rinse the nebulizer cup with tap water after each treatment and to turn it upside down on a clean towel to air dry between treatments. Air drying is preferable to manual towel drying to prevent pieces of lint or dust from entering the unit. Disinfection involves submersion of the entire unit, after scrubbing in mild detergent and hot water, into a disinfectant solution. Both quaternary ammonium compounds (QAC) and acetic acid solutions have been advocated as agents for disinfection of nebulizers in the home setting. If a 1.25% acetic acid solution (1 part white vinegar with 3 parts distilled water) is used, the unit is submerged for 60 minutes; with a QAC bath, prepared according to the manufacturer's directions, the unit is soaked for 10 minutes. The disinfectant procedure is performed routinely at least every three days.

Comparisons of these two disinfectant methods, each incorporating the detergent scrub, have failed to show significant differences in effectiveness between them when used on nebulizers contaminated with *Pseudomonas aeruginosa, Pseudomonas cepacia,* and *Staphylococcus aureus.* The QAC method, however, has some potential advantages, such as being odorless, reusable, more economical (approximately one-half the cost), and more convenient due to the fact that a shorter soak time is necessary than with the acetic acid method.

Pharmacologic Aerosols by Inhaler

Two types of inhalers are commonly used to deliver pharmacologic aerosols. They are the metered dose inhaler (MDI) and the spinhaler. Examples of medications delivered by these methods include bronchodilators of the beta-agonist and anticholinergic classes, cromolyn sulfate, and corticosteroids. (See Appendix A at the back of this book for a discussion of the specific medications.)

Metered Dose Inhaler

The MDI contains the medication and a gas propellant. When the inhaler is activated, a specific dose of the medicine, suspended in the propellant gas, is released from the inhaler. When used correctly, the MDI delivers medication as effectively as small volume nebulizers. However, incorrect use of the inhalers, which is common, dramatically decreases the pharmacologic response. The patient must be carefully instructed in use of the MDI; patients should also periodically be observed using their inhalers and given repeated instruction as necessary. Instruction in use of the inhaler should include the following:

1. Shake the inhaler prior to each activation.
2. Breath out slowly and normally. (Patients should be taught to exhale to a volume just slightly below their resting volume or FRC; they should not exhale forcibly.)

3. Position the inhaler using either the open or closed mouth technique. Recommendations as to the efficacy of the two techniques vary; some experts prefer one technique and some the other. Most likely the differences are due to how the patient actually performs each technique. For both, the inhaler should be held with the mouthpiece end down.

- For the open mouth technique, hold the inhaler approximately 2 inches from the open mouth, with the head tilted back slightly.
- For the closed mouth technique, place the mouthpiece in the mouth with the opening between the teeth and directed over the tongue; tilt the head back slightly.

4. While beginning to slowly inhale through the mouth, activate the inhaler.
5. Continue inhaling slowly to maximal inflation and then do a breath hold (preferably for more than 10 seconds).
6. Wait several minutes and repeat steps 1 through 5 for the second puff.

Patients should be carefully observed to make sure that they shake the MDI prior to each activation, that they are breathing through the mouth, that inspiration is slow, and that there is a breath hold. Improper technique in MDI use or attempts to use the MDI during acute dyspneic episodes without first doing pursed-lip breathing to slow the respiratory rate are major contributors to an inadequate therapeutic effect. Sometimes patients are said to be "abusing" their inhalers when in fact they are trying to obtain a therapeutic response by repeated inhalations. Incorrect technique results in deposition of the drug in the oral cavity rather than in lower airways. Absorption of the drug from the oral mucous membranes results in systemic side effects rather than a significant bronchodilator effect. Clinicians must take time to teach and review proper MDI technique with patients for whom metered dose inhalers are prescribed. Some patients may require other delivery devices, addition of a spacer device, or use of jet nebulization to attain the desired therapeutic response.

The mouthpiece of the MDI should be cleaned periodically and the canister checked to see how full it is. (Float the canister, without the mouthpiece, in water; if it sinks to bottom of the container, it is full; if it bobs in an upright position, it is half full; if it floats on top of the water, it is empty.)

The MDI can also be used to administer bronchodilators to mechanically ventilated and intubated patients. (See Figure 8-2.) The canister is inserted into a small adapter, which can subsequently be directed into the airway (for intubated patients) or attached to a ventilator connector with a suctioning adapter (for ventilated patients). When using the MDI for bronchodilator administration to mechanically ventilated patients, a self-inflating resuscitation bag is usually used

Inhaler

To Patient

Figure 8-2 MDI for intubated patients. Aerosolized bronchodilators can be administered via a metered dose inhaler (MDI) to intubated patients. A funnel-shaped adapter is placed in the diaphragm that is used as a suctioning port. The MDI canister is then placed in the funnel. The MDI is activated and a slow deep breath delivered to the patient via a self-inflating bag.

to deliver the inspired gas, and a tube reservoir is placed between the patient airway and the canister.

Spacers

Even after lengthy instruction, some patients are unable to use the MDI correctly. They demonstrate decreased therapeutic response and increased upper airway irritation. For these patients, a spacer device is extremely helpful. For most patients, using a spacer will increase the dose response (due to increased lower airway deposition), will decrease upper airway irritation, and in the case of inhaled steroids, will decrease the incidence of upper airway infection. Several types of spacers are commercially available; others can be made from usual home materials. (See Figure 8-3.)

All provide a reservoir into which the medication is injected by activating the inhaler, and all intend to decrease the velocity of flow at which the aerosol enters the airway. The decreased velocity decreases upper airway irritation and deposition while increasing the amount of the aerosol that enters the lower airway. Also, the patient does not have to coordinate inhalation and MDI activation as closely as is necessary without the spacer. Use of these devices does not obviate

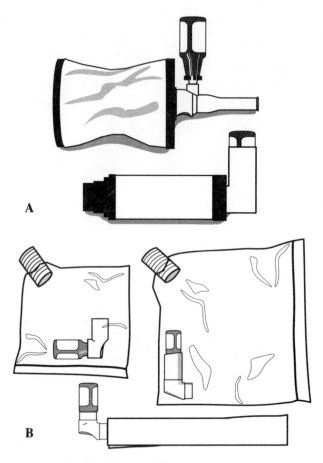

Figure 8-3 Spacers. Both commercial and homemade spacers are shown. The top panel (**A**) shows two commercial spacers. The bottom panel (**B**) shows homemade versions; two are made from baggies (size varies with size and age of individual) and one from a rolled piece of paper.

the need to teach slow, deep inhalation and a breath hold to enhance deposition of the drug in the lung. The devices do add cost to MDI therapy, but generally they are less expensive than opting for jet aerosol therapy as an alternative. Also, because lower airway deposition is improved, the patient may require fewer puffs from the inhaler to achieve a therapeutic effect.

Spinhalers

Spinhalers use medication that is in powder form and contained in a capsule. (Spinhalers are presently available for use with cromolyn sulfate and albuterol.)

The spinhaler contains a mechanism that punctures the capsule. As the patient inhales, his or her inspiratory flow is used to generate an aerosol of the particles of dry medication. The patient inhales slowly one or two times through the spinhaler; the capsule can be checked to see if all the medication has been inhaled. The spinhalers offer the advantage of being small and easily transported. Because the drug is administered only during the patient's inspiration, the clinician can be more assured that the desired dose is delivered.

SUGGESTED READING

Branson RD. Artificial noses: unanswered questions. *Resp Care*. 1989;34:969–971.

Chatburn RL, Kallstrom TJ, Bajaksouzian S. A comparison of acetic acid with a quaternary ammonium compound for disinfection of hand-held nebulizers. *Resp Care*. 1988;33:179–187.

DeBlaquiere P, Christensen DB, Carter WB, Martin TR. Use and misuse of metered dose inhalers by patients with chronic lung disease. *Amer Rev Resp Dis*. 1989;140:910–916.

Kacmarek RM, Stoller JK. *Current Respiratory Care*. Philadelphia: BC Decker Inc; 1988.

Lee DKP, Ingbar DH. Patient education guide. How to use your metered dose inhaler. *J Resp Dis*. 1989;10:117–118.

Luce JM, Tyler ML, Pierson DJ. *Intensive Respiratory Care*. Philadelphia: W B Saunders Company; 1984.

Newhouse MT, Dolovich MB. Control of asthma by aerosols. *N Engl J Med*. 1986; 315:870–873.

Pisut FM. Comparison of medication delivery by T-nebulizer with inspiratory and expiratory reservoirs. *Resp Care*. 1989;34:985–988.

Thompson A, Traver GA. Comparison of three methods of administering a self-propelled bronchodilator. *Am Rev Resp Dis*. 1982;125:140.

Traver GA. *Respiratory Nursing: The Science and the Art*. New York: John Wiley and Sons; 1982.

chapter 9

Oxygen Therapy

Administration of oxygen is a therapeutic intervention common to acute-care settings and home care. The clinician must be aware of the variety of delivery devices and delivery systems available, as well as the differences in oxygen use in the home versus the acute-care setting.

INDICATIONS AND GOALS FOR USE OF OXYGEN THERAPY

Oxygen is an odorless, colorless, tasteless gas that comprises approximately 21% of the total gas in the atmosphere. It is considered a medication when used in clinical settings to alleviate hypoxemia and resulting symptomatology. Clinically significant hypoxemia may be the result of primary pulmonary pathology or a change in pulmonary function due to pathology occurring in another system. For example, hypoxemia may occur with cardiovascular disorders, such as mycocardial infarction or congestive heart failure; central nervous system and neuromuscular problems, such as head injury, cerebral vascular accidents, muscular dystrophy, disturbed sleep (sleep apnea with central respiratory drive etiology), overdoses of narcotics or sedatives, and anesthesia effects. These nonpulmonary disorders may decrease total ventilation and/or impair ventilation-perfusion matching.

Hypoxemia is defined as an arterial oxygen tension (PaO_2) that is less than the expected normal value. It is important to realize that all cases of hypoxemia do not necessitate treatment with supplemental oxygen therapy. A review of the oxyhemoglobin dissociation curve (Figure 5-2 in Chapter 5) reveals that the oxygen saturation (SaO_2) does not fall below a value of 90% until the PaO_2 falls below approximately 60 mm Hg. Generally speaking, an oxyhemoglobin saturation of 90% is sufficient to sustain metabolic and tissue needs without any indication of oxygen starvation, ie, anaerobic metabolism and lactic acid production. Therefore, oxygen therapy is not usually initiated until hypoxemia is severe enough to result in saturation values less than 90% to 93% and symptoms indicative of tissue hypoxia.

The causes of hypoxemia as well as the symptoms associated with hypoxemia are discussed in Chapter 5. The severity of symptoms that develop depends not only on the degree of hypoxemia but also on the period of time over which the hypoxemia developed. Sudden onset of severe hypoxemia is likely to create dramatic symptoms that may include effects on the neurologic, cardiovascular, and respiratory systems, as shown in Table 9-1.

The goal of oxygen therapy in the acutely hypoxemic, previously healthy person is to alleviate the hypoxemic symptomatology and increase the arterial oxygen tension to normal or near normal levels. In the setting of chronic hypoxemia, the goal of therapy is relief of symptomatology, such as cor pulmonale, secondary erythrocytosis, exercise limitation, sleep disturbance, or pulmonary hypertension. Relief of such symptomatology is usually accomplished by maintaining oxyhemoglobin saturation at levels of 90% to 93% (arterial oxygen tension in the 60 mm Hg range) rather than correction to normal levels.

Oxygen therapy in any setting should be monitored. Monitoring is needed to ensure adequate oxygenation without the potential adverse effects of decreasing ventilatory drive (producing progressive hypoventilation and acidemia) and hyperoxia. In adults, arterial blood gas sampling remains the definitive assessment tool. In young children, pulse oximetry is more commonly used. Pulse oximetry is also used in adults to monitor the effects of therapy but must be used cautiously in those patients who may hypoventilate in response to increased PaO_2.

DEVICES FOR OXYGEN ADMINISTRATION

Oxygen can be delivered to the patient with a variety of devices. Factors that determine the choice of a particular oxygen delivery device include the FIO_2

Table 9-1 Symptoms of Hypoxemia

Neurologic	Cardiovascular	Respiratory
headache	tachycardia	dyspnea
confusion	arrhythmias	tachypnea
anxiety	hypertension	
agitation	exacerbation	
depression	of angina	
visual changes		
drowsiness		
impaired judgment		
decreased concentration		
coma		

required, ability of the patient to be cooperative, and the comfort and ease of the patient in wearing the oxygen device. The source of oxygen may be obtained from wall systems, cylinders, liquid systems, concentrators, or enrichers. All of these sources, except for enrichers, supply gas that is dry; therefore, the gas often requires humidification prior to delivery to the patient. Chapter 8 describes the various humidification devices available for use in oxygen delivery.

Low Flow Oxygen Delivery Devices

The most common methods of oxygen administration involve the use of low flow oxygen devices in which the actual concentration of oxygen received by the patient varies with changes in the respiratory pattern. These devices deliver a set flow of 100% oxygen, which is then mixed with room air as the patient inhales. The amount of air entrained, which varies with the patient's respiratory rate and depth, will affect the final concentration delivered. Low flow refers to this variable mixing with room air, not the oxygen flow rate set on the flow meter. Examples of low flow oxygen delivery devices are outlined in Table 9-2 as well as the advantages, disadvantages, and other important considerations for each device.

High Flow Oxygen Delivery Devices

High flow oxygen delivery devices deliver a specific oxygen concentration at total flow rates high enough to completely meet the patient's inspiratory demand (see Table 9-2). Since no additional air dilution takes place, these devices deliver a known, constant oxygen concentration. Venturi or air entrainment masks and mechanical ventilators are considered high flow oxygen delivery devices.

Venturi and air entrainment masks are constructed to produce a specific amount of air entrainment. These masks have specific settings for the desired oxygen concentration. Oxygen is delivered to the device at the flow rate indicated on the mask and then diluted with room air. The construction of the mask determines how much dilution occurs (see Figure 9-1). For example, a 35% mask will entrain less room air than a 25% mask. All of these masks deliver a total flow of approximately 40 L/min at the desired oxygen concentration. This total flow is sufficiently high that the patient's inspiratory demands are met. The source of all inhaled gas is the mask with its known oxygen concentration; additional room air is not drawn into the mask.

Venturi and air entrainment masks are beneficial for oxygen administration to patients in whom small changes in the oxygen concentration may adversely affect ventilatory drive (those patients in whom delivery of high concentrations of

Table 9-2 Devices for Oxygen Administration

Low Flow Devices

Nasal Cannula (Nasal Prong)

- *Advantages:* May be used by a restless client.

  Safe and simple method.

  Relatively comfortable and acceptable.

  Allows client to move about in bed; client can eat, talk, or cough while wearing device.

  With special flow meters, less than 1 L/min can be delivered; in pediatric clients the flow is often less than one liter.

- *Disadvantages:* High flow rates (> 4 L/min) may dry the nasal membranes and cause pain in frontal sinuses.

  Drying and/or breakdown of skin around nose, upper lips, and ears may develop from pressure or reaction to plastic.

- *Comments:* Nasal cannula should be stabilized when caring for a restless client.

  In adults, each liter increment increases FIO_2 approximately 3% to 4%, although there is wide variation.

  O_2 concentration depends on flow rate and client's own breathing pattern.

  New designs have cannula built into eyeglass frame or headband.

  Humidification not necessary for flow rates <3 L/min.

Simple Face Mask

- *Advantages:* With flow rates of 6 to 12 L/min in adult patients, O_2 concentrations of 35% to 50% can be achieved.

- *Disadvantages:* Lack of client tolerance results in inadequate therapy.

  May be uncomfortable since a tight seal must be maintained between face and mask—since mask usually cannot achieve a tight seal, FIO_2 varies.

  Mask may produce a pressure necrosis of the skin.

  Confines heat radiating from the face.

  Must be removed to eat or drink.

- *Comments:* Wash and dry patient's face often.

  Mask needs to fit snugly.

  Nasal cannula may be provided during meals.

  Watch for pressure necrosis at top of ears from elastic straps; may use gauze or other padding to alleviate this.

  In adult patient, at least 5 L/min flow is required to prevent accumulation of expired air in the mask with subsequent increase in inspired CO_2.

Non-rebreathing Mask

- *Advantages:* Bag provides O_2 reservoir.

  High concentrations of O_2 can be delivered—O_2 flows into bag and mask during inhalation; one valve prevents expired air from flowing back into bag, two others prevent inspiration of room air into mask.

  Concentrations of 60% to 90% can be achieved using flow rates of 10 to 15 L/min.

- *Disadvantages:* Same as for simple mask.

continues

Table 9-2 continued

    • *Comments:*   Same as for simple mask.
                                Flow rate must be sufficient to keep bag from collapsing during
                                inspiration.

Partial Rebreathing Mask
    • *Advantages:*   Similar to non-rebreathing mask, except concentrations of only 40%
                                to 60% can be achieved. Same mask as nonrebreathing but all three
valves are removed allowing some dilution of inhaled oxygen by
exhaled gas, therefore decreasing FIO_2.
Also air may be drawn into mask from exhalation ports.
    • *Disadvantages:* Same as for nonrebreathing mask.
    • *Comments:*   Same as for nonrebreathing mask.

Oxygen Conserving Cannula
    • *Advantages:*   Has a built-in reservoir that increases O_2 concentration delivered.
Allows patient to use lower flow, which may lower cost.
    • *Disadvantages:* Cannot be cleaned.
Manufacturer recommends changing cannula every week.
More expensive than standard cannulas.
    • *Comments:*   Client needs to nose breathe for reservoir to be effective.
Available in several styles, including pendant reservoir.
Inflation and deflation of reservoir can be seen.

Transtracheal Catheter
    • *Advantages:*   Lower O_2 flows can be used, allowing smaller portable systems and
lower cost.
May improve patient's self-image.
Eliminates nasal mucosal drying and irritation.
    • *Disadvantages:* Involves minor surgical procedure.
Requires intensive patient education (irrigation, cleaning, catheter
removal, and reinsertion).
Requires alert, oriented, compliant patient for use.

Tracheostomy Collar
    • *Advantages:*   Can deliver high humidity and O_2 via tracheostomy.
    • *Disadvantages:* Condensed fluid in tubing may drain into tracheostomy.
Secretions collect inside collar and around tracheostomy.
FIO_2 variable since collar does not fit tightly.
    • *Comments:*   Attaches to neck with elastic strap.
Should be removed and cleaned frequently.
Tubing should be drained frequently to prevent movement of
accumulated fluid into airway.

Tracheostomy T-Bar (T-Tube, Brigg's Adaptor)
    • *Advantages:*   Allows better O_2 and humidity delivery than tracheostomy collar.
Can be used with both endotracheal and tracheostomy tubes.
    • *Disadvantages:* Condensed fluid in tubing may drain into airway.
Needs to be removed for suctioning.
    • *Comments:*   May use swivel adapter through which suctioning can be done without
removing from supplemental O_2.

Table 9-2 continued

High Flow Devices
Venturi (Air Entrainment Mask)
- *Advantages:*   Can deliver precise concentrations of O_2.
  Lightweight plastic, fitted to face.
  Masks are available for delivery of 24% to 50% O_2.
  Adapters can be applied to increase humidification.
- *Disadvantages:* Mask is uncomfortable.
  Must be removed when client eats.
  Client can talk but voice may be muffled.
  Adapter must be changed to deliver higher concentrations of O_2.
- *Comments:*   Helpful for administering low, constant O_2 concentrations to clients
  with chronic CO_2 retention.
  Air entrainment ports must not be occluded.

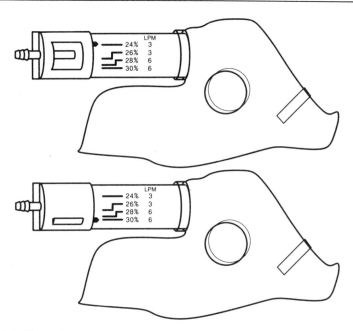

Figure 9-1 Air entrainment mask. Two views of the mask are shown. In the upper panel the mask is set to deliver 24% oxygen; note that the liter flow is indicated as 3 L/min and the entrainment opening is wide. In the lower panel, the mask is set to deliver 30% oxygen; the liter flow is now to be set at 6 L/min and the air entrainment opening is much smaller.

oxygen may cause or intensify hypoventilation). The Venturi mask allows one to deliver an accurate FIO_2 regardless of changes in the patient's ventilatory pattern. The use of a low flow device would have the potential risk of delivering a dangerously high or low FIO_2; the oxygen concentration delivered would increase as the patient's breathing became more shallow and would decrease if minute ventilation increased.

New Devices for Oxygen Delivery

Much of the new technology for oxygen flow delivery is aimed at lowering the oxygen flow requirements; the benefits can be financial as well as providing great patient convenience and therefore better compliance with the prescribed therapy. The types of devices developed to reduce the amount of oxygen used include reservoir-type cannulas (see Figure 9-2), transtracheal cannulas (see Figure 9-3) and intermittent demand flow systems. Devices to make the use of oxygen therapy more convenient or less conspicuous include transtracheal oxygen as well as cannulas built into the frames of eyeglasses and headbands.

Transtracheal oxygen has been receiving greater recognition in both the professional and lay news. Although it is well documented that transtracheal oxygen allows oxygenation at lower flows and often improves patient compliance with both oxygen and exercise programs, it is not without its problems. Patients may have problems maintaining the patency of the catheter (it may become obstructed

Figure 9-2 Oxygen conserving cannulas. These two special oxygen cannulas both contain reservoir systems so that the FIO_2 is increased at any given liter flow of oxygen.

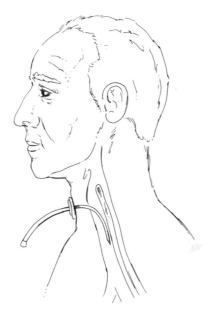

Figure 9-3 Transtracheal oxygen. The position of the transtracheal catheter is schematically depicted. The catheter is held in place by a small chain around the neck.

by "mucus balls"), and some have problems with the manual skills needed in the care of the catheter itself. Therefore, each patient needs to be assessed, in terms of physiologic need as well as ability to care for the catheter, to determine if transtracheal oxygen is appropriate.

OXYGEN THERAPY IN THE ACUTE SETTING

The approaches to oxygen therapy in the acute hospital setting vary. The differences in approach are necessary because of the variability in patient presentation. This section gives a general overview of oxygen therapy in several specific settings, ie, in emergency care of the trauma patient, in the care of the postoperative patient, and the care of the general medical adult or pediatric patient.

During transport and initial treatment of a major trauma victim, oxygen is usually delivered in high concentrations via mask. These patients are frequently severely hypoxemic, have decreased oxygen carrying capacity due to blood loss, and are not able to generate the normal cardiovascular response to increase oxygen delivery to the periphery. Concurrently, these patients are in a setting where they are being closely monitored. Should there be an adverse response to the high oxygen concentration, corrective resuscitative measures, such as intubation and ventilation, can be quickly instituted. As the patient is treated and stabilized, the delivered oxygen concentration is corrected so that adequate oxygen content is attained. (In some patients, the attainment of an adequate oxygen content may require transfusion.) In extreme cases, oxygen concentrations of 100% may be required for extended periods but the goal is to reduce the FIO_2 to less than 0.5 to avoid potential oxygen toxicity. As has been stated but can never be emphasized too much, the optimal oxygen concentration is the lowest one that will maintain an oxyhemoglobin saturation of 90% to 93%.

In the recovery room, oxygen is routinely administered to patients following general anesthesia. These patients are routinely hypoxemic, and the administration of oxygen is often considered normal recovery room procedure. The oxygen is often delivered via an aerosol mask (see discussion of aerosol therapy in Chapter 8), but nasal oxygen via cannula is also frequently given. The use of aerosol with the oxygen is thought to decrease laryngeal irritation subsequent to intubation and administration of dry gas during the operative procedure. In the later postoperative period, some decrease in arterial oxygen tension may be present, but it is usually not of sufficient magnitude to require oxygen therapy unless the patient has an underlying pulmonary problem or has developed a pulmonary complication.

In the general medical adult or pediatric patient population, oxygen is administered according to need as documented by arterial blood gas analysis or oximetry. If the patient was previously healthy, oxygen is frequently administered to maintain normal arterial oxygen tensions. If the patient has underlying chronic hypoxemia, which is more commonly seen in an adult, oxygen therapy is given to maintain the oxygen tension in the patient's usual treated chronic range. This range is usually in the 60s. Higher levels of the PaO_2 may put the patient at risk of decreased ventilatory drive with resulting hypoventilation and respiratory acidemia. It should be noted, however, that the determining factor of how much oxygen to give is the PaO_2 attained—NOT the flow rate administered. For example, one patient may require nasal oxygen at 1 L/min to attain a PaO_2 of 60 mm Hg, while another may require 4 L/min.

For all of these general medical adult and pediatric patients, nasal oxygen, via cannula, is the most common method of oxygen delivery. Some patients will require Venturi masks while others may require higher concentrations via partial or non-rebreathing masks.

CHRONIC HOME OXYGEN THERAPY

Chronic home oxygen therapy is prescribed for those patients in whom the underlying cause of the hypoxemia cannot be corrected. One must then treat the symptom by providing supplemental oxygen to correct the hypoxemia. Included in such a category are those patients with chronic pulmonary disease (chronic obstructive pulmonary disease, interstitial pulmonary fibrosis, cystic fibrosis, bronchopulmonary dysplasia), sleep apnea, and lung cancer. The Nocturnal Oxygen Therapy Trial (NOTT) in 1980 demonstrated the benefit of continuous oxygen therapy versus nocturnal oxygen for patients with chronic obstructive pulmonary disease and chronic hypoxemia. The benefits of continuous oxygen therapy include lower morbidity as well as mortality. Clinically, the sequelae of long-term chronic hypoxemia, eg, cor pulmonale, erythrocytosis and pulmonary hypertension, are reduced.

Prescription for Home Oxygen Therapy

The clinical picture of chronic hypoxemia occurs when hypoxemia develops slowly and persists over a long period of time. As the body attempts to compensate for the chronic hypoxemia, secondary erythrocytosis may occur. Concurrently, chronic hypoxemia may result in cardiovascular changes, including pulmonary hypertension, cor pulmonale, and right-sided heart failure. These secondary effects and symptoms associated with chronic hypoxemia are used, in addition to the actual arterial oxygen tension, as indications for chronic supplemental oxygen therapy (see Table 9-3).

Although the criteria for home oxygen therapy state that an arterial oxygen tension of 55 mm Hg or less is justification for initiating therapy, there are exceptions. For example, an arterial oxygen value slightly less than 55 mm Hg immediately following an acute illness is not necessarily an indication for chronic home oxygen therapy. Another common example is the patient with lung cancer with a PaO_2 of 55 mm Hg and whose shortness of breath is not relieved by oxygen. In both of these examples it may be inappropriate to prescribe continuous home oxygen. The decision of whether or not to prescribe home oxygen must be based on an assessment of the entire clinical picture, including evidence of cardiovascular decompensation, activity level, lifestyle, prognosis, and response to the oxygen therapy.

Prescriptions for use of supplemental oxygen therapy at home should be based upon studies to determine the minimal oxygen flow required to maintain the oxyhemoglobin saturation at or near 90% during rest, sleep, and with exertion. Individuals may require different flows during these various activities due to changes in their oxygenation as a result of modifications in the ventilation-perfusion characteristics in their lungs, alterations in cardiac output, or changes in their respiratory rate and/or respiratory pattern that affect their inspired oxygen concentration.

Table 9-3 Criteria for Chronic Home Oxygen Therapy

1. Patient has received optimal pharmacologic therapy and is in a chronic, stable state of his or her disease.
2. Patient has a primary pulmonary disease resulting in chronic hypoxemia. (Accepted primary diseases include obstructive pulmonary disease, diffuse interstitial lung disease, cystic fibrosis, bronchitis, and pulmonary neoplasm.)
3. Additionally, patients who demonstrate hypoxemia-related symptoms that improve with oxygen therapy may qualify; the signs and symptoms include:
   • pulmonary hypertension
   • recurring congestive heart failure due to cor pulmonale
   • insomnia/nocturnal restlessness
   • morning headache
   • erythrocytosis
   • impairment of cognition
4. Patient has resting room air arterial blood gas values as follows:
   PaO_2 <55 mm Hg or SaO_2 <88%
5. If patient's PaO_2 (SaO_2) is greater than 55 mm Hg (88%), chronic oxygen therapy may be indicated if there is evidence of dependent edema suggestive of congestive heart failure or cor pulmonale ("P" pulmonale on EKG) or erythrocytosis with hematocrit >56%
6. Intermittent oxygen, ie, with exercise and/or with sleep, is indicated if PaO_2 decreases to <55 mm Hg or SaO_2 decreases to <88%; for exercise oxygen, an improvement in exercise tolerance should be demonstrated on oxygen, or the oxygen should have been prescribed as part of an exercise-rehabilitation plan.

Home Oxygen Delivery Systems

The prescription of supplemental oxygen for home use began as early as the 1950s but its widespread use has flourished in the past two decades. As a result, the technology of available delivery systems has improved and continues to strive toward systems that are more convenient as well as functional. Table 9-4 lists the home oxygen delivery systems available, including advantages and disadvantages for each. These systems are usually rented from an oxygen or medical supply company. The company provides instructions concerning how to use the system, how to care for the equipment, how to order refills, and what safety precautions are necessary (eg, no smoking with oxygen on, storing oxygen preferably at least 15 feet from an open flame or heat source). For all oxygen systems used in the home, up to 50 feet of connecting tubing may be used to facilitate ambulation without necessitating moving the oxygen source.

Cost of Home Oxygen

Charges for supplemental oxygen vary with geographic location and the type of delivery system used. The monthly cost is substantial, even when prescribed

Table 9-4 Home Oxygen Delivery Systems

Liquid Oxygen (Reservoir/Portable Unit)

- *Advantages:*   Portable unit can be filled from reservoir.
                   Shoulder pack portable unit gives 6- to 8-hour supply at 2 L/min and is
                   relatively light.
                   Several sizes of reservoirs and portable units are available. Reservoir
                   movable from room to room.
- *Disadvantages:* Generally more expensive.
                   Not available everywhere; generally limited to urban areas.
                   Ambulatory status must be demonstrated.
- *Comments:*   As liquid warms to gas, some is vented from system.
                   In summer evaporation is accelerated and may decrease O_2 supply
                   available, especially for portable unit.
                   Most patients need to have portable unit on a cart.

Compressed Tank Oxygen (H or J Tank/E or A Cylinder for Portable)

- *Advantages:*   Available in most areas.
- *Disadvantages:* The client needs to store four or five large cylinders in the home to
                   have 7- to 10-day supply.
                   Portable cylinder on cart is bulky and heavy.
- *Comments:*   Caution is needed to prevent cylinders from falling, since they are
                   high pressure systems.
                   E cylinder will last four to five hours at 2 L/min.
                   H or J tank at 2 L/min flow will last about 50 hours.
                   Some smaller tanks (D or M) may be used that can be refilled from
                   large cylinders that are at least half full. They weigh about 10 lb and
                   can be carried on a shoulder strap.

Concentrator or Extractor (E or A Cylinder for Portable)

- *Advantages:*   Unit is on wheels; can be moved from room to room.
                   Provides continuous oxygen without periodic deliveries.
                   Compact. Excellent for rural or homebound clients.
- *Disadvantages:* Noisy.
                   May increase client's electricity bill by $20 to $30 per month, which is
                   not reimbursable by insurance.
                   Greater than 4 L/min flow results in significant decrease in oxygen
                   concentration delivered.
                   Some units generate a significant amount of heat.
                   Not good in areas without reliable electrical source.
- *Comments:*   Concentrator should be kept in room other than bedroom if noise
                   disturbs sleep.
                   Some models available in approximately suitcase size; can be used
                   with AC or DC power for travel.
                   Enrichers are a type of concentrator. The enricher provides a high
                   humidity gas (versus dry), but the oxygen concentration is significantly
                   reduced; to equate a normal delivery of 2 L/min, the oxygen enricher
                   must deliver 4 L/min.

at low flow rates. Thus it is imperative that oxygen only be prescribed for patients who have an indicated need and at the lowest flow necessary.

With a prescription for home oxygen and documentation of patient need, most insurance companies will reimburse for approximately 80% of the cost of home oxygen. Many, like Medicare, require at least annual documentation of arterial blood gases and/or oximetry studies demonstrating the patient's continued need for oxygen. In some cases, the insurance provider may choose to purchase equipment, such as a concentrator, rather than pay a monthly rental fee. Some providers also have a limit on the total amount of oxygen coverage. It is advisable to check with the patient's health insurance provider to determine if there is coverage for home oxygen reimbursement or any restrictions on coverage.

Travel with Supplemental Oxygen

Patients who use home oxygen should be encouraged to remain active and to travel normally. If travel is to be via automobile, arrangements should be made for oxygen in the car during the trip as well as at the destination point. Oxygen supply companies may often assist in these arrangements. If a patient wishes to travel by airplane, the airlines require notification of the need for in-flight oxygen when reservations are made.

Since the airplane cabins are pressurized to the equivalent of an elevation of 7000 or 8000 feet, patients who use chronic supplemental oxygen should have oxygen provided during flight. The oxygen system provided by the airline must be used during the flight. Patients may not use their own oxygen systems during the flight because they are not properly pressurized. Most airlines will allow portable reservoirs (liquid or tank) to be carried in the baggage compartment for subsequent use at the point of destination as long as they are empty and the valves are left open during the flight. Arrangements must be made for oxygen in the airport during any layovers between flights.

Travel with oxygen can also be arranged on a bus, train or boat. Generally speaking, patients should be encouraged to avoid prolonged exposure to high elevations during travel. If the high elevation cannot be avoided, patients should have instructions from their physicians on how much to increase their oxygen flows.

POTENTIAL HAZARDS OF OXYGEN THERAPY

While beneficial in the treatment of hypoxemia in acute and chronic settings, oxygen therapy is not without potential problems. These can include combustion, ventilatory depression, and oxygen toxicity.

Combustion

As a combustible gas, oxygen supports combustion and increases the rate of burning. Oxygen is neither explosive nor will it burn spontaneously. Smoking must be prohibited near areas of oxygen use. In the hospital setting, NO SMOKING signs must be clearly posted in areas where oxygen is used. Patients using oxygen at home are cautioned not to smoke or to store oxygen reservoirs near sources of open flame (ie, waterheaters with pilots or fireplaces). Many patients who use oxygen at home cook with gas stoves without any problems but are cautioned not to allow the oxygen tubing to come in contact with the stove surface or flame.

Ventilatory Depression

High oxygen concentrations may prove harmful to individuals who demonstrate chronic carbon dioxide (CO_2) retention. Normally, CO_2 accumulation, as a product of metabolism, is the primary stimulus for ventilation (refer to Chapter 5, Ventilatory Control). Patients with chronic CO_2 retention will have a decreased ventilatory response to increases in arterial CO_2 tension. Instead, the hypoxemic stimulus via peripheral chemoreceptors becomes a significant determinant of respiratory drive. In this situation, elevation of the PaO_2 to high levels, usually greater than 60 mm Hg, may abolish the hypoxic stimulus and aggravate the decreased alveolar ventilation.

In patients with chronic CO_2 retention, oxygen administration should be initiated at low flows and adjusted on the basis of arterial blood gas values. Pulse oximetry may be misleading in these situations because $PaCO_2$ is not measured by oximetry and changes in PCO_2 can shift the position of the oxyhemoglobin curve. Mental status and vital signs should also be assessed frequently to give indications of any developing problems.

Oxygen Toxicity

Pulmonary oxygen toxicity may result from prolonged exposure to high inspired oxygen levels. The development of oxygen toxicity is determined by client tolerance, exposure time, and effective dose delivery. High inspired oxygen concentrations (>50%) may inactivate pulmonary surfactant and lead to the development of the adult respiratory distress syndrome (ARDS).

Early manifestations of oxygen toxicity are a reduced vital capacity, cough, substernal chest pain, nausea and vomiting, paresthesias, nasal stuffiness, sore throat, and malaise. The later stages of oxygen toxicity affect the alveolar-capillary gas exchange unit, causing edema and production of copious sputum. The end stage of oxygen toxicity is progressive fibrosis of the lung. In infants, the retinal capillaries are easily damaged by hyperoxia resulting in retrolental fibroplasia.

Prevention of oxygen toxicity is important for the client receiving oxygen. The amount of oxygen administered should be just enough to maintain the arterial oxygen pressure (PaO_2) within a normal or acceptable range for the client. Arterial blood gases should be monitored frequently to evaluate the effectiveness of therapy as well as to guide the tapering of supplemental oxygen. A safe limit of oxygen concentrations has not yet been established; however, most clinicians consider levels above 50% to 60% to be potentially toxic. Generally, levels of 40% and below are considered relatively nontoxic.

SUGGESTED READING

Campbell EJ, Baker D, Crites-Silver P. Subjective effects of humidification of oxygen for delivery by nasal cannula. *Chest.* 1988;93:289–293.

Fulmer JD, Snider GL. ACCP-NHLBI National Conference of Oxygen Therapy. *Chest.* 1984;86:234–247.

Hoffman LA, Wesmiller SW. Home oxygen. Transtracheal and other options. *Am J Nurs.* 1988;88:464–469.

Kacmarek RM, Stoller JK. *Current Respiratory Care.* Philadelphia: BC Decker Inc; 1988.

Massaro D. Oxygen: toxicity and tolerance. *Hosp Prac.* 1986;15:95–101.

Nocturnal Oxygen Therapy Group. Continuous or nocturnal oxygen therapy in hypoxemic chronic obstructive lung disease. *Ann Int Med.* 1980;93:391–398.

Openbrier DR, Fuoss C, Mall CC. What patients on home oxygen therapy want to know. *Am J Nurs.* 1988;88:198–202.

Openbrier DR, Hoffman LA, Wesmiller SW. Home oxygen therapy. Evaluation and prescription. *Amer J Nurs.* 1988;88:192–197.

Tremper JC, Campbell SC, Kelly SA. Reliability of the oxymatic electronic oxygen conserver. *Am Rev Resp Dis.* 1987;135:A194.

chapter 10

Chest Physiotherapy

Dyspnea and ineffective airway clearance are significant problems to many patients with a variety of medical diagnoses. Chest physiotherapy techniques are frequently incorporated into the total therapeutic regimen as a means of improving airway clearance and assisting the patient to control dyspnea. This chapter discusses modified breathing patterns (hyperinflation techniques, controlled breathing, and inspiratory muscle training), therapeutic cough techniques, and postural drainage, percussion, and vibration as part of chest physiotherapy.

MODIFIED BREATHING PATTERNS

Modifications in breathing patterns designed to improve ventilatory efficiency or increase the patient's comfort level can be achieved by a variety of techniques. An understanding of the patient's altered lung mechanics is needed to ensure selection of the proper technique; interventions vary between the type and severity of mechanical dysfunction.

Hyperinflation Techniques

Hyperinflation therapy encompasses any technique used to encourage patients to take deeper than normal inspirations so that their tidal volume increases to nearly their inspiratory capacity. The primary reasons for using hyperinflation are to prevent or treat atelectasis with its concomitant alterations in gas exchange, surfactant function, and the work of breathing, as well as to improve cough effectiveness.

Voluntary Deep Breathing Maneuver

The simplest way to accomplish hyperinflation is through voluntary deep breathing. This method requires coaching by the clinician to ensure that the patient is performing the technique effectively; the inspiration should be done slowly up to the maximal inflation achievable, which is then held for several seconds as tolerated by the patient. This technique is referred to as sustained maximal inflation (SMI). Slow inspiration achieves better distribution of the volume inhaled because areas with decreased compliance supplied by narrowed airways are allowed to fill.

Many patients who would benefit from hyperinflation are unable to perform the maneuver in response to simple verbal coaching. An example is when lower chest movement is restricted due to pain related to muscular strain, pleuritis, or incisional pain. One successful technique to localize chest movement and improve lower thoracic expansion is to provide proprioceptive feedback. The clinician places his or her hands on the lower lateral chest. As the patient breathes normally, slightly greater pressure is applied to the chest wall during expiration; the hands maintain contact with the chest wall during inspiration but the pressure is released. The clinician will soon feel a change in the patient's ventilatory pattern with increased expansion at the lower chest. The patient is then encouraged to "inhale slowly and deeply, pushing my hands out." Many patients will spontaneously say that this technique helps them take a deep breath. A variation is to have the patient yawn; a yawn is actually a deep breath and a breath hold.

The SMI technique is most commonly associated with the postoperative setting. It is particularly emphasized for patients at greatest risk of developing pulmonary complications because of type of surgery, age, smoking history, and preoperative lung function. Elderly patients who have COPD or who smoke and patients who have had upper abdominal or thoracic surgery are at greatest risk for postoperative pulmonary complications. Generally speaking, hyperinflation therapy is scheduled as 5 to 10 SMI maneuvers every one to two hours in the immediate postoperative period (up to 24 hours); it may be done less frequently (every 3 to 4 hours) for several days until the patient is ambulating freely. The optimal frequency of postoperative deep breathing has not been clearly determined.

Patients who have chronic restrictive ventilatory defects breathe with a rapid, shallow respiratory pattern. Due to low lung volumes and functional residual capacity, there may be an increased tendency toward development of atelectasis in these patients. To expect such a patient to use a respiratory pattern of slow, repetitive, deep breaths is unrealistic and can increase their work of breathing. Therefore, it is preferable to encourage patients with chronic restrictive ventilatory defects to take periodic deep breaths with an inspiratory hold up to their tolerance or to yawn intermittently to achieve hyperinflation.

Intermittent Positive Pressure Breathing (IPPB)

Intermittent positive pressure breathing devices have been used to promote lung inflation by applying positive pressure to the airways. However, except in situations of severe neuromuscular disease, IPPB offers no advantage over other techniques for hyperinflation therapy. IPPB is an expensive therapy, considering the initial cost of the device itself and, in the hospital setting, the continued cost of a qualified clinician to administer the therapy. The expense, when considered in conjunction with the potential problems, has led many institutions to abandon IPPB as a viable routine hyperinflation therapy.

Problems that may be encountered with the use of IPPB for hyperinflation therapy include the following:

- Patients with decreased lung or chest compliance will not achieve adequate lung expansion without using pressures greater than 15 cm H_2O.
- Gastric dilatation may occur, especially when pressures of 15 cm H_2O or greater are used.
- Volumes achieved depend on compliance of the patient's lungs and thorax as well as the patient's ability and willingness to cooperate with instructions.
- Patients with increased lung compliance are susceptible to barotrauma as well as changes in hemodynamic status from transmission of pressures from the lung to other thoracic structures (ie, major blood vessels in heart).

Incentive Spirometry (IS)

Incentive spirometry (IS) has become a widely used and popular method of encouraging patients to perform voluntary deep breathing. The IS devices provide visual feedback of the inspiratory volume that has been achieved. Some devices have the added feature of providing feedback concerning the rate of inspiratory flow to encourage the patient to do a slow maximal inflation.

The preferred volume oriented IS devices usually have some type of a bellows apparatus so that visual feedback to the patient is given based upon the volume inhaled (see Figure 10-1). Most also have a method of marking the volume to be achieved, which provides added incentive. In perioperative situations, a preoperative volume, if known, can be marked on the chamber for comparison with postoperative results. Generally, it can be expected that patients in the early postoperative period should be able to achieve between one-half to three-fourths of their preoperative volume, making allowances for pain, position, and the type of surgery.

When using IS devices that are flow-oriented only, patients must be properly instructed to achieve an SMI rather than merely inhaling quickly. Some flow-oriented devices contain Ping-Pong balls inside chambers. Patients using these

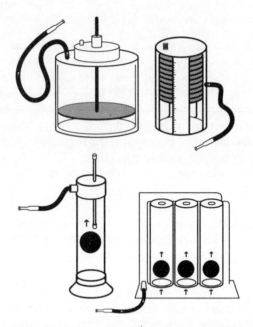

Figure 10-1 Incentive spirometry devices. Several incentive spirometry devices are depicted. The two at the top are volume devices; the two at the bottom are flow devices.

---

flow devices need to be instructed to keep the Ping-Pong balls elevated as long as possible, not merely to raise the Ping-Pong balls to the top of the chamber (see Figure 10-1).

Regardless of the type of IS device used, patient instruction is necessary. Each inhalation maneuver should be preceded by normal exhalation, not forced exhalation. Exhalation is followed by slow inhalation, as deep as possible, with a breath hold at full-lung inhalation for several seconds to the person's tolerance.

While IS devices have become more popular as a method of promoting hyperinflation, it must be remembered that patients will continue to require instruction in deep breathing as well as some degree of assistance and encouragement in the use of the device. The patient's ability and understanding of the proper use of the IS device must be consistently monitored by the clinician.

Continuous Positive Airway Pressure (CPAP)

Another technique designed to achieve hyperinflation is the intermittent use of continuous positive airway pressure (CPAP) administered by mask. This technique is used in some institutions to prevent or treat postoperative atelectasis. It has not been established whether CPAP is more advantageous than other therapies for the prevention and treatment of atelectasis. Continuous positive airway pressure does offer one advantage in that a cooperative patient is not required for its use. (See Chapter 14 for a general discussion of CPAP.)

Controlled Breathing Techniques

Patients with obstructive ventilatory defects tend to breathe at relatively slow respiratory rates due to a prolonged exhalation phase. Many develop severe dyspnea in situations requiring an increased respiratory rate, eg, exertion, emotional stress, or excitement. Often the dyspnea escalates until the patient is in a panic state.

Controlled breathing, or breathing-retraining techniques, are often used for patients with chronic airways obstruction (CAO) as part of rehabilitation therapy, ie, as a method of preventing or controlling the dyspnea or panic reactions. Therefore, labeling the techniques breathing exercises is misleading because that terminology often implies increased energy output and fatigue to patients. Rather, the emphasis should be on relaxed breathing with slow exhalation; the patient should be doing less work, not more!

The primary techniques taught to achieve control are pursed lip breathing (PLB) and diaphragmatic breathing. With either technique, the goal is to assist the patient to slow the respiratory rate. If the patient with CAO breathes rapidly, air trapping ensues. The resting lung volume increases and the diaphragm flattens and becomes less efficient for lung expansion. By breathing slowly and providing adequate time for exhalation, the patient decreases his or her resting lung volume. The diaphragm thus is in a more domed position at end exhalation and becomes a more efficient inspiratory muscle. The end result is a maintenance of alveolar ventilation without an increase in the work of breathing during times of stress.

Whichever technique is taught, it is helpful for the patient to practice during comfortable breathing so that the techniques can be more easily used during periods of increased respiratory rate, eg, with exertion. The techniques can help in preventing dyspnea during activities or in recovering from acute episodes of dyspnea.

Pursed Lip Breathing

Pursed lip breathing is accomplished with slow exhalation through pursed lips. Many patients with CAO can be observed spontaneously utilizing PLB as a physiologic adaptation to their airflow obstruction. In addition to helping the patient slow the respiratory rate, PLB, by increasing airway pressure, is thought to decrease the compression of airways and subsequent air trapping.

To achieve maximal benefit from PLB, the patient is instructed to begin by taking a slow breath and exhaling slowly through pursed lips. At the same time, the patient should count to himself so that the count during exhalation is roughly twice the count during inhalation. The clinician should caution patients that the counts will be shorter when initiated during periods of dyspnea; as they are relaxing and catching their breath, the count may then be extended. If a patient with CAO finds it uncomfortable to do PLB, the result may actually be an increase in the work of breathing and sensation of dyspnea; in such situations, the use of PLB should not be required.

Diaphragmatic Breathing

In the past, this technique stressed exaggerated abdominal movement with no upper chest wall movement during the ventilatory cycle. The assumption was that the observed movement of the abdomen was a direct reflection of the movement of the diaphragm. Patients were taught that the abdominal movement meant they were breathing correctly, ie, they were using their diaphragm and not their accessory muscles. Based on present knowledge of respiratory muscle function, this assumption is no longer valid. As discussed in Chapter 2, diaphragmatic contraction may move the anterior chest wall as well as the abdomen; it therefore does not make sense to tell patients not to move their chests during inhalation. Also, with severe end-stage CAO the lungs are so hyperinflated that the accessory muscles must be used. Another problem with emphasizing abdominal movement is that patients so instructed tend to intentionally push the abdominal wall out during inhalation and perform a Valsalva maneuver; during exhalation they use abdominal contractions. These two maneuvers increase the work of breathing and worsen dyspnea. It is important to recognize that most patients with CAO do breathe with the diaphragm. If the patient is observed during relaxed breathing, the clinician will see a passive bulging of the abdomen during inspiration.

Today it is recognized that concentration on a slow expiratory phase is the best way to maintain diaphragmatic excursion in the patient with CAO. With this change in emphasis, many clinicians no longer use the phrase diaphragmatic breathing but simply refer to a controlled breathing pattern. The technique for a controlled pattern is similar to hyperinflation. The hands are placed on the lower, lateral chest wall or on the abdomen just below the sternum. Gradually increasing pressure is applied during exhalation and the patient is verbally encouraged to breathe out slowly. When the patient begins to inhale, pressure is released. Diaphragmatic or controlled breathing may be used in conjunction with PLB. Both may successfully be applied to aid the patient to prevent or control dyspnea and can be incorporated into an overall rehabilitative plan that includes pacing activities, relaxation therapy, nutrition counseling, and progressive exercise.

Inspiratory Muscle Training (IMT)

The effectiveness of retraining the respiratory muscles through PLB and breathing exercises is often questioned. A newer technique, inspiratory muscle training (IMT), is specifically aimed at increasing the strength and endurance of the inspiratory muscles.

The devices used for this technique produce gradations of resistance to inspiration (see Figure 10-2). The patient begins training with low levels of resistance and gradually, over weeks, increases the amount of resistance. As the resistance increases, so does the work that the inspiratory muscles must perform. As strength and endurance improve, the patient should have increased ability to sustain ventilation during periods of increased stress. Studies have demonstrated that the use of IMT increases exercise performance in patients with CAO.

THERAPEUTIC COUGH TECHNIQUES

Cough, as a normal lung defense mechanism, was discussed in Chapter 1. In the clinical setting, assessment of cough ability is important to indicate appropriate interventions that will enhance cough effectiveness and airway clearance. It is no longer sufficient to simply instruct the patient to take a deep breath and cough. The approach to cough must be adapted to the specific problems presented by the individual patient. General assessment factors and specific clinical conditions that may affect cough effectiveness are shown in Table 10-1.

If thick sputum is determined to be part of the problem leading to decreased cough effectiveness, measures aimed at changing the characteristics of the sputum to make it more easily expectorated can be initiated. The most common and effective measure is to first make sure that the patient has normal hydration. There is no evidence that over-hydration aids in liquefying secretions but adequate hydration is beneficial. Bland aerosol therapy, or in extreme cases mucolytic aerosol therapy, may be considered as an adjunct measure.

Prior to a cough maneuver, the patient should be assisted in taking as deep a breath as possible. The hyperinflation techniques, as previously discussed, should be used to help the patient achieve increased inspiratory volume. For patients in which pain is a limiting factor, pain medication should be administered so it will be maximally effective at the time of cough instruction.

Many patients require some modification of the expiratory phase of the cough and/or cough augmentation techniques to achieve adequate explosive flows. Sev-

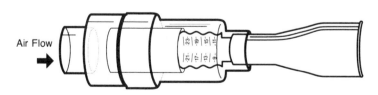

Air Flow

Figure 10-2 Inspiratory muscle trainer.

Table 10-1 Assessment of Cough

General Area of Assessment	Clinical Factors
1. Presence of adequate cough reflex	Sedation Narcotic administration Anesthesia Lung transplantation (loss of vagal innervation to transplanted lung)
2. Mucus transport	Increased volume of secretions Increased vicosity of secretions Impaired ciliary function

3. Ability to take a deep breath	Decreased inspiratory muscle force
	  • Pain
	  • Neuromuscular diagnosis with decreased strength
	  • Malnourishment
	Chest wall stiff
	  • Ankylosing spondylitis
	  • Obesity
	  • Kyphoscoliosis
	Chest wall unstable
	  • Flail chest
	Lung stiff
	  • Parenchymal disease (ARDS, interstitial fibrosis, consolidation)
	  • Pleural disease (Pleural effusion, pneumothorax, pleural scarring)
	Unable to follow directions
	  • Unconscious or decreased mental status
	  • Language barrier

4. Ability to generate high flow and velocity	Low lung recoil
	  • Inability to take deep breath
	  • Pulmonary emphysema
	Increased expiratory airway resistance
	  • Bronchospasm
	  • Bronchial wall edema/scarring
	  • Secretions
	  • Neoplasm
	Decreased expiratory muscle force
	  • Pain
	  • Malnutrition
	  • Fatigue
	  • Paralysis
	  • Neuromuscular disease/weakness
	Unable to follow directions

eral cough techniques may need to be evaluated until one is found to be effective. The techniques are listed in Table 10-2, as well as clinical situations in which they may be useful. Frequently several techniques may be used in combination; for example, end-expiratory cough followed by cascade cough.

In many instances these modified cough techniques may stimulate a normal cough and the patient should be instructed not to suppress the cough if it occurs. In some patients, the techniques move mucus toward the central airways even when the cough is non-productive; in such situations it is not uncommon that the cough will be productive at a later time, sometimes as much as 45 minutes to an hour later.

POSTURAL DRAINAGE, PERCUSSION, AND VIBRATION

Airway clearance may be facilitated by postural drainage alone or in combination with percussion and/or vibration. The addition of these techniques to a patient's treatment regimen must be individualized and evaluated for continuation or modification. In general, start with simpler techniques, such as modified cough with deep breathing, before moving on to these more difficult and time-consuming therapies. Fatigue is a common sequela of patients for whom postural drainage, percussion, and vibration are prescribed. This complaint is understandable when considering that a session of postural drainage, percussion, and vibration, if preceded by an aerosol treatment, can take up to an hour or longer. Fatigue not only makes it less likely that the patient will comply with the therapy, but it can also contribute to a decreased ability to clear secretions from the airways. Therefore, drainage routines must be evaluated and eliminated from the regimen if they are not productive.

Postural drainage is often combined with chest percussion and vibration. This combination is frequently called the ketchup bottle treatment; when you tilt the bottle and the ketchup does not come out, you shake and pound the bottle to loosen it. The rationale for adding percussion and vibration to postural drainage is that vibrations of the chest wall enhance movement of secretions from the area being drained.

Postural Drainage

The basic principle of postural drainage is to place the patient in various positions to utilize gravity to enhance drainage of airways. There are 12 basic positions used in performing postural drainage, each specific to a distinct lung area (see Figure 10-3). The outlined positions are based on normal airway anatomy. Many patients do not require postural drainage of all areas, eg, the ambu-

Table 10-2 Cough Techniques

Cough Technique: Cascade Cough (Normal Cough)
How To Teach: Instruct patient to take a deep breath, followed by a succession of coughs (usually 3 to 4) until it feels as if all the air has been emptied out of the lungs. Repeat several times.
Clinical Indications: Any patient, especially as an initial maneuver.

Cough Technique: Huff Cough
How to Teach: Technique is a modification of the cascade but is performed without closing the glottis; patient performs forced exhalation with mouth open, resulting in a "huff" sound rather than a sharp cough sound. Clinician usually needs to demonstrate the technique.
Clinical Indications:
1. Patient who demonstrates an extreme laryngeal maneuver during cough that results in gagging, squeaky, or high-pitched cough; patient complains of rawness of throat.
2. Patient with compliant airways, ie, sounds like expiratory flow stops due to airway collapse.
3. Postoperative patients who are afraid of cascade cough.

Cough Technique: End-Expiratory Cough
How to Teach: Instruct patient to take several deep inhalations each followed by a prolonged, slow exhalation, through pursed lips if it helps. After three or four repetitions, instruct patient to inhale deeply, exhale to point below normal resting volume, and then cough before inhaling again. Observe to be sure patient does not inhale before coughing.
Clinical Indications: Bronchiectatic conditions, including cystic fibrosis and chronic bronchitis.

Cough Technique: Augmented Cough
How to Teach: Three variations of the augmented cough may be used.
1. Fold a large towel lengthwise in thirds and wrap around the chest with ends crossed in front; pull the ends tightly around the chest during cough.
2. Place hands on lateral chest walls and maintain contact during inhalation; then as patient begins cough, abruptly compress chest wall (lateral chest wall rib spring). Note: It is important to maintain contact with the chest wall during inspiration and not to allow hands to slap or hit the chest.
3. Flat hand is placed on upper abdomen, below xyphoid, with other hand placed on patient's shoulder. As patient coughs, the abdomen is compressed and patient is flexed forward, if possible. As abdomen is compressed, the diaphragm is forced upward, thus increasing expiratory flow.
Clinical Indications: Towel technique—chest wall pain, ie, rib fracture, pleuritis, thoracic surgery. Rib spring technique—fatigue or muscle weakness. Abdominal thrust technique—neuromuscular disease, spinal cord injury or paralysis.

---

latory patient who only requires postural drainage of lower lobes or the patient being treated for middle lobe consolidation. Often the positions require modification due to structural anatomic changes, eg, after surgery or any process resulting in scarring and distortion. It is important to assess which postural drainage positions are necessary or most effective. When dealing with structural

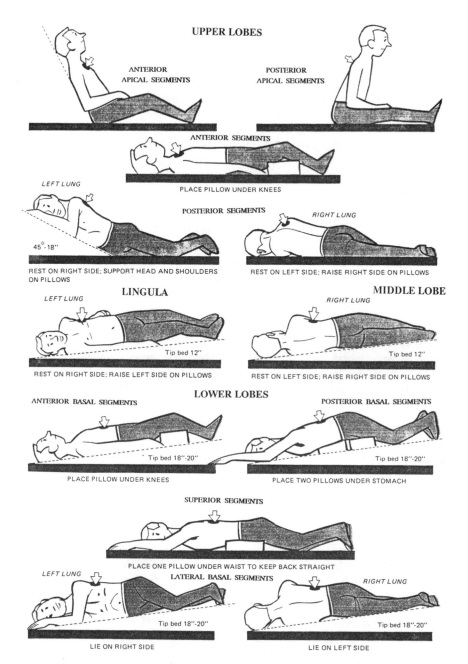

Figure 10-3 Postural drainage positions. The arrows depict the areas over which percussion and vibration are done. *Source:* Reprinted from *Instructor's Guide: Chronic Lung Disease*, ed 2 (p 12) by HD Sigmon with permission of Appleton & Lange, © 1979.

changes of the airways, a chest radiograph or subjective feedback from the patient often can assist in determining the most productive position for drainage.

When postural drainage is done without percussion or vibration, the patient should be in each indicated position for at least five minutes. During the last minute of the drainage, in each position, the patient is instructed to breathe deeply followed by a prolonged exhalation and end-expiratory cough; this breathing maneuver should be repeated several times. Following each position, if cough has not been productive, the patient should return to a sitting position and intentionally cough.

Percussion

Percussion is accomplished by cupping over the area to be drained in a rapid, rhythmic manner for approximately one minute. The hand is held to produce a cup rather than striking the chest wall with a flat palm. The sound produced should be hollow, not a sharp slapping sound. If the chest is slapped, not cupped, the vibrations do not penetrate the chest wall and will not result in the desired effect. In addition, the slapping is uncomfortable for the patient. Percussion should always be done through a layer of clothing, but if the layer is too thick, such as a towel, it can dampen the vibrations. Finally, great force is not necessary to create vibrations that penetrate the chest. The cupping should be accomplished by flexion and extension of the wrists rather than movement of the entire arm. Performed correctly, percussion should not cause discomfort for the patient.

There are mechanical percussors available, primarily for use in institutional settings. The percussors are either powered by electricity or are pneumatic devices powered by compressed air. As with the manual method of percussion, when the caregiver uses a mechanical percussor there should be one layer of clothing between the chest wall and the percussor. During percussion the device should be placed firmly against the chest wall and should not be allowed to "bang" against the patient's chest. Studies have not demonstrated significant differences in effectiveness between mechanical percussors and manual percussion.

Vibration

Vibration of the area to be drained follows percussion. Fine vibrations are set up in the chest at the same time that the chest is being compressed by the hands. Vibration is accomplished by placing flat hands on the patient's chest with arms extended but elbows not locked. The patient is instructed to take a deep breath in and breathe out as slowly as possible. For the duration of the slow exhalation, the chest is vibrated with a fine tremulous movement generated in the shoulder and upper arm. Simultaneously, compression of the chest wall increases gradually until exhalation ends. This maneuver is repeated 3 to 4 times over the area being drained. The patient should be instructed to cough following the vibration if a spontaneous cough has not already been produced. Many patients will require assistance to an upright position to cough and expectorate.

Indications for Postural Drainage, Percussion, and Vibration

Initially, the clinician should determine whether the patient is likely to benefit from postural drainage, with or without percussion and vibration. Too often these measures are ordered and instituted as prophylaxis for pulmonary complications; the effects of the prophylactic use of these therapies has not been documented.

Patients who demonstrate the greatest benefit from postural drainage are those with chronic airway obstruction and large sputum production (>30 cc/day). Patients with cystic fibrosis as well as those with bronchiectasis or chronic bronchitis are potential candidates for this therapy. Studies of patients with cystic fibrosis indicate that exercise or such interventions as end-expiratory or huff coughing may be as beneficial as postural drainage. Postural drainage with percussion and vibration has also been shown to be beneficial for patients with acute atelectatic changes. Drainage techniques are also believed by some clinicians to benefit intubated patients who have compromised mucociliary clearance mechanisms, theoretically a result of bypassing upper airways defenses; this has not been proven in studies.

Evaluation of the effectiveness of postural drainage should not be limited solely to the volume of sputum produced during the therapy. Frequently patients have enhanced expectoration of sputum in one to two hours following the drainage procedure, probably as a result of movement of secretions from smaller, distal airways to large airways where they may be more easily coughed out. Spirometry and flow-volume curves are also used to evaluate the effect of postural drainage.

Special Considerations in the Acute-Care Setting

In some clinical situations, the patient cannot tolerate a Trendelenburg position or percussion of the chest wall. In some cases these therapies may be contraindicated. The head-down positions and forced cough are not appropriate for patients with increased intracranial pressure or patients who have had eye surgery. Obesity or unstable vital signs may make the head-down positions intolerable. Modifications in the acute-care setting include incorporation of the drainage positions into the turning schedule, omitting some positions from the therapy, or changing the degree of head-down positioning so that the head and upper chest are not severely dependent. Percussion and/or vibration are also generally contraindicated in patients with rib fractures or pulmonary hemorrhage.

Hypoxemia can be accentuated during postural drainage due to alterations in ventilation-perfusion matching with positioning. For example, in patients with a unilateral lung process, a decreased oxygen saturation would be expected when the diseased lung is placed in a dependent position. Supplemental oxygen administration may need to be instituted or increased during postural drainage to maintain adequate saturations. Monitoring oxygen saturations with an oximeter is beneficial, when the equipment is available, to ensure oxygenation is maintained during the postural drainage therapy. For patients who are intubated and not able to breathe spontaneously, a self-inflating resuscitation bag connected to oxygen can be used to deep breathe the patient, as well as to provide adequate oxygenation.

Percussion and vibration done in conjunction with postural drainage has been shown to cause bronchospasm in patients with reactive airways disease; therefore, this therapy should be avoided in patients with acute bronchospasm. When postural drainage, percussion, or vibration is required for patients with stable reactive airways disease, it should only be performed following administration of an inhaled bronchodilator to minimize any bronchospastic response.

Special Considerations in the Home Care Setting

Patients with chronic bronchitis, bronchiectasis, or cystic fibrosis may perform postural drainage, percussion, and vibration at home as a routine part of their therapeutic regimen. Some of the special considerations discussed for the acute care setting carry over to the home environment.

For positioning, a tilt board or table may be helpful; many patients prefer simply using multiple pillows or cushions to attain the necessary tilt. For percussion and vibration in the home setting, a second person is required or a mechanical percussor may be used. Several commercial percussors, developed specifically for this therapy, are available. Another effective approach is to add a strap to a massager (see Figure 10-4). The massagers are light and allow the patient to treat posterior as well as anterior lung areas without assistance. If a massager is used, the strength of the vibration against the chest should be strong enough to interrupt the patient's normal voice pattern.

Many patients find that they are able to maintain themselves by performing their pulmonary hygiene measures in the early morning and again approximately an hour prior to sleep. As in the acute setting, the therapy is performed approx-

Figure 10-4 Massager unit. Picture demonstrates how a strap can be attached to a hand-held massager unit for self-administered vibration during postural drainage. The position depicted shows upper lobe drainage, but the same technique can be used for all drainage positions.

imately 15 to 30 minutes after inhaled bronchodilator administration. Clinicians should teach home patients to maintain adequate hydration. If any drainage position is noted to be especially productive of sputum, drainage therapy to that area should be repeated. Patients at home are taught to examine their expectorated mucus and, if changes are noted that are indicative of an infection, ie, a change in color, amount, or consistency, to immediately call their physician or nurse; in some cases patients are taught to immediately begin a course of broad-spectrum antibiotics if signs of infection are noted.

Evaluation of the effectiveness of drainage techniques used in the home setting is very important. Patients may be taught to evaluate the benefit-to-risk or convenience ratio of the therapies applied. Some patients may use the therapies only during episodes of exacerbation with increased sputum production and dyspnea, whereas others may use these techniques on a regular basis.

SUGGESTED READING

Casciari RJ, Fairshter RD, Morrison JT, et al. Effects of breathing retraining in patients with chronic obstructive pulmonary disease. *Chest*. 1981;79:393–398.

Celli BR, Rodriquez KS, Snider GL. A controlled trial of intermittent positive pressure breathing, incentive spirometry, and deep breathing exercises in preventing pulmonary complications after abdominal surgery. *Am Rev Resp Dis*. 1984;130:12–15.

Drain CB, Christoph SS. *The Recovery Room: A Critical Care Approach to Post Anesthesia Nursing*. Philadelphia: W B Saunders Company; 1987.

Feldman J, Traver GA, Taussig LM. Maximal expiratory flows after postural drainage. *Am Resp Dis*. 1979;119:239–245.

Frownfelter DL. *Chest Physical Therapy and Pulmonary Rehabilitation*. Chicago: Year Book Medical Publishers; 1987.

Katz JA. PEEP and CPAP in perioperative respiratory care. *Resp Care*. 1984;29:614–29.

Kirrilloff LH, Owens GR, Rogers RM, et al. Does chest physical therapy work? *Chest*. 1985;88:436–444.

Larson JL, Kim MJ. Ineffective airway clearance related to respiratory muscle fatigue. *Nurs Clin North Am*. 1987;22:207–224.

Larson JL, Kim MJ, Sharp JT. Inspiratory muscle training with a threshold-resistive breathing device in patients with chronic obstructive pulmonary disease. *Am Rev Resp Dis*. 1986;133:A100.

Mackenzie CF, ed. *Chest Physiotherapy in the Intensive Care Unit*. Baltimore: Williams & Wilkins; 1989.

Marini J, Tyler ML, Hudson LD. Influence of head dependent position on lung volume and oxygen saturation in chronic airflow obstruction. *Am Rev Resp Dis*. 1984;129:101–105.

Maxwell M, Redmond A. A comparative trial of manual and mechanical percussion technique with gravity-assisted bronchial drainage in patients with cystic fibrosis. *Arch Dis Child*. 1979;54:542–544.

McCormick KA, Wewers ME, Engel BT. The performance of abdominal breathing in normal persons. *Am Rev Resp Dis*. 1986;133:A163.

O'Donahue WJ. National survey of the usage of lung expansion modalities for the prevention and treatment of postoperative atelectasis following abdominal and thoracic surgery. *Chest*. 1985;87:76–80.

Pardy RL, Rivington RN, Despas PJ, Macklem PT. Inspiratory muscle training compared with physiotherapy in patients with chronic airflow limitation. *Am Rev Resp Dis*. 1981;123:421–425.

Sackner MA, Gonzalez H, Rodriquez M, et al. Assessment of asynchronus and paradoxic motion between rib cage and abdomen in normal subjects and in patients with chronic obstructive pulmonary disease. *Am Rev Resp Dis*. 1984;130:588–593.

Shekelton ME, Nield M. Ineffective airway clearance related to artificial airways. *Nurs Clin North Am*. 1987;22:167–178.

Sonne LJ, Davis JA. Increased exercise performance in patients with severe COPD following inspiratory resistive training. *Chest*. 1982;81:436–439.

Stock MC, Downs JB, Gauer PK, Alster JM, Imrey PB. Prevention of postoperative pulmonary complications with CPAP, incentive spirometry and conservative therapy. *Chest*. 1985;87:151–157.

Traver GA. *Respiratory Nursing: The Science and the Art*. New York: John Wiley and Sons; 1982.

Traver GA. Ineffective airway clearance: physiology and clinical application. *Dimens Crit Care Nurs*. 1985;4:198–208.

Tyler ML. The respiratory effects of body positioning and immobilization. *Resp Care*. 1984;29:472–483.

Willeput R, Vachaudez JP, Lenders D, et al. Thoraco abdominal motion during chest physiotherapy in patients affected by chronic obstructive lung disease. *Resp*. 1983;44:204–214.

chapter 11

Suctioning

The primary purpose of suctioning is to clear the airway of secretions; the secondary purpose is to stimulate cough. Suctioning may be indicated when other treatments and maneuvers are unsuccessful in assisting patients to clear their large airways of secretions. This section discusses assessment of the need for suctioning, suctioning techniques, equipment used, hazards associated with suctioning, special considerations when high levels of positive end-expiratory pressure (PEEP) are being used, and adaptations for home care.

ASSESSMENT OF NEED FOR SUCTIONING

The frequency of suctioning should be decided by an assessment of need rather than a predetermined schedule. Assessment should include the following:

- Chest auscultation to ascertain the presence of retained secretions in the large airways.
- Evaluation of the effectiveness of the patient's cough (see Chapter 10).

While the clinician is auscultating the lung fields, the patient should be instructed to take deep inspirations and to exhale more forcefully than usual. These measures increase the likelihood of generating adventitious sounds.

Suctioning can only remove secretions in the large airways. Secretions in this location can often be heard as gurgling sounds or rhonchi. Removal of secretions from peripheral areas requires other techniques, such as cough, postural drainage, and percussion to mobilize the secretions to larger airways. Auscultatory findings of decreased or absent breath sounds may be due to decreased effort or to secretions that occlude the airways.

Additional sources of data that may support the diagnosis of inadequate airway clearance and indicate a need for suctioning include:

- Chest radiograph with radiographic changes that indicate atelectasis (ie, due to plugging of airways).
- Arterial blood gases with hypoxemia due to low ventilation-perfusion ratio; hypoxemia may also be indicated by pulse oximetry.
- In a mechanically ventilated patient, peak airway pressures that are acutely increased by secretions.

TYPES OF SUCTION CATHETERS

Several designs of suction catheters are available (see Figure 11-1). The most common types include the following:

1. *Whistle-tip catheters.* These can be straight or have a coudé tip. Holes on the surface of the catheter may contribute to mucosal damage.

2. *Mucosal protection design.* Available in various designs, the holes on these catheters are effectively recessed (eg, a mushroom tip) to reduce catheter contact with the airway mucosa and to minimize damage; straight and coudé tip are available.

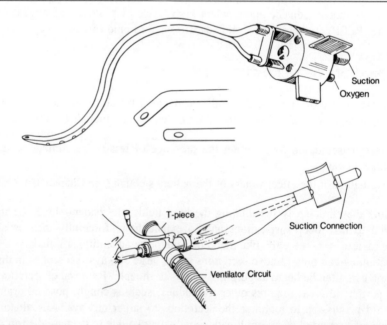

Figure 11-1 Types of suction catheters. Four different types of suction catheters are depicted. The catheter at the top allows for oxygen insufflation during suctioning. The two catheter tips in the center demonstrate a coudé-tipped (curved) catheter and a mucosal protection design. The catheter at the bottom shows a closed-system suctioning apparatus.

3. *Oxygen-insufflation port.* These catheters are designed with an additional side port so that oxygen administration can be maintained during suctioning to minimize hypoxemia.

4. *Closed-system multiuse design.* The catheter is enclosed in a sterile sheath and attached to the universal adapter at the end of the tracheal tube. The catheter unit is replaced every 24 hours. This catheter design may be beneficial for patients with copious secretions requiring frequent suctioning, high levels of PEEP and/or infectious secretions.

TECHNIQUES OF SUCTIONING

Tracheal suctioning can be accomplished with or without an artificial airway in place. The following techniques are common to all types of suctioning.

1. Explain what you will be doing and why to the patient and any family members who may be present; include the fact that the procedure may be uncomfortable.

2. Prevent or minimize hypoxemia by pre-oxygenation or maintenance of supplemental oxygen.

3. Minimize damage to the respiratory mucosa by using the lowest level of suction necessary to remove secretions, and apply suction only while withdrawing the catheter. Most clinicians recommend intermittent suction. The catheter may be gently rotated or rolled between the fingers when suction is applied to minimize damage to tracheal mucosa.

4. Prevent the introduction of pathogens to the lower airway. In the acute-care setting use a new sterile catheter and gloves for each session. Good hand-washing before and after suctioning reduces cross-contamination infection risks. In the hospital setting, Centers for Disease Control guidelines recommend gloves and mask to protect the clinician from infectious secretions.

Additionally, sterile saline irrigation (approximately 5 to 10 cc) may be used to stimulate cough. (Irrigation should not be a routine technique of suctioning.) During endotracheal suctioning, the saline is instilled via the artificial airway, prior to insertion of the catheter. Saline may also be instilled during nasotracheal suctioning after the catheter has been inserted into the trachea; the saline is injected through the catheter. The efficacy of saline irrigation to loosen secretions has not been established. (Irrigation is not necessary if the patient is adequately hydrated and secretions are thin.)

Nasotracheal Suctioning

To suction tracheal secretions in adult patients who do not have an artificial airway in place, the catheter is passed via the nose into the posterior pharynx and past the base of the tongue. The catheter is then maneuvered through the larynx and into the trachea.

Passage of the catheter through the nose may be complicated by anatomic obstruction due to deviated septum, polyps, or edema. When such obstruction is encountered, the catheter should not be forced against resistance. Rather, the opposite naris should be used for insertion; only rarely is the clinician forced to utilize the oral route for catheter insertion. *Gentle* passage of the catheter through the upper airway will enhance patient cooperation and comfort. One must consider the irritation, edema, and nasal sensitivity caused by frequent catheter insertion.

Patients who require frequent suctioning may benefit from placement of a nasal airway or trumpet (see Chapter 12, Artificial Airways). The position of the distal tip must be considered when using nasal airways. An airway that is too short (above the tongue) impedes passage of the suction catheter. If the airway is too long, it may cause gagging.

Successful passage of the catheter through the larynx and into the trachea is often difficult. Attention to the curve of the catheter, repositioning of the patient's head and neck, and a measure of luck will help.

The procedure for nasotracheal suctioning includes the following:

- Maintain oxygen delivery if the patient is receiving supplemental oxygen. A nasal cannula can be left in place. If the patient is on mask oxygen, the mask can be held slightly away from the patient's face or just to the side to allow passage of the suction catheter.
- Lubricate the catheter with sterile water-soluble gel.
- Position the patient's head in a neutral sniffing position (see Figure 11-2).
- Note if the catheter has a natural curve. With the curve pointing down, hold the tip of the nose up and gently pass the catheter through a naris; direct the catheter medially and along the floor of the naris. One can usually feel the catheter pass over the tongue or visualize the pharynx to be certain the catheter is not coiling in the oropharynx.
- Advance the catheter when the glottis is open (during inhalation or exhalation or while the patient coughs). Most patients will cough as the catheter passes through the larynx. If the patient coughs in paroxysms, stop moving the catheter until the patient relaxes, then continue advancing during inspiration. In an adult, the catheter can be inserted to the full length, approximately 18 to 22 inches.
- Apply intermittent suction as the catheter is withdrawn.
- Limit the duration of vacuum application to 10 to 15 seconds. If the patient has large amounts of secretions and requires repeated suctioning, do not completely withdraw the catheter from the airway during the session. With-

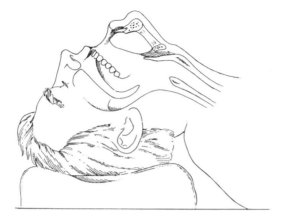

Figure 11-2 Sniff position.

draw the catheter approximately 6 inches so the catheter is between the larynx and major carina. Remove the suction source for a few moments to allow the patient to rest, reinsert the catheter to its full length, and then reapply suction. This technique of repeated lower airway suctioning without complete catheter withdrawal avoids the need for repeated attempts to pass the catheter through the larynx. When done with the session, withdraw the catheter while applying suction during passage through the orpharynx to clear upper airway secretions.

Tracheal Suctioning

Tracheostomies and endotracheal tubes provide direct access to the lower airway for clearing tracheal secretions. In the critical care environment, safe, efficient suctioning is best accomplished by using a two-person technique (eg, one person to suction and observe the patient, the other to hyperoxygenate with a manual resuscitation bag or a ventilator and monitor for arrhythmias and hypoxemia). The procedure includes the following:

- Select the smallest catheter size that will effectively remove secretions, but not larger than one-half the inner diameter of the airway. A catheter that is too large will cause major airway obstruction during suctioning.
- Hyperinflate and hyperoxygenate before and after each insertion and withdrawal of the catheter. (See the section on preventing hypoxemia in this chapter.)

- Gently, but quickly, insert the catheter until resistance is met. Withdraw the catheter one-quarter to one-half inch and apply intermittent suction as the catheter is completely withdrawn. Suction should not be applied at the point of resistance to reduce trauma to mucous membranes. To reduce airway trauma in infants and young children, many pediatricians caution that the catheter should not be advanced beyond the end of the endotracheal or tracheostomy tube.
- Limit the duration of each pass of the catheter to 10 to 15 seconds to minimize risks of hypoxemia; the catheter is completely withdrawn from the airway between passes.
- Suction oral-pharyngeal secretions, if required, *after* completing tracheal suction.

AVOIDING COMPLICATIONS ASSOCIATED WITH SUCTIONING

Although suctioning is a frequently employed technique, it always involves potential hazards, particularly in the acutely ill population. Risks associated with suctioning include:

- hypoxemia
- bronchospasm
- increased intracranial pressure
- cardiac dysrhythmias
- vomiting and aspiration
- lower airway contamination
- mucosal injury

An understanding of the causes of these suctioning complications and careful technique can reduce the risk of serious injury.

Preventing or Minimizing Hypoxemia

Suctioning will cause a fall in PaO_2. The exact mechanism is not known but involves removal of gas and/or oxygen from the lung, bronchospasm, and changes in lung volume that alter the $\dot{V}/\dot{Q}$ ratio. The severity of the hypoxemia and the degree of risk posed depend on the patient's baseline oxygenation, dependence on supplemental oxygen, and associated risk factors (eg, propensity for arrhythmias).

The techniques selected to prevent hypoxemia should be appropriate for the patient's condition. For example, not all patients require hyperinflation with a manual resuscitation bag. Stable patients with adequate ventilation and gas exchange, eg, a patient with a laryngectomy, can be instructed to take several deep breaths before and after suctioning.

Suction-induced hypoxemia is particularly dangerous for the critically ill patient who is dependent on supplemental oxygen. Several techniques have been suggested to minimize this hazard, such as suction catheters that have a supplemental oxygen sideport. The two most common techniques used to prevent hypoxemia in intubated patients are hyperinflation and hyperoxygenation.

Hyperinflation

Using either the ventilator or a manual resuscitation bag, administer 100% oxygen in volumes slightly larger than the patient's normal ventilator-delivered tidal volume. Clinicians should be aware that delivered volumes vary greatly when using manual resuscitation bags. It is generally recommended that at least three to five breaths be delivered before and after each catheter insertion, although the optimal number of breaths has not yet been determined. An exception to this recommendation is when the artificial airway is filled with secretions: suction first. Attempts to hyperinflate initially only result in forcing secretions back into the lung.

Hyperoxygenation

The goal of pre-oxygenation is to raise the PaO_2 above baseline so that the inevitable decrease during suctioning will not be to dangerous levels. Although an FIO_2 of 1.0 is generally recommended, it may not be essential for patients who require a low to moderate FIO_2. An FIO_2 20% higher than the maintenance level is sufficient for some patients.

Clinicians should be aware that manual resuscitation bags may not deliver 100% oxygen. The actual FIO_2 delivered varies with the design of the bag; bags with a reservoir provide the highest percentage of oxygen. Hyperoxygenation can also be provided via the ventilator. However, depending on the ventilator model, several minutes may be required for the tubing near the patient to be flushed with the 100% concentration. If 100% oxygen is used, the clinician must remember to return the ventilator to the ordered FIO_2.

Minimizing Bronchospasm

Bronchospasm may be induced by catheter irritation of reactive airways. Techniques to decrease mucosal irritation should be employed (see section on endotracheal suctioning). Patients with suction-induced bronchospasm may also benefit from bronchodilators.

Preventing Increased Intracranial Pressure

The risks posed by suctioning are magnified in patients with increased intracranial pressure (ICP), as seen in patients with closed head trauma or anoxic brain injury. Coughing and gagging, Valsalva maneuvers, discomfort, hypoxemia, and hypercapnia resulting from suctioning and interruption of mechanical ventilation may all increase ICP.

Pre- and postsuctioning hyperinflation with 100% oxygen is recommended as a protective measure against suctioning-induced increases in ICP. The optimal duration of the hyperinflation and hyperoxygenation has not been determined. The duration of each catheter insertion should be limited to 10 seconds and each session should be limited to 2 to 3 insertions, with generous oxygenation between insertions.

Patient response can be assessed by ICP monitoring, heart rate, and blood pressure. Extreme or sustained elevations in ICP or blood pressure are indications to discontinue suctioning until the patient's vital signs return to baseline. The need for pulmonary hygiene must be carefully balanced against the risks of increased ICP.

Preventing and Reducing Cardiac Dysrhythmias

Cardiac dysrhythmias during suctioning are common, especially in the acutely and critically ill population. They range from sinus tachycardia to lethal ventricular arrhythmias. The pre- and postoxygenation techniques described previously are used to protect the patient from dysrhythmia-producing hypoxemia.

Preventing Aspiration

Massive aspiration of gastric contents is a life-threatening event. Gagging and vomiting are commonly triggered by nasotracheal and oral suction. Patients with a decreased level of consciousness or impaired gag and cough reflexes are at increased risk for aspiration. The following methods decrease the risk of aspiration:

1. Elevate the head of the bed at least 30 degrees.
2. Check feeding tube placement prior to administering bolus feedings. Tube placement should be verified every four hours and after suctioning when patients

receive continuous feeding. Feeding tubes, especially the small-bore flexible tubes can become displaced into the esophagus by the suction catheter and by retching and coughing.

3. If the patient has a cuffed artificial airway in place and is unable to protect his or her airway, the cuff may be inflated during and for one hour after feeding.

4. If suctioning can be anticipated (eg, following aerosols and postural drainage), schedule treatments before or one hour after meals so that the stomach is not full. If the patient is receiving continuous feedings, stopping the feeding one-half hour before the drainage treatment may reduce the risk of aspiration.

5. When suctioning is required during or shortly after tube feedings, remove residual prior to suctioning, if possible. The feedings can be returned when suctioning is completed.

Should vomiting and aspiration occur, immediately turn the patient to a lateral position and suction the upper airway using a Yankauer tonsillar suction device. Clear the lower airway using the techniques described previously.

Preventing Lower Airway Contamination

Infection control is a concern for both the patient and clinician, particularly in the hospital setting. Aseptic or sterile technique must be maintained and cross-contamination avoided. Good handwashing technique must always be used before and after suctioning.

Sterile suction catheters, gloves, and lubricant are to be used and discarded after each session or if inadvertently contaminated while suctioning. Care should be taken to prevent contamination of the airway-ventilator connection. Sterile saline or water may be used to clear the suction catheter of secretions between passes; this solution, too, must be discarded after each session. Large bottles of sterile saline and water should be dated and discarded after 24 hours.

The Centers for Disease Control guidelines recommend that all body fluids and secretions be considered contaminated and that clinicians employ proper isolation techniques. Gloves must be worn while suctioning. Masks, gowns, and goggles may be appropriate to prevent contamination with sputum.

Preventing Mucosal Injury

Mucosal injury from suction catheters can result in airway edema, increased secretions, and hemorrhage. Techniques to minimize this risk are discussed in the previous section on endotracheal suctioning.

SUCTIONING WITH HIGH POSITIVE END-EXPIRATORY PRESSURE

Many authors caution that removing high PEEP (eg, disconnecting the patient from the ventilator), even momentarily for suctioning, causes airway closure and hypoxemia. This risk is primarily a concern when using PEEP levels greater than 10 cm H_2O.

One method suggested to maintain PEEP during suctioning is the use of a tube/ventilator adapter that has a catheter port or resealing diaphragm. The suction catheter is passed through this opening; the ventilator does not need to be disconnected and PEEP is maintained during the procedure. There is a potential risk of increased airway closure with use of the suction adapter if the ventilator does not have continuous flow.

Manual resuscitation bags used for patients on PEEP should be adapted to maintain the appropriate level of PEEP. These bags can also be used with the suction port. A continuous pulse oximeter may be helpful to judge the relative risks and benefits of using a manual resuscitation bag or using the ventilator and whether or not to disconnect during suctioning.

SPECIAL CONSIDERATIONS IN HOME CARE

In the home setting, several modifications of tracheal suctioning technique are often used. Patients who require tracheal suctioning usually have a tracheostomy in place. If the home setting is adequate, the patient does not have an infection, and the caregiver (patient or family member) understands and follows the technique meticulously, clean technique with handwashing is frequently used. (Note that the patient or family member is instructed *not* to touch that part of the catheter that is passed into the tracheal tube.) In other situations—due to aesthetic concerns, the home setting, or the presence of secretions—the patient or family member wears gloves when suctioning. In the home setting, clean rather than sterile gloves are frequently used.

Because of cost problems, many patients reuse suction catheters. The same catheter may be reused over several hours (no more than eight); between suctioning sessions the catheter is rinsed, wiped, and stored between layers of a dry towel. Catheters may then be cleaned and disinfected for future use. To clean the catheter, suction clear water through it until it is cleared of all mucus. (If the catheter cannot be cleared or if the patient has a bronchial infection, the catheter is discarded and not reused or disinfected.) After several cleared catheters have accumulated, the catheters are washed in a mild soap, rinsed, and soaked in a disinfectant solution (follow manufacturer's instructions); the catheter is rinsed, dried, and stored in a sealed container (Baggie).

In addition to the actual technique of home suctioning, the clinician must also consider approaches to teaching the patient or family member to suction. Suctioning is a frightening experience for many and the person needs an opportunity to practice before actually passing a catheter into his or her own or a family member's trachea. After demonstrating correct technique, discussing technique, and providing written material, the clinician should observe and supervise while the patient or family member practices on a model. A simple model that can be used is to place a tracheostomy tube in a glass of water. The tube is held at an angle that simulates normal anatomic position. The patient or family member then suctions the water out of the glass via the tracheostomy tube. Use of the model allows familiarity with the feel of passing the catheter through the tube, the resistance felt before withdrawing the catheter, and the use of intermittent suction. For those providing care to pediatric patients, the use of the model also allows them to determine how far the catheter should be passed because they can visualize the catheter when it passes beyond the end of the tube.

SUGGESTED READING

Ackerman M. The use of bolus normal saline instillations in artificial airways: Is it useful or necessary? *Heart Lung*. 1985;14:505–506.

Barnes CA, Kirchhoff KT. Minimizing hypoxemia due to endotracheal suctioning: a review of the literature. *Heart Lung*. 1986;15:164–176.

Bodai B, Walton C, Briggs S, Goldstein M. A clinical evaluation of an oxygen insufflation/suction catheter. *Heart Lung*. 1987;16:39–46.

Bostick J, Wendelgass S. Normal saline instillation as part of the suctioning procedure: effects on PaO₂ and amount of secretions. *Heart Lung*. 1987;16:532–537.

Buchanan LM, Baun MM. The effect of hyperinflation, inspiratory hold, and oxygenation on cardiopulmonary status during suctioning in a lung-injured model. *Heart Lung*. 1986;15:127–134.

Chulay M, Graeber G. Efficacy of hyperinflation and hyperoxygenation suctioning intervention. *Heart Lung*. 1988;17:15–22.

Demers RR, Saklad M. Minimizing the harmful effects of mechanical aspiration. *Heart Lung*. 1973;2:542–545.

Elpern E, Jacobs E, Bone R. Incidence of aspiration in tracheally intubated adults. *Heart Lung*. 1987;16:527–531.

Fell T, Cheney F. Prevention of hypoxia during endotracheal suction. *Ann Surg*. 1971;174:124.

Goodnough S. The effects of oxygen and hyperinflation on arterial oxygen tension after endotracheal suctioning. *Heart Lung*. 1985;14:11–17.

Hanley M, Rudd T, Butler J. What happens to intratracheal saline instillations? *Am Rev Respir Dis*. 1987;117:124.

Hess D, Goff G, Johnson K. The effect of hand size, resuscitator brand, and use of two hands on volumes delivered during adult bag-valve ventilation. *Resp Care*. 1989;34:805–809.

Kleiber C, Krutzfield N, Rose E. Acute histologic changes in the tracheobronchial tree associated with different suction catheter insertion techniques. *Heart Lung.* 1988;17:10–14.

Methany, N, Eisenberg P, Spies M. Aspiration pneumonia in patients fed through nasoenteral tubes. *Heart Lung.* 1986;15:256–261.

Preusser BA, Stone KS, Gonyon DS, Winningham ML, Groch KF, Karl JE. Effects of two methods of preoxygenation on mean arterial pressure, cardiac output, peak airway pressure, and postsuctioning hypoxemia. *Heart Lung.* 1988;17:290–299.

Rogge JA, Bunde L, Baun MM. Effectiveness of oxygen concentrations of less than 100% before and after endotracheal suction in patients with chronic obstructive pulmonary disease. *Heart Lung.* 1989;18:64–71.

Rudy EB, Baun M, Stone K, Turner B. The relationship between endotracheal suctioning and changes in intracranial pressure: a review of the literature. *Heart Lung.* 1986;15:488–494.

Stone KS, Vorst EC, Lanham B, Zahn S. Effects of lung hyperinflation on mean arterial pressure and postsuctioning hypoxemia. *Heart Lung.* 1989;18:377–385.

Taggart J, Dorinsky N, Sheahan J. Airway pressures during closed system suctioning. *Heart Lung.* 1988:17;536–42.

chapter 12

Artificial Airway Care

Artificial airways are used to maintain a patent airway and facilitate pulmonary hygiene when other measures are unsuccessful, and they are necessary for most types of positive pressure ventilation. This chapter describes different types of artificial airways and their indications for use.

UPPER AIRWAY DEVICES

Upper airway devices are used to maintain patency of the upper airway. If the patient cannot maintain patency of the lower airway, then an upper airway device alone would be inappropriate. The most commonly used devices are oral and nasal airways. In emergency out-of-hospital situations, an esophageal airway may be used.

Oral Airways

Oral airways are curved plastic devices designed to slide over the tongue and hold the tongue down and forward (see Figure 12-1). These tubes are most commonly used in comatose or semi-comatose patients to relieve airway obstruction caused by the tongue falling posteriorly. They are also a useful adjunct to mask-bag ventilation in a nonintubated patient because they reduce or alleviate upper airway obstruction, which could prevent adequate ventilation.

To insert an oral airway, the caregiver should hold the airway with the distal end pointing up. The airway is inserted at the side of the mouth, between the teeth. Once the airway is over the tongue, it is rotated over and down to the correct position. This insertion technique protects against pushing the tongue back with the airway.

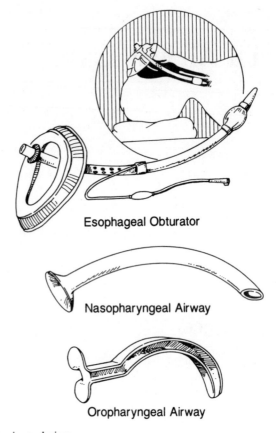

Esophageal Obturator

Nasopharyngeal Airway

Oropharyngeal Airway

Figure 12-1 Upper airway devices.

Oral airways may stimulate gag and cough reflexes, especially if they are too long and positioned incorrectly. It is often difficult to keep them in the proper position, ie, maintaining tongue position without stimulating a gag reflex. Consequently, these airways are not well tolerated in the conscious patient. The comatose patient must also be closely observed so that, if misplaced, the airway does not cause gagging, vomiting, and aspiration.

Nasal Airways

A nasal airway is a trumpet-shaped device inserted through the nares (see Figure 12-1). It must extend to the base of the tongue, holding the tongue forward, to effectively relieve obstruction. Passage of the airway through the nasal passage is facilitated by lubricating the airway with a water-soluble lubricant. These airways are most commonly used when a patient requires frequent naso-tracheal suctioning and when passage of the catheter through the nasal passage is difficult or has caused irritation and edema.

Nasal airways can cause trauma and ischemia to the nares. For this reason, nasal airways should be rotated from one naris to the other as necessary to prevent tissue breakdown. As with oral airways, one must make sure that the tube is holding the tongue in the correct position but is not causing a gag reflex.

Esophageal Airways

Esophageal airways are primarily used in prehospital care and transport of patients who require ventilation via a self-inflating resuscitation bag (see Figure 12-1). The purpose of the tube is to prevent aspiration of stomach contents during resuscitation and to prevent gas insufflation of the stomach.

The esophageal airway resembles an endotracheal tube in appearance but is inserted into the esophagus rather than the trachea. The distal end of the tube is sealed and an inflatable balloon prevents air from entering the stomach and causing regurgitation of stomach contents into the pharynx. Because the tube prohibits air flow into the esophagus, air delivered by positive pressure goes through the side openings and into the trachea. Before an esophageal tube is removed, an endotracheal tube must be inserted to ensure that the patient does not aspirate.

Esophageal tubes carry the risk of esophageal or gastric perforation and inadvertent endotracheal placement. They are only used on adults.

LOWER AIRWAY DEVICES

Lower airway devices include endotracheal and tracheostomy tubes, which may be cuffed or uncuffed. These tubes are used to bypass the upper airway in patients for whom the upper airway obstruction cannot be relieved by an upper airway device, to protect against aspiration, to provide access to the lower airway for positive pressure ventilation, and to facilitate lower airway suctioning.

Cuffed Tubes

Cuffs are located on the distal end of endotracheal and tracheostomy tubes and, when inflated, occlude the space between the outer surface of the tube and the tracheal mucosa (see Figure 12-2). Cuffed tubes are not used in infants because the tracheal diameter is so small that the space between the airway and the

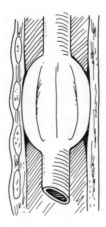

Figure 12-2 Airway cuff. The position of an inflated, cuffed tube in the trachea is depicted. When the cuff is inflated, a closed system with the ventilator is created, and aspiration of secretions from the upper airway into the lower trachea is prohibited.

tracheal wall is insignificant. In older children (usually six years or older) and adults, the space around the tube becomes significant. The cuff is therefore necessary when the purpose of the tube is to prevent aspiration or to allow positive pressure mechanical ventilation.

Most tubes used today have large volume, low pressure cuffs. This type of cuff reduces the amount of pressure exerted on the tracheal mucosa. The majority of cuffed tubes are inflated with air via a pilot balloon. Self-inflating foam cuffs are also available. The foam cuffs are *deflated* for insertion and allowed to self-inflate when positioned correctly.

Monitoring Cuff Volume and Pressure

The volume of air used to inflate the cuff and the pressure the cuff exerts on the tracheal mucosa should be monitored to prevent tracheal damage. Even with the use of low pressure cuffs, tracheal stenosis at the cuff site may occur.

Capillary closing pressure occurs at 25 to 30 mm Hg in the normotensive individual. Cuff pressures that exceed the capillary closing pressure can cause tissue ischemia and necrosis. The goal of airway cuff management is to maintain an effective seal for positive pressure ventilation using the lowest possible pressure—less than 20 mm Hg or 25 cm H_2O pressure. Measuring the back pressure from the cuff is usually a reflection of the pressure exerted by the cuff on the tracheal mucosa.

Monitoring the volume of air used to inflate the cuff is a way to assess the potential development of tracheomalacia—weakening of the tracheal support structures with gradual expansion of the trachea. An increasing volume of air needed to obtain a seal reflects distention of the trachea (this distention may also be seen on chest radiograph). The following is a recommended procedure for monitoring cuff volumes and pressures.

1. Explain the procedure to the patient. Because cuff deflation often induces coughing and triggering of ventilator alarms (due to cough and loss of return volumes), the patient should be prepared.

2. Suction the trachea if needed, then the oropharynx to remove excessive secretions. (Upper airway secretions can be aspirated when the cuff is deflated.)

3. Deflate the cuff during a ventilator breath or manually ventilate the patient with a manual resuscitation bag. Any secretions above cuff will be blown up into the pharynx and may need to be suctioned. Removal of the secretions pooled above the cuff is important because they can contribute to the development of local infection and subglottic stenosis.

4. Reinflate the cuff slowly. Auscultate over the trachea, listening for the air leak to disappear during inspiration. The smallest amount of air in the cuff needed to attain the seal is called the minimal occlusive volume. In some institutions a minimal leak technique is used to inflate the cuff. In this method, the cuff is inflated to a full seal, then a small amount of air is withdrawn (¼ to ½ cc). Ventilator volumes are measured so that a leak of approximately 50 cc is allowed around the cuff. The ventilator is adjusted so that the desired volume is delivered to the patient. (For example, if a tidal volume of 850 cc was desired and a 50 cc leak was allowed, the ventilator would be set to deliver 900 cc.)

5. The frequency of cuff volume monitoring varies widely among institutions. The volume needed to attain a full seal should be recorded at least once or twice a day. The need for increasingly larger volumes indicates an expanding trachea.

6. The cuff pressure may also be measured. Ideally, the pressure is kept at levels less than 20 mm Hg. Cuff pressure greater than 20 mm Hg may be unavoidable for ventilated patients with non-compliant lungs who require high peak pressures and high levels of PEEP.

Inability to Maintain a Cuff Seal

A cuff that is not properly sealed produces an air leak. An air leak can produce several findings, eg, exhaled tidal volume less than that delivered by a ventilator, a patient who is able to phonate, and the sound of secretions bubbling in the pharynx. A persistent air leak around the tube that cannot be obliterated by adding air to the cuff can be caused by three problems: actual air loss from the cuff (the cuff is leaking), a tube that is too small for the airway (a leak around the inflated cuff), or, in the case of an endotracheal tube, tube displacement upward into the larynx (a leak around the inflated cuff). Clinical techniques will allow one to discriminate between a leak around the cuff and a leak in the cuff itself. First, inflate the cuff to full seal with a known amount of air. When the air leak is again detected, deflate the cuff and note the volume of air withdrawn. If the entire volume originally used to inflate the cuff is obtained, then there is a leak around the cuff. If the tube is positioned properly (checked by x-ray and by noting that tube has been inserted to the proper depth), a new larger tube may be required. If the tube has been displaced into the larynx, the cuff should be fully deflated and the tube advanced to its proper position and reinflated.

If, on cuff deflation, less air is retrieved than was originally used to inflate the cuff, the clinician can conclude that there is an air leak in the cuff or cuff inflation system, eg, valve, pilot balloon, or tubing. To aid in locating the actual site of the leak, reinflate the cuff via a stopcock. If the leak was in the valve, closing the stopcock after inflation should prevent the leak from recurring. For leaks in the pilot balloon or tubing, inflate the cuff and then clamp the tubing at various points until a leak no longer occurs. When the site of the leak has been localized, the tubing can be cut at that point and a blunt-end 20-gauge needle, attached to a stopcock, can be inserted into the tubing. The cuff can then be inflated via the needle and stopcock. These techniques to bypass a leak in the inflation system can prevent the need for emergency reintubation.

In all cases of persistent air leak, reintubation may be avoided if the goals of intubation are being met. For example, if the ventilator can be set to compensate for the leak, the patient may not need to be reintubated. If significant aspiration or inadequate ventilation are present, a new tube needs to be inserted.

Endotracheal Tubes

Endotracheal tubes are preferred over tracheostomy in situations where quick access to the lower airway is required (eg, emergency situations, such as respiratory arrest) or when the defined need for the tube is anticipated to be of a relatively short duration. By present clinical practice, short duration includes intraoperative use of intubation as well as instances in which the need for mechanical ventilation is anticipated to be not more than two to three weeks. In some clinical situations, however, the use of an endotracheal tube may go on for more than a month (eg, the patient is expected to be weaned from the ventilator in several days and the disadvantages of tracheostomy do not warrant doing the procedure when weighed against the disadvantages of several additional days of endotracheal intubation.)

Endotracheal tubes are inserted via the upper airway through the glottis and terminate above the major carina (with the exception of endobronchial tubes). Endotracheal tubes are usually described in terms of their route of insertion: nasal and oral. In addition, there are endobronchial tubes that terminate in a bronchus versus the trachea (see Figure 12-3). Each of these tubes has advantages and disadvantages.

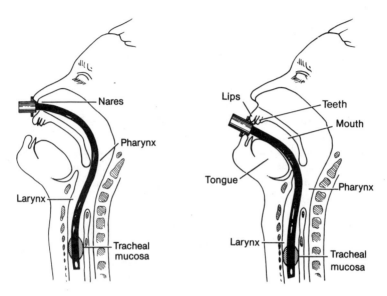

Figure 12-3A Endotracheal tubes. Lateral views of oro- and naso-endotracheal tubes are shown. *Source:* Reprinted from *Respiratory Nursing: the Science and the Art* (p 267) by GA Traver (Ed) with permission of John Wiley & Sons, Inc, © 1982.

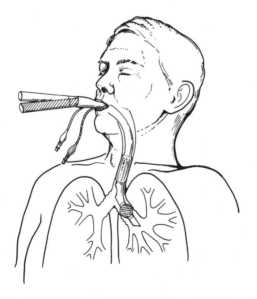

Figure 12-3B Endobronchial tube. *Source:* Reprinted with permission from *Critical Care Nurse* (1986;6:46), Copyright © 1986, Hospital Publications, Inc.

Types of Endotracheal Tubes

1. *Nasal tubes.* These tubes can usually be inserted without visualization when the patient is breathing spontaneously, and they are usually more comfortable than an oral tube for long-term intubation. They are also easier to stabilize and secure than oral endotracheal tubes.

Due to the anatomy of the insertion route, in any one specific individual, nasal tubes are longer and often of a smaller diameter than an oral tube. The smaller diameter of nasal tubes may also dictate the need for smaller suction catheters, which could impair the retrieval of very thick airway secretions. Irritation and even necrosis of the nasal passages may result from the pressure of these tubes. In addition, they may block sinus drainage. Sinus infection, a sequela of blocked sinus drainage, is an infrequent but potentially serious complication of nasal intubation. The incidence of this infection as well as blockage of the eustachian tubes with potential inner ear infection is increased by the presence of a nasogastric tube. A final caution is that placement of a nasal tube is contraindicated when basilar skull fracture is suspected due to the risk of additional neurologic trauma.

2. *Oral tubes.* Insertion of an oral endotracheal tube usually requires glottic visualization with a laryngoscope. The oral tube can be of larger diameter but is often more difficult to secure and less comfortable than a nasal tube. Obstruction is also a greater problem with oral tubes. Patients can bite these tubes (a bite block may be needed) and the tubes can kink in the posterior pharynx. Possible or known cervical neck injury requires additional precautions and produces greater difficulty during insertion because the injury dictates that the patient's neck not be hyperextended.

3. *Endobronchial or double lumen tubes.* This special type of endotracheal tube is available for the unique situation in which the right and left lung must be ventilated independently (differential lung ventilation). The endobronchial tube is a larger tube that encloses two lumens, one providing access to one lung, and the other to the opposite lung. This special tube is most commonly used for situations of severe unilateral lung disease (pneumonia, contusion) and to provide access and ventilation to the nonoperative side during thoracic surgery.

General Care Measures

This section discusses the measures required in caring for any patient intubated via the oral or nasal route. Care measures unique to cuffed tubes have been previously discussed.

1. *Care following intubation procedure.* It is extremely important to verify the position of the endotracheal tube immediately following its insertion. Note the distance the tube has been inserted (endotracheal tubes have centimeter

markings that indicate the depth of the tube in the airway). Then, with someone holding the tube in place, auscultate the lungs to ensure that there are breath sounds bilaterally. When the tube is inserted too far, it usually enters the right mainstem bronchus. Breath sounds will be absent or decreased over the left lung and possibly over the right upper lobe (blockage of the right upper lobe bronchus may occur because its point of departure from the right mainstem bronchus is very close to the major carina). If auscultation indicates that the tube has been inserted too far, the tube needs to be pulled back until breath sounds are heard over all lung areas.

The endotracheal tube is then secured in place. A common method is to use adhesive tape. The tape is double-backed behind the head with the adhesive across the face; the ends are wrapped around the endotracheal tube. Commercial devices that use Velcro are also available for securing these tubes. Whatever technique is used, the tubes must be properly secured to prevent accidental extubation, tube movement that irritates the tracheal mucosal, and inadvertent right mainstem intubation due to the tube slipping to a greater depth. At the time the tube is secured, the centimeter marking denoting the depth to which the tube was inserted should be recorded. In adults, the average depth is 22 to 24 cm for oral tubes.

A chest radiograph is then obtained to confirm placement. The tip of the endotracheal tube should be positioned approximately 3 cm above the major carina.

Once correct placement of the tube is confirmed, any excess length of the endotracheal tube should be trimmed to a distance of approximately 1 inch beyond the lip or naris. The excess length protruding from the nose or mouth presents a greater risk of the tube position being inadvertently changed. It can be pulled out from traction by the ventilator or slip further down the airway.

Trimming the excess tubing to 1 inch is not recommended initially in situations where severe facial edema is expected (eg, facial trauma, large volume fluid resuscitation in shock). While the distal position of the tube does not change in the trachea, edema of oropharyngeal and facial tissues may require that the tube be secured at a marking proximal to the original level (eg, 20 cm at the lip rather than 22 cm). If the edema develops rapidly, an oral endotracheal tube may need to be resecured at a more proximal level to prevent upward tube displacement.

2. *Airway care measures.* Because the upper airway has been bypassed, the upper airway functions of heating and humidifying the inspired air must be provided. (See Chapter 8 on humidity and aerosol.) In addition, endotracheal intubation reduces cough effectiveness and impairs normal mucociliary clearance. There is also the risk of the tube itself becoming occluded. Therefore, patients with an endotracheal tube in place will require suctioning, frequent position changes and, possibly, postural drainage.

3. *Insertion site care.* The site of insertion, nasal or oral, should be checked for irritation and necrosis. In addition, unusual purulent drainage from the nose or in the oropharynx of a nasally intubated patient may indicate sinus infection. As a preventive measure, oral tubes should be repositioned daily to the opposite side of the mouth.

4. *Oral care.* Oral hygiene should be provided frequently (eg, every four hours and as needed) to remove oral secretions and prevent infection. During oral care, the oral cavity should be inspected for lesions, bleeding, loose teeth and infection.

5. *Providing communication.* Because these tubes pass through the vocal cords, normal speech is not possible. The patient and significant others need to know that this loss of speech is temporary and, when appropriate, alternative means of communication must be provided (eg, a picture board or magic slate for writing). Special endotracheal tubes designed to facilitate speech are available.

Disadvantages/Risks of Endotracheal Tubes

There are a number of disadvantages and risks in the use of endotracheal tubes.

1. *Discomfort.* Endotracheal tubes are generally less comfortable than tracheostomy tubes. The discomfort can be minimized by properly securing the tube and providing frequent oral care. In addition, patients with an endotracheal tube in place usually need to be restrained (initially, all are restrained). This limitation of movement adds to the patient's discomfort both physically and psychologically.

2. *Laryngeal injury.* Because the tube passes through the vocal cords, injury may occur during intubation or as a result of prolonged tube placement. The trauma to the larynx may be aggravated by excessive head movement and the patient's attempts to speak. If the chosen method of communication is lip reading, patients should be encouraged to mouth words rather than trying to speak.

3. *Silent aspiration.* While endotracheal tubes do offer protection against massive aspiration, aspiration does occur even around an inflated cuff. Precautions should be taken to prevent aspiration (ie, intestinal versus gastric feeding, elevating the head of bed when possible).

4. *Accidental extubation.* Explain the purpose and importance of the airway as frequently as needed. Confused, agitated patients may require sedation and restraints to protect against self-extubation.

Tracheostomy Tubes

The indications for tracheostomy and the insertion of a tracheostomy tube are similar to those cited for endotracheal intubation. Tracheostomy is required as an initial procedure when upper airway obstruction or facial trauma prevents the passage of an endotracheal tube, or when oral or pharyngeal surgery requires visualization of the oropharynx. Tracheostomy is also used initially or to replace oral or nasal intubation for patients in whom prolonged protection of the airway or prolonged mechanical ventilation is anticipated (eg, positive pressure mechanical ventilation exceeding three to four weeks, sleep apnea, or chronic aspiration). The major advantages of tracheostomy tubes over endotracheal tubes are avoiding laryngeal damage and permitting the patient, if appropriate, to have an oral intake.

Types of Tracheostomy Tubes

The specific designs of tracheostomy tubes vary among manufacturers. As with endotracheal tubes, tracheostomy tubes may be cuffed or uncuffed. Most tracheostomy tubes have an outer cannula and a neck plate that provides a means of securing the tube. Most tubes also have a universal adapter (as part of either the outer or inner cannula) to allow connection to self-inflating resuscitation bags and ventilators. Finally, all tubes will have an accompanying obturator that is used to insert the tracheostomy tube.

Some tubes have an inner cannula. Tubes with an inner cannula are the type most frequently used for adults. The inner cannula can be periodically removed for cleaning, so that secretions do not reduce the size of or occlude the lumen. Smaller pediatric tracheostomy tubes do not have an inner cannula. When very small tracheostomy tubes are used, as in pediatrics, the presence of an inner cannula would dramatically affect available lumen space.

In addition to the basic types of tracheostomy tubes, there are also several tubes that are designed for special purposes, such as facilitating speech. Examples of the various tracheostomy tubes can be seen in Figure 12-4.

1. *Fenestrated tracheostomy tube.* The fenestrated tracheostomy tube has one or more openings on the upper curve of the outer cannula (see Figure 12-4). When the inner cannula is removed and the opening of the outer cannula occluded, a route for air flow between the lower and upper airway is created. In other words, air flow follows the normal passageway via the fenestration rather than bypassing the upper airway. Since air is now flowing over the vocal cords, the patient can speak. It should be noted that when the inner cannula is in place, the fenestration is blocked and the tracheostomy becomes the major route for air flow. The fenestrated tube may also be used in weaning from the tracheostomy.

2. *Talking tracheostomy tube.* The "talking" tracheostomy tube is also designed to allow speech, especially in clinical situations where a cuffed tracheostomy tube and mechanical ventilation are required. This tube has an additional small air port that terminates just above the cuff (see Figure 12-4). An outside air source is connected to the port; the additional air flow is controlled by a Y connector. When air is allowed to flow, it is released in the airway, just above

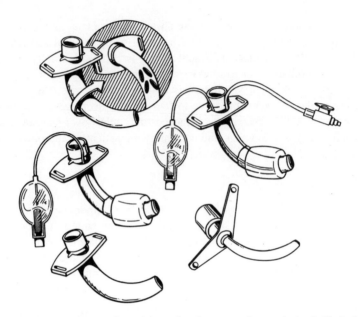

Figure 12-4 Tracheostomy tubes. Several types of tracheostomy tubes are depicted. Clockwise from the top, they are fenestrated tracheostomy tube, talking tracheostomy tube, pediatric tracheostomy tube, plain (uncuffed) adult tracheostomy tube, and a cuffed tracheostomy tube.

the cuff, and then flows up through the larynx. Flows are usually set at 4 to 6 L/minute. Speech is then possible. It is important to clear the upper airway of secretions prior to using the air port. If not cleared, secretions will be blown up into the pharynx; the resulting sensation is uncomfortable to many patients. Care should also be taken to avoid continuous flow through the air port; air in the pharynx could be swallowed and result in gastric insufflation.

3. *Tracheostomy button.* A button is simply a short tube that extends from the neck into trachea to keep the stoma patent (see Figure 12-5). It does not extend down the trachea. The button can be plugged to allow the patient to breathe normally and to talk and can be opened to allow access to the trachea for suctioning. A tracheostomy button, when required, is used primarily as the last phase in weaning from a tracheostomy, before the stoma is allowed to close.

4. *Cricothyrotomy.* When an airway is needed emergently and the endotracheal route is not possible (due to facial or neck trauma, laryngospasm, or laryngeal obstruction), an endotracheal tube may be inserted through a surgical incision in the cricothyroid membrane. Cricothyrotomy carries a high risk of subglottic stenosis and is only used emergently.

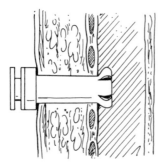

Figure 12-5 Tracheostomy button. The button maintains the track through the soft tissues of the neck but does not extend down the trachea.

General Care Measures

There are a number of measures for the general care of tracheostomy patients that caregivers must keep in mind.

1. ***Securing tracheostomy tubes.*** A recommended method for securing tracheostomies is shown in Figure 12-6. Tracheostomy ties or twill tape should be cut long enough to circle around the patient's neck in a double fold with an additional six to eight inches for tying. The ends are cut at a tapered angle. One end is inserted up through the neck plate; the tape is pulled through to the middle of the tape. Bringing both ends around the patient's neck, slide one end up through the other side of the neck plate. The ends are then tied in a square knot (not a bow) at the side of the patient's neck. After tying the tapes securely, check that there is room to slip only one finger under the ties. If looser, the tube could become dislodged or movement could be excessive, causing airway irritation and cough. Commercial tracheostomy ties made with Velcro are also available.

The risk of extubation is most serious in the first two to three days after tracheostomy. In this early period, the tract is not established and reinsertion of the tube may be impossible. Many surgeons suture the tracheostomy tube in place to avoid or minimize the risks of accidental extubation.

2. ***Inner cannula care.*** It is becoming increasingly common in the hospital setting for tracheostomy tubes to have disposable inner cannulas so that routine cleaning is not necessary. A new inner cannula is simply inserted. When a non-disposable inner cannula is used (usually when the patient has a long-term tracheostomy), inner cannula care is carried out using strict aseptic or sterile technique. Necessary equipment includes sterile gloves, basins, half-strength hydrogen peroxide, and brushes and/or cotton-tipped applicators. (Some manufacturers recommend that brushes not be used to clean their inner cannula.) For mechanically ventilated patients, when the cannula is removed for cleaning, a

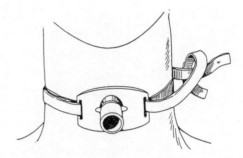

Figure 12-6 Securing a tracheostomy tube. This double tape technique makes removal of the tapes much easier and safer than untying or cutting knots.

special connector or spare cannula may be needed to attach the ventilator tubing while the inner cannula is being cleaned. The tube should be cleaned with the hydrogen peroxide solution, inspected to ensure that no mucus is attached to the inner lumen, rinsed with sterile water or saline, and reinserted. When removing or inserting an inner cannula, the tracheostomy tube should be stabilized so that movement that could irritate the airway and cause coughing is minimized. In addition, the person providing the care must be sure that the inner cannula is in a locked position after reinsertion. (Lock styles vary among manufacturers.) The inner cannula should be cleaned as frequently as necessary. In older well-established tracheostomies with minimal airway secretions, the inner cannula may only need to be cleaned twice a day.

3. **Stoma care.** Stoma care, which is usually done after cleaning the inner cannula, is done in the hospital setting with aseptic technique to decrease contamination risks. The skin around the stoma is cleaned with half-strength hydrogen peroxide. This solution will facilitate the removal of dried blood and secretions. It is also important to visually inspect the stoma site. When tracheostomy tubes are sutured in place, visual inspection is often difficult, but it is necessary to ensure that the site has no signs of infection, eg, unusual redness, swelling, or purulent drainage. Following cleaning of the stoma site, a pre-slit tracheostomy dressing may be applied. (A tracheostomy dressing is usually not used in pediatric patients and is optional in adults.) Avoid using 4 × 4 gauze pads cut to fit around the stoma. These pads can fray and shed small fragments into the wound. Site care is done as frequently as necessary to keep the skin clean and dry. Patients with a large amount of secretions draining from the stoma will need additional skin care to prevent excoriation of the surrounding intact skin. If the routine skin cleansing is not adequate, benzoin or commercial skin barrier products should be applied to the intact skin around the stoma.

4. **Airway care measures.** In the hospital setting, humidification of the inspired air should be provided. In addition, suctioning is usually required. When

a new tracheostomy has been performed, suctioning is usually needed at very short intervals (every one or two hours). If the tracheostomy has been present for a prolonged period, the patient must be assessed to determine the frequency of suctioning.

Risks and Complications of Tracheostomies

Tracheostomies are not without their risks and complications. Among the risks are:

1. **Surgical complications.** The major complications are pneumothorax and bleeding due to vascular injury.

2. **Extubation before the tract is formed.** In cases of early extubation, reinsertion of the tracheostomy tube may be difficult, especially in patients with heavy necks. During reinsertion there is also the risk of cannulation of the mediastinum or subcutaneous tissue when the tract is not mature.

3. **Infection.** The tracheostomy provides direct access to the lower airway and therefore the patient is prone to infection, especially during the immediate postoperative period. Infection of the stoma site and mediastinum may also occur.

4. **Hemorrhage.** Bleeding may occur at the time of surgery or anytime following the tracheostomy. New or unusual bleeding from the stoma or trachea needs further investigation. A rare but potentially fatal hemorrhage can occur from erosion of the innominate artery. If the bleeding site can be located, direct pressure or further inflation of the cuff may control the hemorrhage en route to the operating room.

5. **Damage to the tracheal mucosa.** If the patient has a cuffed tube in place, the cuff can cause damage. With both cuffed and uncuffed tubes, the position of the tube in the trachea may result in damage to the mucosa. The most frequent site of erosion is the anterior wall of the trachea caused by the tip of the tracheostomy tube. A tracheal erosion posteriorly creates a tracheoesophageal fistula. The risk of this complication is increased when the patient also has a nasogastric tube in place.

Home Tracheostomy Care

Many patients are discharged from the hospital with a tracheostomy tube in place. It is extremely important that these patients and their families be taught self-care measures. Components of a teaching program should include:

1. **Need.** Explanation of why the individual has the tracheostomy.

2. **Equipment.** Description of the specific tube the individual has, including the component parts and the purpose of each.

3. **Stoma care.** In the home setting, the use of hydrogen peroxide may no longer be necessary. The area is simply washed with soap and water.

4. *Inner cannula care.* If the patient's tracheostomy tube has an inner cannula, it is usually more economical in the home setting to use a nondisposable inner cannula. The technique used is similar to that used in the hospital setting except that clean rather than sterile technique is used.

5. *Airway care.* The amount of humidification needed will vary. Some patients who have had a tracheostomy for an extended period may need no additional humidity, whereas others will need only a room humidifier at night, and still others may require aerosol. Some patients also use small saline instillations (four or five drops) when away from home to prevent dryness and promote comfort. *All* patients with tracheostomies need to know how to suction. In the home setting, clean technique versus sterile technique is usually used. During periods when the patient is away from home and suction apparatus, tracheal irrigation with 5 cc normal saline is often helpful to stimulate expulsive cough and maintain airway clearance.

6. *Changing the entire tracheostomy tube.* The patient needs to know how to change the tube for several reasons. First, it is necessary to periodically change the tube (some recommend every one to two weeks, others every one to two months) simply to keep it clean, especially if the tube is used without an inner cannula. In addition, knowing how to insert a new tube alleviates fear about what will happen should the tube come out.

7. *Cuff care.* If the individual requires a cuffed tube at home, several modifications can be made to simplify cuff care techniques. A tube with a pressure release valve can be used to prevent overinflation of the cuff. Other approaches to checking for minimal occlusive volume include listening for air at the mouth and having the patient blow lightly onto his hand. If air can be felt or heard the cuff is not sealed.

8. *Knowledge of modifications in lifestyle.* Patients need to know how they can bathe without getting water into the tracheostomy. (For example, use a bib with plastic on one side to shield the tracheostomy opening.) They need to know how to avoid constipation (a Valsalva maneuver is not possible with a tracheostomy.)

It is important that all of the skills be practiced sufficiently in a protected, supervised environment. When patients have sufficient time for learning of the need for care and the skills required, care does not have to be burdensome or stressful.

SUGGESTED READING

Berlauk JF. Prolonged endotracheal intubation vs. tracheostomy. *Crit Care Med.* 1986;14:742–745.

Bone RC, George RB, Hudson LD. *Acute Respiratory Failure.* New York: Churchill Livingstone; 1987.

Civeta JM, Taylor RW, Kirby RR. *Critical Care.* Philadelphia: J B Lippincott Company; 1988.

Colice GL, Stukel TA, Dain B. Laryngeal complications of prolonged intubation. *Chest.* 1989;96:877–884.

Demers RR, Saklad M. Intratracheal inflatable cuffs: a review. *Respir Care.* 1977;22:29–36.

Habib MP. Physiologic implications of artificial airways. *Chest.* 1989;96:180–184.

Keane WM, Rowe LD, Denneny JC, Atkins JP. Complications of intubation. *Ann Otol Rhinol Laryngol.* 1982;91:584–587.

Lewis RF, Scholobohm RM, Thomas AN. Prevention of complications from prolonged tracheal intubation. *Am J Surg.* 1978;135:452–457.

Luce JM, Tyler ML, Pierson DJ. *Intensive Respiratory Care.* Philadelphia: W B Saunders Company; 1984.

Marsh HM, Gillespie DJ, Baumgartner AE. Timing of tracheostomy in the critically ill patient. *Chest.* 1989;96:190–193.

Millar S, Sampson LK, Soukup M. *AACN Procedure Manual for Critical Care.* Philadelphia: W B Saunders Company; 1985.

Plummer AL, Gracey DR. Consensus conference on artificial airways in patients receiving mechanical ventilation. *Chest.* 1989;96:178–180.

Snowberger P. Decreasing tracheal damage due to excessive cuff pressures. *DCCN.* 1986;5:136–142.

Stauffer JL, Olson DE, Petty TL. Complications and consequences of endotracheal intubation and tracheostomy. *Am J Med.* 1981;70:65–76.

Traver GA, Flodquist-Priestley G. Management problems in unilateral lung disease with emphasis on differential lung ventilation. *Crit Care Nurse.* 1986;6:40–50.

Wu W, Lim I, Simpson FA, Turndorf H. Pressure dynamics of endotracheal and tracheostomy cuffs. *Crit Care Med.* 1973;1:197–202.

chapter 13

Pleural Drainage

Pleural drainage is required when air or fluid or both collect in the pleural space and restrict adequate lung expansion and gas exchange. This chapter discusses conditions that require pleural drainage and the various techniques available.

THE PLEURAL SPACE

The pleural cavity is a potential space between the visceral pleura, which is a membrane that covers the lung, and the parietal pleura, which lines the thoracic cavity. The pleural cavity normally contains a small amount of fluid that acts as a lubricant allowing the membranes to slide easily as the lungs and chest move with breathing. Normally, the pressure in the pleural cavity is negative—the result of tension between the tendency of the thoracic cage to expand and the tendency of the lungs to recoil. The degree of this negativity fluctuates slightly with respiration. Negative pleural pressure keeps the lungs from collapsing from the natural recoil of the lung.

CONDITIONS REQUIRING PLEURAL DRAINAGE

Air or fluid in the pleural space disrupts the balance between expansion and recoil. Accumulation of fluid in the pleural space (eg, pleural effusions or empyema) gradually compresses the lung. Air accumulation (from disruption of either pleural membrane) causes loss of negative pressure and lung collapse.

Pneumothorax

Pneumothorax is the term for air in the pleural space. Specific subtypes of pneumothorax designate the source of air entry and the effect on the lung.

A *closed pneumothorax* develops when air enters from a tear in the lung and visceral pleura (see Figure 13-1). A spontaneous closed pneumothorax can occur, most frequently in patients with underlying lung disease and in tall, young men. The risk of closed pneumothorax increases when patients with underlying lung disease are placed on positive pressure ventilation.

Tension pneumothorax is the term given to a large closed collection of pleural air that is under positive pressure (see Figure 13-1). The pressure increases due to a ball-valve effect that allows air to enter the pleural space with inhalation but prevents air from leaving during exhalation. As more and more air is trapped in the pleural space, lung tissue is severely compressed and the heart and great vessels are pushed toward the unaffected side. Ventilation is then compromised in both lungs and cardiac output falls with the reduction in venous return. Tension pneumothorax is a medical emergency that requires prompt treatment to prevent cardiorespiratory collapse.

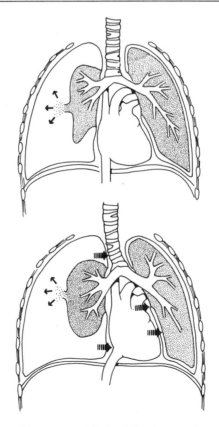

Figure 13-1 Pneumothorax. The upper panel depicts a closed pneumothorax; the lower panel depicts the mediastinal shift that occurs with a tension pneumothorax.

Air can also enter the pleural space from an opening in the chest wall that penetrates the parietal pleura creating an *open pneumothorax.* Air is drawn into the pleural space during inspiration when pleural pressure is less than atmospheric pressure. Open pneumothorax is most commonly associated with chest trauma (eg, stab wounds and gunshot wounds).

Pleural Fluid Accumulation

Several types of fluid can collect in the pleural space. Blood, usually from traumatic injury, is termed *hemothorax.* Hemo-pneumothorax can also occur as an iatrogenic complication of invasive procedures, such as central line placement and thoracentesis. Serous fluid collections, or *pleural effusions,* are associated with a number of pathologic conditions, such as heart failure, atelectasis, and cancer. Lymph collection is termed *chylothorax. Empyema* is purulent fluid associated with such states as pneumonia and lung abscess. It is important to remove this type of fluid before adhesions develop that loculate the purulent fluid, making drainage difficult.

APPROACHES TO PLEURAL DRAINAGE

A variety of techniques are available for pleural drainage. The technique to use depends on the substance to be drained, the relative emergency of treatment, and whether the problem is acute or chronic in nature. Several techniques are described in this section. Chest tubes are discussed in more detail in the following section.

Not all air or fluid collections need to be drained. An otherwise healthy person may tolerate up to a 20% pneumothorax without significant symptoms. Similarly, a pleural effusion may reabsorb without drainage when the underlying lung process resolves.

Thoracentesis

Thoracentesis involves inserting a needle into the pleural space and aspirating air or fluid into a syringe or vacuum bottle. This technique is used to treat pneumothorax and pleural fluid collections, to obtain fluid samples for diagnostic analysis, and to instill medications into the pleural space. Three approaches are commonly used. Anterior thoracentesis is used to remove air; this technique is described in the next section. Pleural fluid can be removed by a posterior approach, in which the patient is sitting upright, or by the mid-axillary approach, in which the patient is supine.

The risks associated with thoracentesis include:

- Bleeding from punctured vessels at the bottom of the rib or a punctured liver or spleen.
- Pneumothorax from inadvertent puncture of the lung.
- Lung laceration should the patient move or cough while the needle is in place.

Patients should be closely monitored for these complications during and following the thoracentesis. A post-thoracentesis chest radiograph is done to evaluate residual air or fluid collections and lung re-expansion and to rule out inadvertent pneumothorax.

Emergency Needle Aspiration

Air in the pleural space moves to the highest area. Needle aspiration of air is done anteriorly at the second interspace mid-clavicular line. This technique can be used emergently when tension pneumothorax is suspected. For example, tension pneumothorax should be suspected when a ventilated patient suddenly develops cyanosis, tachycardia, hypotension, or decreased breath sounds. Cardiopulmonary deterioration may be rapid and preclude radiographic confirmation and elective chest tube insertion.

Long-Term Approaches for Pleural Drainage

Alternative methods for pleural drainage are needed for treatment of recurrent fluid collections and to deal with purulent, loculated infections. Several approaches are available.

Pleurodesis

When pleural effusions recur despite repeated thoracentesis, the pleural space may be eliminated by pleurodesis. After evacuating all of the fluid from the pleural space, a sclerosing agent, such as tetracycline, is instilled via a pleural catheter. The medication creates a severe inflammatory reaction causing the pleural membranes to adhere to each other. Thus, the space for fluid accumulation is eliminated.

Pleurodesis is a painful procedure; patients should be prepared to expect discomfort and should be adequately medicated. For 30 to 60 minutes after the sclerosing agent is instilled, the patient is placed in various positions to facilitate full dispersement of the medication throughout the pleural space. The sclerosing agent is then drained from the pleural space.

Decortication

Adhesions that develop around the purulent fluid of an empyema may prevent the lung from reexpanding when the fluid is removed. Surgical decortication, or peeling of the membrane, may be done to reexpand the lung. The end result is similar to that of pleurodesis: The lung and the chest wall adhere to each other and the potential pleural space is eliminated.

Open Lung Drainage

In rare situations in which pus continues to accumulate in the pleural space and the patient cannot tolerate a thoracotomy, drainage of the pleural space may be accomplished by surgically creating a cutaneous fistula. Thus, the pleural fluid or pus drains to the outside. The wound is packed and handled as any open surgical wound. Usually, granulation tissue will eventually fill the space.

CHEST TUBES

Chest tubes are radiopaque catheters (approximately 20 inches long for adults) with drainage holes along the distal end. They are inserted into the pleural space through a small incision in the chest wall and connected to the drainage system. Chest tube sizes for adults range from 12 French for pneumothorax to large 36 French for removal of blood and purulent fluid.

Chest tubes connected to a closed drainage system serve three general purposes:

1. continuous drainage of air or fluid from the pleural space
2. reexpansion of the lung when collapse is due to loss of negative pleural pressure
3. protection against the reentry of air into the pleural cavity.

Apparatus for Chest Tube Drainage

In conjunction with the chest tube, some type of drainage system must be used to prevent air entry into the pleural space. Two options are discussed in the following section: a 3-bottle drainage system, which is used most frequently, and a Heimlich valve.

Three-Bottle Drainage Systems

There are three basic components to most chest drainage systems—a collection bottle for fluid drained from the chest, a water seal to prevent air from reentering the chest, and a method to control suction. Figures 13-2 and 13-3 demonstrate these components.

In Figure 13-2, fluid drains into a collection bottle (#1). As the fluid accumulates, air in bottle #1 leaves via the connection to bottle #2. Bottle #2 is a water seal acting as a one-way valve. The connection from bottle #1 is partially submerged under water in the second bottle. Air can be vented out (seen as bubbling in the water-seal chamber) but can not reenter through the submerged opening.

Commonly, a third bottle is used to apply controlled suction to the system. Bottle #3 contains water and a straw partially submerged under the water and vented to the outside air; suction is applied to this bottle. The amount of suction actually created in the system is regulated by the depth to which the straw is submerged (or in commercial drainage systems, the depth of fluid in the chamber, eg, 20 cm H_2O). Increasing the suction source does not increase the amount of negative pressure applied to the drainage system; excess suction will draw air through the vented straw (seen as more vigorous bubbling in bottle #3). Bottle #3 serves as a safety device against excessive negative pressure applied to the pleural cavity.

In most clinical situations, one of the commercially available pleural drainage systems is used. These systems utilize three-bottle systems (see Figure 13-3).

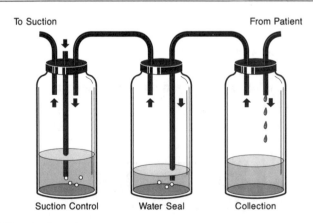

Figure 13-2 Three-bottle suction apparatus.

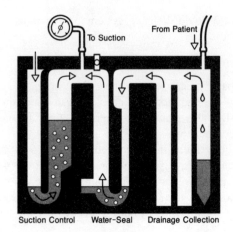

Suction Control   Water–Seal   Drainage Collection

Figure 13-3 Commercial pleural suction apparatus.

Heimlich Valve

In situations in which a chest drainage system is too inconvenient (eg, during ambulation or emergency transport), the external end of the chest tube can be attached to a Heimlich valve (Figure 13-4). This device is essentially a short flexible tube that acts as a one-way valve; excess air or fluid is allowed to escape from the pleural cavity but is prevented from reentering. If fluid is being drained, a collection device (eg, a sterile glove) is placed on the end of the valve. The collection device should be vented to prevent increased pressure. The Heimlich valve is useful during patient transport and has been used when chronic chest drainage (eg, in cases of empyema) is needed outside the hospital setting.

Care of the Patient with Chest-Tube Drainage

Close monitoring of the patient and drainage system are required to ensure effective drainage of the pleural space.

To Patient

Figure 13-4 Heimlich valve.

Patient Assessment

Many of the signs and symptoms of inadequate chest drainage or obstruction in the chest tube are similar to those created by the original problem. The following are signs and symptoms of pleural air or fluid accumulation that indicate either the need for pleural drainage or inadequate drainage after chest tube placement:

- shortness of breath
- tachycardia
- decreased breath sounds on the affected side
- change in sounds over the lung field with percussion: hyperresonance over an air collection, dullness over a fluid collection
- decreased excursion on the affected side
- presence of subcutaneous air
- hypoxemia

A patient developing a *tension* pneumo- or pneumohemothorax may display the signs listed above as well as evidence of mediastinal shift and cardiopulmonary decompensation:

- tracheal deviation
- hypotension
- pulsus paradoxus
- increase in peak inspiratory pressures if mechanically ventilated.

Tube Insertion Site Care

The chest tube is usually sutured in place to prevent it from being dislodged. The dressing over the insertion site is changed daily. Using sterile technique, the surrounding skin is cleansed with an antiseptic, usually providone-iodine. Commonly, petroleum gauze is wrapped around the tube to form an occulsive seal. (This practice is controversial because it frequently leads to maceration of the skin.) Four-by-four gauze pads, which support and protect the tube, are then covered with an airtight dressing. The tubing should be securely taped to the patient's skin to prevent accidental dislodgment. (Specific protocols may vary among institutions.)

Drainage System Assessment and Monitoring

In order to assess and monitor the effectiveness of the drainage system, the following things should be checked:

1. *Connecting tubing.* Tubing connections between the chest tube and the drainage system must be secure and airtight. The connections are usually wrapped with adhesive tape or banding strips.

The collection system must be below the patient's chest at all times to prevent backflow. The long drainage tubing should be coiled on the bed, not hanging down in a loop, which impedes drainage. Patients must be carefully positioned to avoid lying on the tubing or creating kinks that obstruct flow.

2. *Air leaks.* Air leaks are detected by bubbling in the water-seal chamber. Some drainage systems provide estimates of the amount of air leakage by a scale (liters per minute).

If the patient has air accumulation in the pleural space, one would expect to observe bubbling in the water-seal chamber. However, air leaks other than at the level of the pleural space may also cause bubbling. These leaks may occur at connections, in the collection system, or at the skin entry site from improper tube placement. A procedure for identifying the source of the leakage is as follows:

- *Momentarily* clamp the tubing beginning at chest site. If the leak stops, air is coming from the pleural space. (A hissing sound at the insertion site likely means that the drainage holes are too near the skin surface and are drawing in atmospheric air.)
- If the leak continues, move the clamp progressively down the tubing until the bubbling in the water-seal chamber stops. For example, if the leak stops with the clamp below the connection between the chest tube and the drainage tubing, the leak is at that connection.
- Persistent air leakage when the clamp is next to the collection bottle indicates a leak in that system; the collection system should be replaced.

Chest tubes should *never* be clamped other than momentarily for this procedure and during removal. Prolonged clamping may cause a life-threatening tension pneumothorax.

Bubbling in the water-seal chamber often fluctuates with breathing. If the patient is breathing spontaneously, the air leak may increase during exhalation. A ventilated patient may have increased leakage during inspiration when the lungs are inflated with positive pressure. Constant bubbling in the water-seal chamber indicates either a large pleural air leak or a system leak.

3. *Tube patency.* When there is no air leak or drainage, normal pleural pressure variations should cause fluctuations in the water-seal chamber. The water level in the submerged tube in the water-seal bottle (or small column between bottles #1 and #2 on many of the commercial systems) should rise with spontaneous inhalation and fall during mechanical ventilator breaths. Lack of fluc-

tuation may be caused by fibrin or blood clots, kinks in the tubing, or lung tissue occluding the holes in the chest tube.

Milking and stripping are techniques used to move fluid through the tubing and maintain patency. Milking involves alternately compressing and releasing the long drainage tubing. Stripping, which is a controversial technique, is done by grasping and occluding the drainage tubing with one hand and sliding the other hand down the drainage tubing, thus compressing the tubing. Stripping moves clots and fluid into the collection chamber but also creates increased negative pressure in the system. The longer the segment of tubing stripped, the greater the amount of negative pressure created. The excessive negative pressure can damage lung tissue, is painful, and may draw lung tissue against the chest tube holes and occlude them. If stripping is needed to maintain tube patency (eg, to prevent obstruction from blood clots), it should be done gently to avoid creating excessive negative pressure. Many drainage systems have a pressure release valve that will allow atmospheric pressure to enter the drainage chamber to relieve the excess negativity.

4. ***Suction and water-seal chambers.*** Maintain appropriate water levels in both the water-seal and suction chambers. The suction source should be regulated to cause continual, not vigorous bubbling. If suction is not used (ie, the system is placed on water seal), the tubing from the suction chamber to the suction source should be left open to air, not clamped. Clamping this tubing closes the system so air accumulations in the chest cannot escape, creating a risk of tension pneumothorax.

5. ***Portable suction.*** While most patients can be safely disconnected from chest suction and the system placed on water seal for transport, some situations, such as a very large air leak (eg, a bronchopleural fistula), may require continual suction. Clinicians should be aware that lightweight portable suction units are available.

Discontinuing Chest Tubes

Prior to chest tube removal, the chest drainage system is usually placed on water seal and the patient is assessed for air accumulation by chest radiograph. Some physicians prefer to clamp the chest tube prior to removal to rule out small pleural air leaks. If the chest tube is clamped prior to removal, the patient must be observed closely for the signs and symptoms of tension pneumothorax.

Chest tube removal is usually painful; patients should be prepared for the discomfort. Patients should be instructed to exhale (the Valsalva maneuver, if not contraindicated); the chest tube is rapidly pulled during exhalation while the sutures are simultaneously tightened, thus closing the skin incision site. (If bifurcated tubes are in place, the second chest tube must be clamped to prevent air from entering the pleural space when the first tube is removed.) The insertion site is immediately covered with an occlusive dressing that can be removed within 48 to 72 hours. Patients must be closely monitored for signs of pneumothorax following removal of the chest tube. A chest radiograph is usually done to rule out pleural air accumulation.

Special Problem: Patient with a Bronchopleural Fistula on Mechanical Ventilation

The term bronchopleural fistula is usually used to refer to those patients who have a large continuous air leak. When these patients are receiving mechanical positive pressure ventilation, the increased pressure during inspiration enlarges the fistula. Much of the delivered tidal volume will be delivered to the pleural space through the bronchopleural fistula, and then evacuated by the chest drainage system. The result is a severe decrease in effective ventilation and difficulty in maintaining lung expansion.

Control of ventilation in the face of such a large fistula is extremely difficult. Techniques such as high frequency ventilation may be used in an effort to reduce airway pressure and therefore the amount of volume lost through the fistula. Pleural suction levels may also be increased to evacuate the space. Because the pleural suction approach does not lessen the amount of air lost through the fistula, an increase in delivered tidal volume may be required.

SUGGESTED READING

Duncan C, Erickson R. Pressures associated with chest tube stripping. *Heart Lung.* 1982;11:166–171.

Duncan CR, Erickson RS, Weigel RM. Effect of chest tube management on drainage after cardiac surgery. *Heart Lung.* 1987;16:1–9.

Erickson RS. Mastering the ins and outs of chest drainage: part 1. *Nursing.* 1989;19:37–44.

Fishman NH. *Thoracic Drainage: A Manual of Procedures.* Chicago: Year Book Medical Publishers, Inc.; 1983.

Lim-Levy F, Babler SA, De Groot-Kosolcharoen J, Kosolcharoen P, Kroncke GM. Is milking and stripping chest tubes really necessary? *Ann Thorac Surg.* 1986;42:77–80.

Luce JM, Tyler ML, Pierson DJ. *Intensive Respiratory Care.* Philadelphia: W B Saunders Company; 1984.

Millar S, Sampson L, Soukup M. *AACN Procedure Manual for Critical Care.* Philadelphia: W B Saunders Company; 1985.

Miller K, Sahn S. Chest tubes: indications, technique, management, and complications. *Chest.* 1987;91:258–264.

Waxman KS. Pleural disorders. In: Shoemaker W, Ayres S, Grevnik A, Holbrook P, Thompson W, eds. *Textbook of Critical Care.* Philadelphia: W B Saunders Company; 1989.

chapter 14

Mechanical Ventilation

Mechanical ventilation is a supportive therapy used to treat respiratory failure in both the acute-care and home-care settings. This chapter discusses the indications for mechanical ventilation, approaches to mechanical ventilation (including basic types of ventilators and their application), and special care concerns. Specific problems of both the acute- and home-care settings are included in the discussion.

INDICATIONS FOR MECHANICAL VENTILATION

The criteria used as the basis for instituting mechanical ventilation are widely cited (see Table 14-1). These criteria provide measures of the patient's ability to maintain ventilation, including ventilatory muscle strength, as well as measures of the efficiency of oxygenation. Although the criteria may at first glance appear clear cut, the actual clinical decision is frequently not so easily made.

The need for mechanical ventilation in the acutely apneic patient, as for example during a surgical procedure, is clear cut. Mechanical ventilation is also used to treat acute respiratory failure when other conservative approaches to improving ventilation and oxygenation have not been successful. When the patient was previously healthy, the criteria listed in Table 14-1 are most easily applied. Before mechanical ventilation is instituted, the patient usually demonstrates severe impairment as measured by several of the criteria. In addition, the general clinical impression supports the decision that the patient is and will be unable to maintain ventilation and oxygenation. When the patient demonstrates acute respiratory failure superimposed upon chronic pulmonary dysfunction, the decision to institute mechanical ventilation becomes more difficult. The philosophical problem of whether or not mechanical ventilation is appropriate becomes a significant dilemma. A medical judgment must be made to decide if the

Table 14-1 Criteria For Initiation of Mechanical Ventilation

Measurement	Criteria	Normal Values
Ventilation		
PaCO$_2$	>60 mm Hg*	35–45 mm Hg
pH	<7.25	7.35–7.45
Mechanics		
VC	>10–15 mL/kg*	65–75 mL/kg
VT	<5 mL/kg	
MIF	<−20 cm H$_2$O	−50 to −100 cm H$_2$O
Oxygenation		
PaO$_2$	<60 mm Hg on FIO$_2$ > 0.6	
A-a DO$_2$	>350 mm Hg on FIO$_2$ = 1.0	<100 mm Hg
Qs/QT	>20%	<5%

*These values reflect critical values for previously healthy patients with acute respiratory failure. Note that patients with chronic failure may exhibit values in this range as their normal values.

acute respiratory failure is a response to a specific insult or if it is the result of the chronic progression of the underlying disorder. This decision also includes the patient's ultimate prognosis—Will the patient, after treatment, be able to maintain adequate spontaneous ventilation? Philosophically, clinicians must be aware of their own prejudices and the patient's wishes regarding the possibility of ultimate ventilator dependence. Physiologic criteria are also applied. As noted in the table, however, the criteria must be interpreted relative to the patient's normal baseline state and not simply to normal values.

Once the decision to institute mechanical ventilation has been made, the decision concerning what type of ventilation will be used must be made. There are basically two types of mechanical ventilators, the negative pressure ventilators and the positive pressure ventilators.

NEGATIVE PRESSURE VENTILATION

Negative pressure ventilators apply a negative pressure to the chest during inspiration. The negative pressure expands the thorax, creating a pressure difference between the lung and the atmosphere, and air is drawn into the lung. When the pressure is released, the patient exhales normally; the force is lung recoil. Some negative pressure ventilators allow the application of positive pressure during exhalation so that expiratory time can be shortened. The basic settings on the negative pressure ventilators are simply pressure and rate. The iron lung is a classic example of a negative pressure ventilator.

Within the last decade negative pressure ventilators have received renewed interest. Instead of the cumbersome iron lung, negative pressure ventilation is now usually applied using a cuirass or shell ventilator or the poncho wrap. The most common type of shell ventilator consists of a hard shell (often referred to as a turtle shell) that encloses the anterior and lateral chest. The shell is held in place by straps and has cushioned edges to facilitate obtaining a seal between the chest wall and the device. Various sizes of shells are available so that they fit the patient. The poncho wrap uses a cage device over the anterior and lateral chest, but the cage is then covered with a plastic wrap or poncho. The poncho may enclose the entire body or just the upper torso.

These negative pressure ventilators are reserved for patients who do not require continuous mechanical ventilation and who have a compliant chest wall. They are usually not effective in patients who have very stiff lungs or markedly increased airway resistance. Negative pressure ventilation offers the advantage that the patient does not require an artificial airway, but at the same time the patient must be able to maintain airway patency. For these reasons, negative pressure ventilation is most frequently seen in patients with muscle dysfunction leading to respiratory failure.

Care of the patient receiving negative pressure ventilation presents some special concerns. Those of major importance include:

- Observation of the ventilatory pattern demonstrates a downward movement of the shell as the thorax expands; with exhalation, the shell moves outward. (As the negative pressure is applied between the shell and the chest wall, the two move toward each other.)
- A tight seal between the shell and the chest wall (or poncho wrap and body) must be maintained or a negative pressure will not be created around the chest. The skin must be checked for areas of irritation, abrasion due to movement of the shell.
- The negative pressure, especially with the poncho wrap, may cause pooling of the blood in the abdomen leading to changes in hemodynamics (decreased cardiac output and its sequelae).
- Patient immobility may result in anxiety.
- Patients may complain of feeling chilled due to the continuous movement of air over the chest.

POSITIVE PRESSURE VENTILATION

Positive pressure ventilation applies positive pressure to the airway during inspiration. The pressure gradient thereby pushes air into the lung. (It is obvious that the pressure gradient is the opposite of that occuring during spontaneous ventilation or during negative pressure ventilation.) When the positive pressure is withdrawn, the patient exhales normally. Positive pressure ventilation is the most common approach to mechanical ventilation. When used for continuous mechanical ventilation, positive pressure ventilation requires intubation; except in small children, the tube must be cuffed (see Chapter 12).

Positive pressure ventilators are classified by the method of terminating the inspiratory cycle. The two most common types are the pressure-limited and volume-limited ventilators. These two classes of positive pressure ventilators will be discussed separately.

Pressure-Limited Ventilators

Pressure-limited ventilators deliver gas to the lung until a preset pressure is met. At that point, the machine cycles off and exhalation is accomplished by withdrawal of the positive pressure from the airway. The actual volume delivered to the patient is variable depending on the pressure set and the mechanical characteristics of the lung. For example, if lung stiffness or airway resistance increases, the volume delivered to the patient will decrease as the inspiratory pressure remains constant. For this reason, volume must be closely monitored when using a pressure-limited ventilator. Examples of pressure-limited ventilators include the Bennett PR2 and the Bird Mark series.

These ventilators are most commonly used for intermittent positive pressure breathing (IPPB) treatments. When used for intermittent treatments, intubation of the patient is not required but the clinician must ensure airway patency and correct use of the apparatus so that the patient does not generate high oral pressures that would cycle the machine; for example, holding air in the mouth and blowing back. (Some of the uses of the IPPB treatments have been discussed in Chapter 10, in the section on hyperinflation, and in Chapter 8, in the section on delivery of aerosolized medications. In addition, IPPB treatments may be used to acutely lower a patient's $PaCO_2$ when an attempt is being made to avoid intubation and continuous mechanical ventilation.) In some settings, pressure-limited ventilators are also used for continuous mechanical ventilation.

Volume-Limited Ventilators

The volume-limited ventilators deliver a predetermined volume of gas to the lung, regardless of the pressure required. Therefore, as the lung compliance or airway resistance varies, volume delivery remains constant. As a safety device, these ventilators also incorporate a pressure limit. The pressure limit prevents pressure from exceeding a level determined by the clinician. (When the pressure limit is met, an alarm will sound and any additional volume will be vented and not delivered to the patient.) Ventilators of the volume-limited class are the most common type of ventilator used for continuous mechanical ventilation. Examples are the Bennett MA1, Bennett 7200, Servo, and Bear.

INSTITUTING VOLUME VENTILATION

The initiation of volume ventilation requires that certain basic settings be made on the ventilator. These settings determine how deep a breath is delivered, how fast the breath is delivered, how frequently breaths are delivered, and the concentration of oxygen in the inspired gas. Although the labels on the various controls may vary among different ventilators, all allow these basic settings. There are general guidelines for setting these ventilator controls when a patient is initially placed on a ventilator. As subsequent arterial blood gases are analyzed, adjustments are made in the settings to achieve the level of ventilation and oxygenation support needed by the patient. Each parameter should be specifically determined for each patient. The usual ranges of the initial ventilator settings are as follows:

1. *FIO_2*. In most situations the oxygen concentration is usually set at high levels (80 to 100%) initially. Arterial blood for blood-gas analysis is drawn within 15 to 20 minutes and the FIO_2 is adjusted downward according to the blood-gas results.

2. *Tidal volume*. A volume of 10 to 12 mL/kg is initially set. This setting provides large volume ventilation so that periodic sighs are not necessary.

3. *Inspiratory flow rate*. The inspiratory flow rate allows the clinician to adjust how fast the patient will receive the desired tidal volume; the higher the flow rate, the shorter the inspiratory time. Inspiratory flows should be adjusted according to the patient's ventilatory pattern and peak airway pressures. If the patient is breathing spontaneously, inspiratory flows must be sufficient to meet demand, and the inspiratory time should be adjusted so that the inspiratory to expiratory time (I:E) ratio allows for an expiratory time that is approximately twice that of inspiratory time.

4. *Respiratory rate*. Initially the ventilator is set at 12 to 16 breaths per minute. The ventilator may have a specific rate control, or the respiratory rate may be determined by the inspiratory and expiratory times.

These basic settings provide immediate ventilation. Observation of the patient and blood-gas results are then used to make adjustments and additional settings. Several additional settings are usually made immediately. These settings are discussed in the following sections and include the mode of ventilation, setting the pressure limit (discussed under alarms), and the level of positive end-expiratory pressure (PEEP).

MODES OF VENTILATION

The mode of ventilation determines the pattern by which mechanical breaths are delivered. Which mode is used will depend upon the specific clinical presentation of the patient. Figure 14-1 presents the pressure-time relationships produced by the various modes of ventilation.

Controlled ventilation refers to the situation in which all breaths are delivered by the ventilator at a preset rate. This mode of ventilation is reserved for the apneic patient or the patient who is sedated or paralyzed to suppress spontaneous inspiratory efforts. Some patients have such rapid spontaneous rates that they

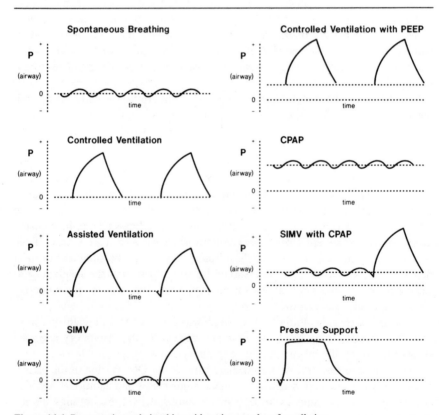

Figure 14-1 Pressure-time relationships with various modes of ventilation.

"buck" the ventilator; bucking or fighting the ventilator refers to the situation in which the patient is attempting to exhale before the total inspired volume is delivered. This situation results in excessively high airway pressures and an inability to successfully ventilate the patient. Sedation or paralysis with such agents as *Versed* or pancuronium suppress the spontaneous efforts so that ventilation can be controlled.

Assisted ventilation refers to setting the ventilator so that it responds to the patient's spontaneous inspiratory efforts. As the patient inhales, the ventilator detects the fall in airway pressure and delivers a mechanical inspiration. Thus the patient's spontaneous inspiration is assisted by the machine. Mechanical ventilators have a sensitivity control whereby the ventilator can be made more or less sensitive to the patient's spontaneous efforts. In the assist mode the respiratory rate is dependent on the patient's spontaneous rate. The assist mode is usually instituted as an assist–control mode. Assist–control means that a back-up control rate is set on the ventilator. The back-up rate is less than the patient's spontaneous rate. Should the patient become apneic or dramatically slow his spontaneous rate, the ventilator will deliver the tidal volume at the preset control rate. Many ventilators have a monitor that allows the clinician to know if the ventilator breath has been initiated by the patient's inspiratory effort or by the machine. Observing the airway pressure monitor will also allow the clinician to detect if the breath was initiated by spontaneous effort or not; if initiated by a spontaneous effort, there will be a slight fall in airway pressure just prior to the positive pressure breath delivered by the ventilator. A drop in airway pressure that is not followed by a machine breath indicates that the sensitivity is not set high enough to detect the patient's spontaneous effort.

Intermittent mandatory ventilation (IMV) is a mode that combines ventilator delivered breaths with spontaneous, unassisted breaths. This mode has been used extensively in weaning patients from mechanical ventilation. It is also used when obliteration of the patient's ventilatory drive by sedation is not desired but the mechanical assistance of all spontaneous efforts would result in excessive alveolar ventilation. When IMV is used, a ventilator rate is set that is less than the spontaneous rate. The patient is assured of receiving the number of ventilator initiated breaths set on the rate control. Additional spontaneous breaths are allowed without mechanical assistance; the tidal volume of these unassisted rates is determined by the amount of inspiratory force the patient's inspiratory muscles can generate. IMV may also be referred to as synchronized IMV (SIMV) or demand IMV (DIMV); SIMV and DIMV refer to those settings whereby the preset number of mechanical breaths are provided in response to the patient's spontaneous efforts. Another variation of IMV is mandatory minute ventilation (MMV), which provides a predetermined minimal minute volume. When the patient's spontaneous minute volume is lower than the value set, the ventilator will deliver a sufficient number of machine breaths to maintain the minute volume. Therefore, when MMV is used, the number of machine-delivered tidal volumes is variable.

When IMV is used, it is important that the patient's work of breathing is not increased too much—to the level at which respiratory muscle fatigue or decreased ventilation or both result. Several factors need to be considered. One is the number and depth of spontaneous breaths. For example, if an IMV rate was set at six breaths per minute and the spontaneous rate is 30, there would be concern about the patient's increased ventilatory drive and work of breathing. Another consideration is the size of the artificial airway. Endotracheal tubes with small lumens (size seven or less in the adult) add significantly to the work of breathing; if the IMV rate is set very low, the work of breathing spontaneously through the endotracheal tube to sustain total ventilation may put an unwarranted burden on the patient's inspiratory muscles. Finally, the mechanical apparatus by which IMV is delivered must be considered. Continuous flow systems provide gas in response to a spontaneous inspiration after minimal airway pressure changes. Demand systems provide gas after a valve has been opened. Many of the demand systems require a relatively large drop in airway pressure before the valve opens; thus the work of breathing may be dramatically increased.

VENTILATOR ALARMS

Ventilators are usually equipped with a combination of audible and visual alarms; some alarms are built into the ventilator while on some types of ventilators the alarms that are necessary must be added. (This is particularly true in settings in which earlier models of mechanical ventilators are used.) While some alarms can be silenced for periods of time (ie, low pressure alarms can be silenced during circuit disconnection for suctioning), care must be taken to turn all alarms on and make sure that they are operable prior to leaving the patient's bedside. The basic alarms found on most mechanical ventilators are:

- *Oxygen.* Alarm sounds if oxygen supply to the ventilator is interrupted. An in-line oxygen, monitor can be added to detect changes in delivered FIO_2.
- *Pressure limit.* Alarm sounds if set value is exceeded during inspiration.
- *Inverse ratio.* Alarm sounds if expiratory time is less than inspiratory time (I:E ratio less than 1).
- *Low pressure.* Alarm sounds if peak inspiratory pressure is less than alarm level set. The alarm is usually set 10 cm H_2O lower than peak inspiratory pressure. It functions as a disconnect alarm and an apnea alarm. Units that are added to ventilators often monitor a time period within which a certain minimal pressure must be met; on these units, both time and minimal pressure are set.

One of these alarms, the pressure limit, requires special attention. The airway pressure is continually monitored during volume ventilation (preferably the pressure is monitored at a point close to the endotracheal or tracheostomy tube). The peak inspiratory pressure will vary with the volume delivered as well as the mechanical properties of the lung and chest wall. A limit can be set for the peak inspiratory pressure—a level that will not be exceeded during delivery of a mechanical breath. Usually this level is set approximately 10 cm H_2O above the level that the patient usually attains with a ventilator breath. Therefore, the pressure limit alarm (usually audible and visual) provides the clinician with information about the mechanical properties of the lung; if the pressure limit is met, assuming volume has not been changed, it means that resistance or stiffness has increased. The pressure limit is usually set to facilitate monitoring and care, not as a safety limit. Of course, excessive pressures could lead to complications, but pressure limits are usually set below the safety level. For the clinician, it is also important to realize that when the pressure limit is met, additional volume is not delivered to the patient. For example, if a tidal volume of 900 mL is set but the pressure limit is met after 500 mL has been delivered, the remaining 400 mL will not be delivered to the patient.

Additional alarms may also be used. Examples are a low PEEP alarm and a high temperature alarm.

POSITIVE END-EXPIRATORY PRESSURE

Positive End-Expiratory Pressure (PEEP) refers to the maintenance of a positive pressure plateau at end expiration. Instead of airway pressure returning to zero (atmospheric) at end exhalation, the pressure is maintained at some level greater than atmospheric. The level of pressure may be set; if PEEP is desired, it is usually set initially at 5 cm H_2O and slowly increased according to the patient's response and tolerance. The direct effect of the addition of PEEP is to increase the FRC, or functional residual capacity. PEEP is usually added when a patient has very stiff, noncompliant lungs. The very stiff lung becomes so small that airway closure and alveolar collapse occur with resulting shunt and low $\dot{V}/\dot{Q}$ abnormalities (there is no ventilation but perfusion continues). Increasing the FRC increases the lung volume, opening nonventilated areas, and improves oxygenation by reducing the shunt fraction. Therefore, the desired clinical response to PEEP is improved oxygenation and an ability to reduce the FIO_2 to acceptable levels. When used to improve oxygenation in patients with stiff, noncompliant lungs and a large shunt fraction, PEEP levels of 10 to 15 cm H_2O are usual; levels may occasionally, in very severely ill patients, be in the 20 to 30 cm H_2O range.

In many settings, 5 cm H_2O PEEP is used routinely on patients who are mechanically ventilated. This level is termed *physiologic PEEP.* With a normal, intact airway, most people sigh and yawn periodically. The yawn maneuver is actually a means of producing increased intrathoracic pressure and is similar to the application of PEEP. When the ability to yawn is removed by placement of an artificial airway (the patient can no longer increase intrathoracic pressure against a closed glottis), it is believed that the addition of 5 cm H_2O PEEP mimics the effect of a closed glottis and prevents alveolar collapse.

Continuous positive airway pressure (CPAP) is a form of PEEP and refers to the use of PEEP in the spontaneously breathing patient. A continuous positive pressure is maintained over the airway. As the patient inhales spontaneously, the pressure drops slightly but remains positive; as the patient exhales, pressures rise. (Figure 14-1 includes a time/pressure tracing of CPAP.) CPAP is used for the spontaneous breaths when a patient is on PEEP and IMV. It is also frequently used for weaning from mechanical ventilation.

Some ventilators have a CPAP mode that allows the patient to remain connected to the ventilator circuitry while ventilating spontaneously. Actually the use of the term CPAP is often a misnomer in this situation because the CPAP mode can be used without PEEP.

NEW APPROACHES TO MECHANICAL VENTILATION

Several new approaches to mechanical ventilation are available. Four are briefly described. For those interested in a more extensive discussion of these techniques, there are sources listed in the suggested reading list at the end of this chapter.

Differential lung ventilation refers to the technique in which the right and left lung are ventilated separately. This technique is used in unilateral lung disease when ventilation with one ventilator results in worsening of the $\dot{V}/\dot{Q}$ relationships; the ventilator breath goes preferentially to the good lung. Differential lung ventilation requires the placement of an endobronchial tube. The two lumens are then connected to two ventilators. The two ventilators do not need to be synchronized; each can be set to deliver a different tidal volume at different flow rates, different respiratory rates, and different PEEP levels. The FIO_2 is set at the same level on each ventilator.

High frequency ventilation is a technique that has greater usage in the neonatal population than in children and adults. It has been used in adult patients with large bronchopleural fistulas. Several subtypes of high frequency ventilation are available. All utilize small tidal volumes (less than anatomic dead space) at rapid respiratory rates (greater than 60 breaths per minute). The goal is to maintain gas exchange with decreased intrathoracic pressures.

Pressure support is a new modification of mechanical ventilation that is receiving widespread attention. It is primarily used to decrease the work of breathing on spontaneous breaths (with either CPAP or IMV). Pressure support refers to the application of a positive pressure (similar to pressure-limited ventilators) to the spontaneous breaths. As the patient inhales spontaneously, the gas is delivered at a constant pressure, until the inspiratory flow rates fall below a specified level. The higher the level of pressure support, the greater the proportion of the total work of breathing that is done by the ventilator. When used to facilitate weaning, the level of pressure support is usually at the 5 to 10 H_2O level.

Another new approach is pressure control, inverse ratio ventilation (PC-IRV). In this type of mechanical ventilation, inspiration is pressure- and time-limited. The ventilator is set so that inspiration is longer than expiration (inspiration may be four times longer than expiration). The level of inspiratory pressure held for that time is controlled (a pressure limit). The rationale is to decrease peak intrathoracic pressures, prolong alveolar filling time so that poorly ventilated areas can be filled, and prevent complete recoil and emptying of the lung on exhalation (thus increasing FRC). The number of ventilators that can be used for this type of ventilation is limited. Also, this type of ventilator is presently reserved for acutely ill patients when other conventional means of ventilation have not been successful, and it usually requires that the patient be sedated and paralyzed.

COMPLICATIONS OF MECHANICAL VENTILATION

Complications of mechanical ventilation include those related to problems with the airway and mechanical problems with the ventilator itself, as well as the physiologic side effects of therapy.

Airway Complications

Airway complications are usually related to right main-stem intubation and cuff malfunction resulting in inadequate ventilation. Long-term complications of intubation also include laryngeal damage and potential tracheal stenosis. These airway problems are discussed more fully in Chapter 12, Artificial Airway Care.

Ventilator Problems

Problems with the mechanical function of the ventilator may be actual malfunction of the apparatus or iatrogenic. The ventilator circuitry is the most common source of malfunction, ie, leaks in the expiratory valve or leaks in the circuitry connections. There may also be failures of the controls and electrical system. More common than true ventilator malfunction are iatrogenic problems—in other words, human error. The ventilator controls may be incorrectly set, but most commonly, alarms are turned off or do not evoke a response. The results can be disastrous!

Pulmonary Complications

The most common complications are hyperventilation and respiratory alkalemia. These problems are usually iatrogenic and due to the level of ventilation provided.

Barotrauma (air in the pleural space, mediastinum, or peritoneum) may result from mechanical ventilation. Barotrauma is most commonly seen when mechanical ventilation results in hyperinflation (the hyperinflation may be regional rather than generalized) and when there is alveolar damage (eg, area of infection or decreased pulmonary capillary blood flow). Although a small pneumothorax may not be clinically apparent, most pneumothoraces that occur during mechanical ventilation do produce symptoms, eg, increased peak pressures and increased respiratory rate. When a pneumothorax occurs, a chest tube must be inserted; the presence of a bronchopleural fistula with positive pressure ventilation can quickly lead to a tension pneumothorax.

Hemodynamic Complications

The application of positive pressure to the lung can result in a variety of changes in cardiovascular function. Most often cited is a decrease in cardiac output. Decreased cardiac output is most common when high pressures are transmitted to the pleural space. The transmission of high pleural pressures is related to lung hyperinflation and chest wall stiffness, not simply to the pressures used to ventilate the patient. Because PEEP is more likely to hyperinflate the lung, the clinician should be more aware of these hemodynamic changes when PEEP is used. The changes in cardiac output and other related cardiovascular problems are discussed more fully in Chapter 16, Hemodynamic Monitoring.

Complications in Other Systems

Other complications associated with mechanical ventilation include the following: malnourishment, increased risk for venous thrombosis and emboli, stress ulcers and gastrointestinal hemorrhage, infection, renal malfunction, and psychologic disturbances. These complications have led to the routine institution of such prophylactic measures as low dose heparin (unless contraindicated), antacid therapy, and early institution of enteral feedings.

CARE OF THE PATIENT REQUIRING MECHANICAL VENTILATION

In addition to ongoing monitoring of patients requiring mechanical ventilation to ensure adequacy of ventilation as well as to detect potential complications of mechanical ventilation (see Chapter 15), there are several areas of care that require special attention. Special areas of concern include airway care, positioning, nutrition, communication, and environmental factors. Airway care, which includes suctioning technique, airway clearance, and the care of patient in relation to use of endotracheal or tracheal tubes with cuffs, is discussed in Chapters 11 and 12. The remaining areas are discussed in this chapter.

Positioning

The complications of immobility, and the need for turning and positioning are well known. In the mechanically ventilated patient, the problem of immobility is related to both the underlying disease and its treatment. Frequent turning and changing of position are often difficult due to the limitations imposed by equipment, infusion lines, and treatment schedules. In addition, many of these patients have cardiovascular instability that may result in dramatic hemodynamic changes when the patient is turned. It is imperative, however, that the patient be turned. Not only should the patient be turned side to side, but especially for patients with adult respiratory distress syndrome (ARDS), the prone position should also be used if possible. For patients with cardiovascular instability or trauma, side-to-side turning may be facilitated by the use of one of the new rotating beds, such as the Rotorest®; with these special beds, turning is continuous but so slow that cardiovascular changes are minimized. As the patient's condition improves, the patient should be out of bed, in a chair, and eventually ambulated as soon as possible. The patient is manually ventilated (using a self-inflating bag and oxygen) during ambulation.

Nutrition

Nutritional support of critically ill patients, including those being supported with mechanical ventilation, is a major concern. Much information is available examining various aspects of nutritional support for ventilated patients, including when to begin nutritional support, what types of nutrients to supply, and the effects of the nutritional support on the patient's course on mechanical ventilation.

The initial step in beginning nutritional support is an assessment of the patient's nutritional status. Standard anthropometric measurements (triceps skinfold, percent ideal body weight [%IBW], and mid-arm circumference), biochemical tests (serum transferrin, prealbumin, albumin, and iron-binding capacity), or immunological indicators (lymphocyte count and delayed hypersensitivity) can be used in the nutritional assessment.

However, most of these parameters are not sensitive to changes in acute negative nitrogen balance. The clinician usually bases the decision to begin nutritional support on assessment of several interrelated factors: (1) the patient's premorbid nutritional status, ie, does the patient have a chronic illness that has depleted the energy stores available; (2) %IBW, with consideration of possible positive fluid balance; (3) prealbumin or transferrin levels. Sometimes an estimate of energy expenditure is also calculated using an equation such as the Harris-Benedict equation, which attempts to factor in weight, age, and height of the person. The equation is as follows:

Resting Energy Expenditure (REE)

MALES = 66.473 + (13.7516 × weight in kg) + 5.0033 × height in
cm − (6.755 × age in yrs)
FEMALES = 65.0955 + (9.5634 × weight in kg) + 1.8496 × height in
cm − (4.6756 × age in yrs)

The problem associated with any equation that uses weight as a variable is that in critically ill catabolic patients, weight becomes an unreliable reading due to the occurrence of increases in intracellular volume or third spacing. Therefore, the equation may be helpful in the critically ill patient to estimate energy requirements, but additional adjustments may need to be made. To accommodate for increases in metabolic requirements due to severe illness and stress, the REE is usually multiplied by a factor of 1.2, representing an increase of 20% over the resting requirements.

Generally, patients who clearly demonstrate malnutrition, based on the assessment, should, as soon as possible (within 24 to 48 hours), receive nutritional supplementation aimed at repletion. In trauma patients who are admitted without clear malnutrition but in whom mechanical support is anticipated to exceed five to seven days, nutritional supplementation is usually begun within 24 to 48 hours to maintain nutritional status rather than trying to catch up at a later time. For patients who are not clearly in poor nutritional status and who are expected to require mechanical ventilation for only a few days (five to seven), nutritional supplementation may not be required.

Once the decision to institute nutritional support is made, a determination must be made regarding which nutrients, including vitamins, minerals, and trace elements, to include. Carbohydrates, fats, and proteins are given in sufficient quantity and proportions, as determined during the initial assessment, to meet the energy requirements of the patient and to restore or maintain nitrogen balance. Generally, for patients with acute respiratory failure who require supplementation, 20% of the calories should be supplied by protein and the remaining 80% supplied by carbohydrate and fat in equal proportions. Increased CO_2 production can be observed with a high carbohydrate load, making weaning from mechanical ventilation difficult. There are special dietary formulas available, such as *Pulmocare,* which have the carbohydrate-to-fat proportion adjusted to minimize increased CO_2 production. Additionally, it is recommended not to exceed the individual's estimated caloric requirements since overfeeding can stimulate lipogenesis resulting in an increased respiratory quotient and increased CO_2 production.

Whenever possible, the enteral route for feeding (versus total parenteral nutrition) should be used. When the patient's gastrointestinal tract is functional, enteral feedings have the added advantage of reducing gastrointestinal complications, such as mucosal breakdown and the development of stress ulcers. Enteral feedings are, however, associated with additional care problems, such as increased risks of aspiration and increased incidence of diarrhea (which can often be severe). Slowly increasing the amount and concentration of the enteral feedings can help to reduce diarrhea. The problem with giving reduced strengths of the feedings is that nutritional requirements are only being partially met. The use of duodenal tubes rather than gastric tubes can help reduce the possibility of aspiration of feedings; elevating the head of the bed during and immediately after feedings is also helpful.

Communication

One of the most difficult and frustrating aspects of caring for mechanically ventilated patients is the area of communication. Much time is often spent in attempts to assess the etiology of a patient's discomfort or anxiety. Often the anxiety stems from the patient's inability to understand the reason that they are unable to speak. The anxiety can be intensified by fear of all the machines in the surroundings with their accompanying array of lights and sounds. Every patient should be reminded often that they cannot speak and should not try to speak while intubated; they also need to be reassured that they will be able to speak later when the endotracheal tube is removed.

A great deal of necessary communication can be accomplished by posing closed-ended questions to which the patients can respond by shaking or nodding their heads. When the patient needs to ask for something or communicate in a manner other than responding to a question, the clinician needs to be more creative. Letter boards are sometimes used; they enable the patient to point to letters and form words. Some patients are able to write as a means of communication when provided with a magic slate or paper and pencil.

If the patient is tracheotomized, periodically deflating the cuff on the tracheostomy tube may allow the patient to speak. The ability to speak will vary with the amount of air flow around the tracheostomy tube and the existence of any cord trauma due to prior intubation. Use of a fenestrated tube is more helpful. When the fenestration is used, the patient cannot be mechanically ventilated; the inner cannula must be removed to open the fenestration, and the cuff deflated. When the patient is placed back on mechanical ventilation, the cuff is reinflated and the inner cannula inserted. For patients who cannot tolerate any time off mechanical ventilation, a talking tracheostomy tube may be used. (These special tracheostomy tubes are described in Chapter 12.)

The technique of deflating the cuff is rarely helpful in patients with oral or nasal endotracheal tubes. It is also not encouraged due to the potential for injury to the vocal cords (due to cord movement against the endotracheal tube).

Other alternative and less frequently used methods are available. They include talking endotracheal tubes. These tubes are similar to the talking tracheostomy tubes. In addition, they include a tone-generating device; the device creates the vibrating column of air, not the vocal cords, and the words are formed by oral movements. Other devices, such as the Venti-Voice® provide, via a small tube inserted into the nasopharynx, a vibrating column of air; words are formed by mouth movement. The patient controls the flow through the small tube by a finger control or a magnetic forehead switch for quadraplegics.

Environment

Much has been written concerning the effect of the intensive care environment on the patient. There is a spectrum of effects of sensory overload and sleep deprivation that can be noted in most patients in an intensive care setting, ranging from mild disorientation to place or time to the full blown *ICU psychosis* syndrome. Even patients requiring only short-term mechanical ventilation for respiratory failure have reported hallucinations and delusions. These psychologic disturbances frequently result in combative behavior that complicates general care and may result in an erroneous labeling of the patient, which regretfully may follow him throughout his hospitalization.

In addition to the physiologic factors such as hypoxia, there are multiple environmental factors that contribute to disorientation. These factors include lights that are on at all times, noise from various machines and alarms, often no windows or the curtains pulled around the patient's bed for privacy, and frequently no indication of time orientation (ie, a clock or calendar). An effort should be made to modify these factors whenever possible to allow patients to achieve adequate rest and minimize the effect of sleep deprivation and sensory overload.

As the technology of mechanical ventilation has improved, patients who require ventilation on a chronic basis have become more common. To avoid the problems of the intensive care environment, those patients who are medically stable can be transferred to other settings. Many patients progress from an intensive care unit to a step-down unit to a general unit to a home or chronic care facility. Similarly, other patients who receive chronic ventilation at home and require admission for a non-ventilation problem are often admitted to a non-intensive care setting. Institutions have policies describing the circumstances under which ventilator patients can receive care outside of the intensive care unit.

MECHANICAL VENTILATION IN THE HOME SETTING

Although most patients are able to be weaned from mechanical ventilation, some require chronic mechanical ventilation. Few institutional settings are able to care for these patients. As a result, in the last decade, home ventilation has become more common. The number of patients who do require such prolonged ventilatory support is relatively small, however.

The complexity of a home ventilation program is such that patients to whom this alternative is offered must be carefully selected. Experience has demonstrated that such a program is more likely to be successful if the patient's basic diagnosis is a neuromuscular or skeletal problem versus a primary pulmonary disorder. Other factors that help to predict success include the patient's ability to sustain spontaneous ventilation for at least several hours a day, the absence of severe dyspnea, and, of major importance, strong, available family support.

Determining Clinical Stability

Any patient who is a candidate for home mechanical ventilation must be clinically stable. Factors that must be considered include:

- absence of acute, severe dyspnea and/or tachypnea
- acceptable blood gases on an FIO_2 less than 0.4

- excessive airway pressures (> 35 cm H_2O) not required to maintain ventilation
- ventilator settings have been stable for several weeks and no major changes anticipated
- cardiovascular stability, ie, absence of life-threatening arrythmias or severe congestive heart failure
- ability to maintain airway clearance (with use of suctioning)
- healed tracheostomy in place if positive pressure ventilation is to be used
- adequate nutritional status; includes adequate growth for pediatric patients
- psychologic stability

Planning for Home Discharge

A variety of factors and people are included in the preparation for discharge of a patient on a mechanical ventilator. Although this section emphasizes discharge to home, the same planning is required for patients discharged to long-term facilities. The factors outlined present the preferred approach to discharge; some of the factors may not always be possible.

Evaluation of the Patient and Family Potential for Home Care

This evaluation requires input from a variety of professionals—social workers, respiratory therapists, nurses, and physicians. In addition to the input of individuals, group meetings that include the patient and proposed caregivers are needed. The patient's physical capabilities as well as motivation and psychologic preparedness must be considered. Financial capability is also a major question; although third-party payers may cover the cost of equipment, they may not cover the cost of supplemental nursing visits to the home.

Home Evaluation

The home setting needs to be evaluated to determine if providing home ventilation is feasible. For example, is the electrical circuitry adequate, is the size of the room adequate, are bathrooms accessible (with wheelchair)? In addition to the structure of the home, the clinician must consider the availability of emergency services and the dependability of electrical service. Prior to discharge to home, time must be allowed for preparing the home environment.

Selection of Home Ventilator

Both positive pressure and negative pressure ventilators are available for home use. The most commonly used are small volume-limited positive pressure ventilators. These home ventilators are small and light, and are usually able to be placed on a bedside stand or on a wheelchair. Most have an internal battery backup system, as well as an external battery supply which, when fully charged, can power the ventilator for up to 24 hours. Alarm systems are included, specifically for patient-disconnect, low-system-pressure, high-system-pressure, and machine failure situations. Most home-care ventilators are capable of IMV and assist/control modes of ventilation in order to have application to clinical situations ranging from complete control of ventilation to those that may only require partial assistance, ie, during sleep. The specific ventilator selected will depend on the patient's requirements. The patient should be placed on the ventilator that he or she will be using at home during the transition period when patient and family teaching is being done.

Patient and Family Education

Extensive patient and family education is required. Areas to be covered include:

- tracheal suctioning
- tracheostomy care, including changing the tube
- operation and care of the ventilator
- emergency procedures, including manual ventilation, obtaining outside help, and response in power failure
- use of supplemental oxygen equipment, as necessary
- assessment of pulmonary status
- use of any special equipment (monitoring equipment, etc.)
- administration of medications

As teaching is done, the patient and family must become progressively more involved in actually providing the care within the hospital setting. It is preferable that the patient not be in the intensive care unit at this time; the best location is a unit where the staff has specialized knowledge and skill in working with patients requiring prolonged ventilation. Some institutions have chronic units, where families may actually move in and provide care in a setting that approximates the home. Finally, prior to discharge, it is helpful if the patient can move to the home setting on leave. It is much easier to face going home the first time when it is only for several days. If the on-leave home experiences are positive and successful, discharge to the home is then accomplished. In some instances, patients will be highly successful with a direct discharge to home without the on-leave experience.

Home Follow-Up

Follow-up care can be accomplished utilizing community resources, such as home-care nurses or respiratory therapists and physicians. Home-care vendors should be able to provide 24-hour service and have backup equipment available. Assessment of the patient's and family's adjustment to the routines of care, procedures, and additional responsibilities is important. Physiologic monitoring of arterial blood gases and/or oximetry should be performed routinely. Readmission to the acute-care setting should be possible if any problems arise.

SUGGESTED READING

Abraham E, Yoshihara G. Cardiorespiratory effects of pressure controlled inverse ratio ventilation in severe respiratory failure. *Chest*. 1989;96:1356–1359.

Berger R, Adams L. Nutritional support in the critical care setting *Chest*. 1989;96 (pts 1 and 2):139–150,372–380.

Byra C. High frequency ventilation. *Crit Care Nurs*. 1985;5:42–47.

Earl J. Should we support pressure support?(editorial) *Resp Care*. 1989;34:125–129.

Hodgekin JE, Webster JS. IPPB: worthwhile for which patients? *J Resp Dis*. 1982;3: 97–102.

Johnson DL, Giovannoni RM, Driscoll SA. *Ventilator-Assisted Patient Care: Planning for Hospital Discharge and Home Care*. Rockville, Md: Aspen Publishers, Inc.; 1986.

Kacmarek RM, Pierson DJ, eds. Positive end-expiratory pressure (PEEP). *Resp Care*. 1988;33(special issue, pt 2):523–637.

Kacmarek RM, Stoller JK. *Current Respiratory Care*. Philadelphia: BC Decker Inc.; 1988.

Kaplow R, Fromme LR. Nursing care plan for the patient receiving high frequency jet ventilation. *Crit Care Nurs*. 1985;5:25–27.

Lain DC, DiBenedetto R, Morris SL, Nguyen AV, Saulters R, Causey D. Pressure control inverse ratio ventilation as a method to reduce peak inspiratory pressure and provide adequate ventilation and oxygenation. *Chest*. 1989;95:1081–1088.

Make BJ, Gilmartin ME. Rehabilitation and home care for ventilator-assisted individuals. *Clin Chest Med*. 1986;7:679–691.

Nochomovitz ML, Montenegro HD. *Ventilatory Support in Respiratory Failure*. Mt. Kisco, NY: Futura Publishing Co.; 1987.

O'Donohue WJ. Long-term mechanical ventilation. *Chest*. 90:1S-37S.

Openbrier DR, Covey M. Ineffective breathing pattern related to malnutrition. *Nurs Clin North Am*. 1987;22:225–247.

Schreiner MS, Donar ME, Kettrick RG. Pediatric home mechanical ventilation. *Pediatr Clin North Am*. 1987;34:47–60.

Shelledy DC, Mikles SP. Newer modes of mechanical ventilation. Part I: pressure support. Part II: mandatory minute volume ventilation. *Resp Management*. 1988;18: 14–28.

Tobin MJ, Perez W, Guenther SM, et al. Pattern of breathing during successful and unsuccessful trials of weaning from mechanical ventilation. *Am Rev Resp Dis*. 1986;134:1111–1118.

Traver GA. *Respiratory Nursing: The Science and the Art*. Philadelphia: John Wiley and Sons; 1982.

Traver GA, Flodquist-Priestley G. Management problems in unilateral lung disease with emphasis on differential lung ventilation. *Crit Care Nurs*. 1986;6:198–208.

Vasbinder-Dillon D. Understanding mechanical ventilation. *Crit Care Nurse*. 1988;8:42–56.

chapter 15

Ventilatory and Gas Exchange Monitoring

Monitoring of the patient's ventilatory mechanics and gas exchange is important not only to assess the patient's present status but also to determine the effectiveness of interventions. Although the term monitoring often implies the critical care setting, it is important to consider monitoring techniques in all settings. The techniques used depend on the information required for management of the specific patient, the risk to the patient, the accuracy of the measurement, and the practicality of obtaining the measure. Basically, the clinician must always ask, "What is the risk-benefit ratio?" This chapter covers the basic monitoring techniques available, the purpose of the various techniques, the means of obtaining data, and the practicality of their use in different settings.

MONITORING OF PULMONARY MECHANICS

As discussed in Chapter 2, pulmonary mechanics is the study of the forces and resistances involved in moving air in and out of the lung. The most common measures seen as part of routine monitoring include assessment of pattern and rate, measures of volume and flow, compliance, and muscle strength.

Assessment of the Ventilatory Pattern and Rate

The most common technique of monitoring the patient's ability to move air is simple observation of the ventilatory pattern. As discussed in Chapter 2, observation of the ventilatory pattern can provide much significant data. In the spontaneously breathing patient, changes in the muscles used and the pattern of movement should be documented at rest and with activity. In the mechanically ventilated patient, documentation of the pattern during both spontaneous breaths and mechanically delivered breaths should be made.

Accurate measurement of the respiratory rate is extremely important. Changes in the respiratory rate are admittedly nonspecific, but they often indicate changes in the patient's status prior to the development of other signs and symptoms. Measurements of rate obtained after stressful activities (eg, exercise at home or suctioning in the intensive care unit) should be noted as such and not confused with the resting, baseline respiratory rate. The respiratory rate should also be counted over a sufficient time period so that variations in rate do not cause one to calculate an inaccurate respiratory rate. For example, if the patient has periods of apnea lasting 10 seconds, the rate must be counted for at least a full minute; if the rate had only been counted for 15 seconds and then multiplied by four, the rate recorded would not reflect the true rate. In the mechanically ventilated patient who also has a spontaneous breathing effort, it is important to record the patient's spontaneous rate, the number of mechanically delivered breaths, and the total rate per minute.

In the critical care area, in addition to counting the patient's respiratory rate via observation of actual respiratory movement, various technologies may also be used. Impedance techniques (via the leads used for EKG monitoring) or inductance (via wires embedded in a mesh vest) may be used to monitor respiratory rate. (The same technology is used for apnea monitoring of infants in the home setting.) Some of these newer technologies allow one to compartmentalize the amount of chest and abdominal movement during each breath. Thus, in addition to a rate measurement, one is able to document the presence of asynchrony, alternans, and paradox. As has been previously discussed in Chapter 2, these patterns, especially when accompanied by rapid respiratory rates (greater than 30 breaths per minute) often denote impending respiratory muscle fatigue. Some of these technologies, with proper calibration, will provide volume measurement as well as rate and pattern displays.

Measuring Volume and Flow

A wide variety of approaches to monitoring volume and flow are available. Major differences are seen in the approaches used in intubated, mechanically ventilated patients versus patients breathing spontaneously.

Spirometry

Spirometry is the most common technique used to measure volume and flow in the non-critically ill patient. Because of the degree of patient cooperation required, spirometry is not usually used in critical care settings, with the possible exception of monitoring the acute asthmatic. In the outpatient with pulmonary disease, a measurement of forced vital capacity (FVC) and forced expiratory volume in one second (FEV_1) is often done as part of routine vital signs. This measurement provides basic information about the patient's present ventilatory status by assessing changes over time, the effect of interventions, and the progression of the patient's disease.

For the home setting, small, inexpensive portable devices that provide an FVC and FEV_1 measurement are now becoming available. Until such devices are more readily accessible, other techniques may be used. Small disposable peak flow meters can be used by patients to measure peak flow at home. Although peak flow is a less sensitive measure than spirometry, it allows a gross measure of obstruction in appropriate patients, mainly asthmatics.

Other techniques that require no special equipment are also used. Although admittedly lacking in sensitivity and specificity, the following techniques are often helpful in assessing a patient's status. Estimating the time it takes a patient to perform an FVC maneuver provides some evaluation of airways obstruction. Normally, the vital capacity can be exhaled in three seconds. If the time required is significantly longer, the caregiver can make the assumption that there is expiratory slowing or airways obstruction present. This technique can even be used over the phone by requesting the patient to take a deep breath and, with his mouth open, breath out rapidly as much as he can into the phone. (This method also aids in documenting the presence of wheeze.) Another approach to obtaining an estimate of the vital capacity (VC) in patients with restrictive disease, is to use "count VC." The patient is requested to take as deep a breath as possible, and then to count as far as he can before having to take another breath. The assumption is made that the higher the patient can count, the larger the VC. (Needless to say this is a very gross qualitative, not quantitative, estimate of changes over time, and it requires good patient cooperation.)

Volume Measures in Critically Ill or Intubated Patients

Measures of *vital capacity* using a Wright respirometer or other electronic devices are commonly employed to monitor lung mechanics in patients who are intubated or critically ill. The respirometer can be used with a mouthpiece or mask or attached to the universal adapter of a tracheal tube. In the non-intubated patient, there must be a good seal between the device and the patient so that all of the exhaled gas flows through the respirometer. In the intubated patient, the patient must have a cuffed tube, which is properly inflated, in place. In all instances, the patient must be alert and cooperative (measurement of the VC requires maximal patient effort). The patient is instructed to take as deep a breath as possible and then to exhale as much as possible; the volume of gas exhaled is measured. The person obtaining the measure should ensure that the patient is in an optimal position (preferably in a semi-Fowler's position or sitting) and should provide vigorous, verbal encouragement so that a maximal effort is obtained. A slow rather than forced vital capacity is obtained. A normal vital capacity is approximately 65 to 75 mL/kg; values less that 15 mL/kg are associated with the need for mechanical ventilation.

Other measures used commonly in the intubated patient are the *tidal volume* and *minute volume*. These measures are obtained with the same equipment used to measure vital capacity. The measures are used to determine the volumes that the patient attains spontaneously as well as to verify volumes delivered by the ventilator. (Although many ventilators provide a digital readout of tidal volume—spontaneous and mechanical—and minute volume, these values should be periodically checked for validity.) The minute volume is a measure of the volume exhaled over a one-minute period, or tidal volume multiplied by respiratory rate. When obtained on a spontaneously breathing patient, the volume exhaled is measured over a 30- to 60-second period. The average tidal volume is then obtained by dividing the total volume measured by the number of breaths taken during the measurement. Because the tidal volume is usually variable, the clinician should not just measure one exhaled breath. It is often helpful, however, to note the volume of each breath exhaled. For example, when a patient is removed from ventilatory support, does he initially have large tidal volumes which then gradually decrease? Does the patient take mainly small breaths interspersed only occasionally by large breaths? Such observations will contribute to assessment of the patient's ventilatory strength, ventilatory drive, and ability to maintain spontaneous ventilation.

Another volume measurement that would be helpful in patient management is the *functional residual capacity (FRC)*, but the techniques for measuring the FRC are too complicated to be used in routine monitoring. In the mechanically ventilated patient, however, one simple clinical observation correlates with an increased FRC. This observation is the presence of *auto PEEP,* which refers to the observation of positive pressure at end expiration on mechanically ventilated patients who are *not* receiving mechanical PEEP or an end-expiratory pressure that is higher than the set PEEP level. (See Chapter 14 for a discussion of PEEP.) The interpretation of this finding is that the patient has insufficient expiratory time, usually observed in patients with obstructive disease, and therefore cannot exhale as much gas as usual. The result is elevation of the FRC. The pressure data are obtained from the pressure monitor on the ventilator and the observation is made at end expiration. It should be noted that the absence of auto PEEP does not rule out a larger than normal FRC.

Measures of Compliance

Routine monitoring of compliance is not done in the nonintubated patient but can be easily accomplished in the intubated patient who is mechanically ventilated. Because no additional special equipment is required, these measurements can be done in the critical care or home setting. This compliance measurement is usually referred to as the effective compliance because it includes factors related to the ventilatory equipment used. The basic concept is that the relationship between airway pressure generated during a mechanical breath and volume delivered provides information as to the distensibility of the lung and chest.

Simply noting the change in peak inspiratory pressure (PIP) in patients being ventilated with a volume ventilator provides an indication of the ease with which a breath is delivered. In other words, the more pressure that is required to deliver a given tidal volume, the stiffer the system must be. (If the patient is being ventilated with a pressure-limited ventilator, a decrease in the volume delivered at the preset pressure would indicate increasing stiffness of the system.) The observation of increasing stiffness then requires further assessment to delineate the factors involved. For example, if peak pressure rises without a change in delivered volume in a patient on a volume ventilator, the change may be due to either an increase in airway resistance *or* an increase in lung or chest-wall stiffness. Clinical examples of an increase in airway resistance are increased secretions and bronchospasm; high airway resistance may also be due to a small diameter endotracheal tube. Examples of factors resulting in increased lung stiffness are: pneumothorax, pulmonary edema, atelectasis, and intubation of the right main-stem bronchus. Examples of factors resulting in increased stiffness of the chest wall are: abdominal distention and pain. Measures of compliance are most helpful when they are used to follow the patient's condition over time.

Static and Dynamic Measures

More specific information can be gained by measuring the effective static and effective dynamic compliance. Effective dynamic compliance is measured by determining the change in volume divided by the change in airway pressure (peak airway pressure minus PEEP level) required to deliver that breath (see Figure 15-1A).

To measure effective static compliance, the tidal volume is delivered followed by a breath-hold at end inspiration. The breath-hold can be accomplished by using an inspiratory pause (if included on the ventilator controls) or by preventing exhalation (occluding the expiratory port). Because the ventilator is no longer required to generate pressure to push gas through the airways but only has to generate enough pressure to hold the lung open, the peak pressure will fall slightly to a plateau level. The effective static compliance is then calculated by using the volume delivered and the difference between the plateau pressure and PEEP level, including auto PEEP (see Figure 15-1B).

Another factor that is considered when calculating these compliance measurements is the distensibility of the ventilator tubing. When simply observing the mechanically ventilated patient, it should become obvious to the clinician that

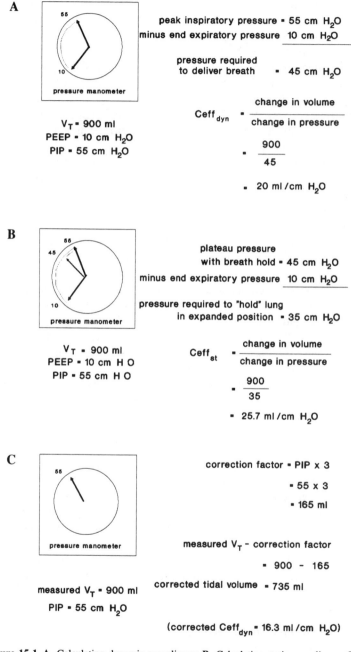

A, Calculating dynamic compliance:

peak inspiratory pressure = 55 cm H_2O
minus end expiratory pressure 10 cm H_2O
———————————
pressure required
to deliver breath   = 45 cm H_2O

V_T = 900 ml
PEEP = 10 cm H_2O
PIP = 55 cm H_2O

$Ceff_{dyn}$ = $\dfrac{\text{change in volume}}{\text{change in pressure}}$

= $\dfrac{900}{45}$

= 20 ml/cm H_2O

B, Calculating static compliance:

plateau pressure
with breath hold = 45 cm H_2O
minus end expiratory pressure 10 cm H_2O
———————————
pressure required to "hold" lung
in expanded position = 35 cm H_2O

V_T = 900 ml
PEEP = 10 cm H O
PIP = 55 cm H O

$Ceff_{st}$ = $\dfrac{\text{change in volume}}{\text{change in pressure}}$

= $\dfrac{900}{35}$

= 25.7 ml/cm H_2O

C, Correcting tidal volume:

correction factor = PIP x 3

= 55 x 3

= 165 ml

measured V_T - correction factor

= 900 - 165

corrected tidal volume = 735 ml

measured V_T = 900 ml

PIP = 55 cm H_2O

(corrected $Ceff_{dyn}$ = 16.3 ml/cm H_2O)

Figure 15-1 A, Calculating dynamic compliance; **B,** Calculating static compliance; **C,** Correcting tidal volume.

the greater the pressure required to ventilate the patient, the greater the distention of the ventilator circuitry during inspiration. This distention then affects the delivered tidal volume; the greater the distention, the more the reduction of the tidal volume actually received by the patient. Although this effect may not be significant in patients requiring modest peak pressures, in those patients who have very stiff lungs and require very high peak pressures, there can be a marked effect on the volume delivered. To correct for this effect, the tidal volume minus the factor of peak pressure × 3 cc is used to calculate compliance (see Figure 15-1C). Some clinicians do not routinely make this correction unless there is a dramatic change in the peak pressure.

Finally, the measurements of compliance are best obtained when the patient is making no spontaneous breathing efforts. If the patient spontaneously inhales to trigger the machine breath, the pressure required to effect the delivered tidal volume is actually greater than that measured on the ventilator pressure manometer. This effect is disregarded by many clinicians.

Once the measures of effective static and dynamic compliance have been made, the clinician can then determine if the patient has a significant component of increased airway resistance, or if the problem is solely one of lung or chest-wall stiffness. If the static compliance is significantly lower than the dynamic, the clinician can then assume a major airway resistance problem. For example, peak pressures rise and dynamic compliance falls without a significant change in static compliance. If both measures are elevated but there is little difference between them, then the clinician can assume there is a major problem of lung or chest-wall stiffness rather than an airway resistance problem.

To aid in the interpretation of the system compliance measurements, the following values should be kept in mind. The normal effective static compliance is 60 to 99 mL/cm H_2O. A value that is 25 mL/cm H_2O or less indicates severe disease.

The relationship between pressure and volume can also be used to construct a pressure volume curve for the patient. Machine delivered breaths of different volumes are provided. For each breath, the required static and dynamic pressure changes are recorded. By plotting volume against pressure, a static and dynamic curve can be constructed. Information derived from such curves provides additional discrimination for separating airway problems from lung and chest-wall changes. The data are also used in conjunction with hemodynamic data to determine optimal tidal volumes and PEEP levels. For more information on the use of these curves, the reader is referred to the suggested reading list at the end of this chapter.

Monitoring Respiratory Muscle Strength

Monitoring of respiratory muscle strength includes periodic measurement of vital capacity. The additional measurement frequently used is the maximal inspiratory force (MIF). This measure may also be referred to as the negative inspiratory force (NIF). The measure provides information as to how much negative pressure the inspiratory muscles can generate; the stronger the muscles, the more negative the pressure.

For measurement of the MIF, the patient inhales through a pressure manometer. As the patient inhales, the access to room air is occluded so that the airway pressure drops. Some experts specify that the inhalation begin at residual volume (RV), while others use a volume slightly less than FRC based on the rationale that inhalation from FRC is a better indicator of muscle strength during normal breathing. Another advantage to this measure is that inspiration from FRC can be attained from non-cooperative patients—occluding the airway for several breaths provides stacking so that a maximal inspiration is attained. A normal MIF is in the range of -90 to -130 cm H_2O; the values are less in females and they decrease with age in all subjects. The minimal level considered sufficient to maintain spontaneous breathing is -20 to -30 cm H_2O.

Monitoring Work of Breathing

Monitoring the work of breathing is receiving greater emphasis as a measure of a patient's ability to sustain spontaneous ventilation. However, because the measurement involves invasive techniques (an esophageal balloon), it has not become a routine measure. Usually the work of breathing is qualitatively estimated from observations of the respiratory rate, use of accessory muscles, retractions, and paradox.

MONITORING GAS EXCHANGE AND TRANSPORT

The first step in monitoring gas exchange is to be aware of those clinical situations that may result in a gas exchange abnormality, and to be alert to signs and symptoms that may indicate a gas exchange abnormality. These factors have been discussed in Chapter 5. This section concentrates on the approach to monitoring those patients in whom a gas exchange abnormality is known to exist.

The primary method of monitoring gas exchange abnormalities is by arterial blood sampling. In the critically ill patient who has an arterial line in place, the samples are drawn via the arterial line. (An arterial line is often placed when there is a need for repeated frequent arterial blood sampling—more than four samples per day.) In patients who do not require repeated samples over several days, it is usually much safer to do individual percutaneous arterial punctures. Whenever arterial blood is obtained for blood gases, the status of the patient at the time the blood was drawn should be noted. For nonventilated patients, that status includes the FIO_2 or the liters per minute (L/min) of oxygen the patient is receiving, and whether the blood was drawn at rest, exercise, or in the supine position. For mechanically ventilated patients, notation of the following should be made: patient's temperature, FIO_2, tidal volume, PEEP level, total respiratory rate, and mechanical rate; measurement of the minute volume is also helpful. All of these status conditions, in all clinical settings, are needed to correctly interpret the blood gas results and to compare the results with those obtained previously or subsequently. Even when status is unchanged, there may be marked variability (5 to 10 mm Hg) in the blood gases of stable patients; therefore, it is important to follow trends rather than individual gases.

Monitoring Oxygenation

A variety of approaches to monitoring oxygenation are now available. Not only may different expressions of oxygenation be monitored (PaO_2 versus $\dot{V}/\dot{Q}$), but there are also a variety of technical approaches that may be used.

Oximetry

Although blood gas analysis is the primary means of assessing oxygenation, oximetry, a method that provides the percent oxyhemoglobin saturation, is a technique that is becoming increasingly popular in all settings—home, hospital and intensive care unit. A sensor probe is attached to the finger or ear, and the oximeter provides a continuous display of percent saturation, and in many models, the pulse rate. Although extremely useful for continuous monitoring in unstable patients, for evaluating changes in oxygenation with exercise, and as an aid in determining requirements for supplemental oxygen, the disadvantages and potential inaccuracies of pulse oximetry must be considered. Some of these are:

- The accuracy of different oximeters varies, with the most accurate being ± 4% saturation.
- Oximeters lack sensitivity to changes in PaO_2 if the patient has a high baseline PaO_2 (> 60 mm Hg) due to the flat upper limb of the oxyhemoglobin dissociation curve.
- Accuracy is decreased at very low saturations.
- Readings are affected by jaundice, cardiac output dyes, high levels of carboxyhemoglobin, nail polish on finger to which probe is attached, skin pigmentation, impaired regional perfusion (at site of probe), and severe anemia.
- Readings are influenced by shifts in oxyhemoglobin curve due to changes in PCO_2 and pH and may not therefore accurately reflect the PO_2.

The above potential inaccuracies do not, however, negate the value of oximetry. One must, however, periodically compare oximetry with arterial blood gases and must be aware of those situations that could possibly influence the accuracy of the oximetry reading.

Transcutaneous Oxygen (Ptco$_2$)

Transcutaneous oxygen monitoring uses an electrode placed on the skin to monitor the Pao$_2$. The technique has been most successfully used for neonates whose dermis is thin and well supplied with capillaries and who have few problems of tissue perfusion. In the neonate, the readings correlate well with the actual Pao$_2$. In the adult, transcutaneous monitoring has been less successful, with changes often being related to perfusion rather than to the Pao$_2$. When transcutaneous monitoring is used, the equipment must be carefully calibrated, and the skin and electrode must be properly prepared; because the skin must be warmed, the electrode site should be changed frequently to prevent a burn.

Assessing Ventilation Perfusion Abnormalities

In addition to monitoring changes in Pao$_2$, especially in the critical care area, it is important to monitor the efficiency of oxygen exchange (changes related to $\dot{V}/\dot{Q}$ matching). Several different approaches may be used. One of the simplest is to use the ratio of Pao$_2$ to Fio$_2$ or P/F ratio. A normal value is greater than 400. Values less than 350 are definitely abnormal. The P/F ratio does not account for changes in Paco$_2$, but it is helpful in comparing Pao$_2$ values obtained with varying levels of inspired oxygen. When the inspired oxygen is changed, the P/F ratio also allows the clinician to predict the resulting Pao$_2$ (see Figure 15-2).

The ratio between the arterial and calculated alveolar oxygen (a/A ratio) is also used to assess $\dot{V}/\dot{Q}$ mismatching. This measurement accounts for changes in the Paco$_2$ as well as the inspired oxygen. The normal value for an a/A ratio is 0.8 to 0.85. Ratios below 0.7 are definitely abnormal (see Figure 15-3).

The classic measurement to examine differences between the alveolar and arterial oxygen tensions is the (A-a)o$_2$ gradient. (Chapter 5 discusses calculation of the alveolar oxygen tension.) As with the a/A ratio, this measurement considers changes in Paco$_2$ but is less reliable in situations of changing Fio$_2$. The normal gradient in an adult should be less than 10 to 15 mm Hg when breathing room air. (The gradient is larger in the elderly.) When breathing 100% oxygen, the gradient may increase to as high as 100 mm Hg .

In practice the P/F ratio is frequently used if the Paco$_2$ is stable because the ratio can be quickly calculated and it provides a good estimate of the anticipated Pao$_2$ when the Fio$_2$ is changed. The a/A ratio is more helpful if the Paco$_2$ is showing marked fluctuation. Both measures, however, have the disadvantage of becoming less reliable as the shunt fraction becomes large (eg, ARDS).

$$P/F \text{ ratio} = \frac{PaO_2}{F_IO_2} \qquad \text{normal} = \, \text{›} \, 400$$

if, $PaO_2 = 50$ mm Hg

$F_IO_2 = 0.45$

then, P/F ratio $= \dfrac{50}{.45} = 111$

if F_IO_2 changed to 0.5, anticipate PaO_2 55.6 mm Hg

$$111 = \frac{x}{0.5}$$

$$x = 55.6$$

Figure 15-2 P/F ratio. Calculation of the P/F ratio and its use with changing oxygen concentrations is shown.

$$a/A \text{ ratio} = \frac{P_aO_2}{P_AO_2} \qquad \text{normal} = 0.8 - 0.85$$

if, $PaO_2 = 50$ mm Hg

$PaCO_2 = 40$ mm Hg

$F_IO_2 = 0.45$

$$P_AO_2 = (\text{barometric pressure} - 47) \times F_IO_2 - \frac{PaCO_2}{0.8}$$

$$= 713 \times .45 - \frac{40}{0.8}$$

$$= 321 - 50$$

$$= 271$$

$$a/A \text{ ratio} = \frac{50}{271} = 0.18$$

Figure 15-3 a/A ratio.

The most reliable measure of the efficiency of oxygen exchange is the calculation of venous admixture. When it is necessary to determine shunt versus simply low $\dot{V}/\dot{Q}$, venous admixture is calculated on an FIO_2 of 1.0; because of the potential hazards of this FIO_2, absolute shunt is frequently not measured. Rather, if the patient's PaO_2 does not improve to levels above 60 mm Hg with an FIO_2 of 0.5 or greater, it is assumed that a shunt fraction greater than 25% is present; in other words, 25% of the cardiac output does not see a ventilated alveolus. The measurement of venous admixture is mathematically cumbersome (although that is not a problem with the newer monitoring systems that have built-in computer computations). It requires that a pulmonary artery catheter be in place for the sampling of mixed venous blood.

To actually calculate venous admixture, the following information must be available: PaO_2, SaO_2, $P\bar{v}O_2$, $S\bar{v}O_2$, $PaCO_2$, FIO_2, barometric pressure, and grams hemoglobin. Figure 15-4 presents the actual calculations performed. For reference, the normal shunt fraction while the patient is breathing room air is approximately 2.5%.

Monitoring Mixed Venous Oxygen

Monitoring changes in mixed venous oxygen tensions provides the clinician with information about oxygen delivery and oxygen consumption. Especially in critically ill patients, changes in oxygen delivery or oxygen consumption may be a major factor in the development of generalized tissue hypoxia. For example, the lungs may adequately oxygenate the blood, but if the oxygen is not delivered to the tissues (decreased cardiac output), tissue hypoxia will ensue. Such a change would be reflected in a decreased mixed venous oxygen tension. (Due to decreased delivery, more oxygen would be extracted from the blood available to the tissues.)

In the past, mixed venous oxygen tension was monitored as an indicator of cardiac output. It is now recognized that in many critically ill patients, there may be dramatic increases in oxygen consumption (especially in the septic patient) that can also cause a decrease in mixed venous oxygen. It has also been shown that oxygen consumption may vary with oxygen availability. In the latter instance, a fall in cardiac output would also result in decreased oxygen consumption. The end result would be that the cardiac output would be lower than expected from the change in mixed venous oxygen.

In many institutions, mixed venous oxygenation is monitored continuously via oximetry. Pulmonary artery catheters in which sensors have been placed to

$$\frac{\dot{Q}_S}{\dot{Q}_T} = \frac{C_cO_2 - C_aO_2}{C_cO_2 - C_{\bar{v}}O_2}$$

shunt is measured on 100% oxygen

for calculation, assume capillary and alveolar tensions are equal

Figure 15-4 Shunt calculation.

monitor mixed venous saturations are now available. When monitoring mixed venous oxygenation, the $P\bar{v}O_2$ of the blood is low, which places it on the steep part of the oxyhemoglobin dissociation curve. Therefore, large changes in saturation result from relatively small changes in the $P\bar{v}O_2$. The mixed venous saturation ($S\bar{v}O_2$) has also been used for shunt calculations without actually drawing blood from the pulmonary artery. Since most of the oxygen content is in the form of oxyhemoglobin, the amount carried in the dissolved form is negligible, especially in venous blood.

For basic reference, the normal mixed venous oxygen tension is 40 mm Hg with an oxyhemoglobin saturation of 75%. Values below this level are considered abnormal. (Even with a decreased arterial oxygen tension, the mixed venous oxygen level should be maintained due to the shape of the oxyhemoglobin dissociation curve and its relationship to oxygen content.) The monitoring of mixed venous oxygen is discussed further in Chapter 16.

Monitoring PCO_2

The continuous monitoring of PCO_2 is not done as frequently as monitoring of oxygenation. In neonates, transcutaneous monitoring is possible. An electrode placed on the skin senses the changes in PCO_2 of the capillary blood flow. The $PtcCO_2$ is always slightly higher than the $PaCO_2$. In adults, transcutaneous monitoring is much less reliable and therefore seldom done.

Another method, which can be used in adults, is the monitoring of the exhaled carbon dioxide by capnography. In the normal individual, the end tidal CO_2 ($PetCO_2$) is equivalent to the alveolar PCO_2 and therefore the arterial PCO_2. Conceptually that last aliquot of air in a tidal exhalation is coming from alveoli. In patients with increased dead space or prolonged expiration, the last bit of air exhaled during normal breathing may not be coming from a perfused alveolus and therefore the measure cannot be used to estimate alveolar PCO_2.

Collection of all of the exhaled gas is sometimes analyzed for carbon dioxide. The result is the mixed expired PCO_2 ($PeCO_2$). (The first gas exhaled did not come in contact with a perfused alveolus and contains no carbon dioxide while the last gas exhaled contains the highest amount of carbon dioxide.) This measure of mixed expired CO_2 is used to calculate the ratio of dead space to tidal volume. Normally the Vd/Vt is 0.3 (one-third of each tidal breath is deadspace). Values greater than 0.4 indicate increased dead space ventilation. Often, instead of directly measuring dead space, a qualitative estimate is made based on the minute volume required to maintain a normal $PaCO_2$. Normally a minute volume of 7 L will maintain a normal $PaCO_2$. If the patient's minute volume is 20 L and the $PaCO_2$ is 40 mm Hg, it is obvious that much of the minute volume is wasted ventilation (not taking part in gas exchange) or dead space.

SUGGESTED READINGS

Ahrens T. Blood gas assessment of intrapulmonary shunting and deadspace. *Crit Care Nurs Clinics North Am.* 1989;1:641–648.

Bone RC. Monitoring ventilatory mechanics in acute respiratory failure. *Resp Care.* 1983;28:597–604.

Capps JS, Hicks GH. Monitoring non-gas respiratory variables during mechanical ventilation. *Resp Care.* 1987;32:558–571.

Civetta JM, Taylor RW, Kirby RR. *Critical Care.* Philadelphia: J B Lippincott Company; 1988.

Covelli HD, Nessan VJ, Tuttle WK. Oxygen derived variables in acute respiratory failure. *Crit Care Med.* 1983;1:646–649.

Glauser FL, Polatly RC, Sessler CN. Worsening oxygenation in the mechanically ventilated patient: causes, mechanisms, and early detection. *Am Rev Respir Dis.* 1988;138:458–465.

Harris K. Noninvasive monitoring of gas exchange. *Resp Care.* 1987;32:544–557.

Hess D. Bedside monitoring of the patient on a ventilator. *Crit Care Quart.* 1983;6:23–32.

Kram H. Noninvasive tissue oxygen monitoring in surgical and critical care medicine. *Surg Clin North Am.* 1985;65:1005–1022.

Krieger BP, Chediak A, Gazeroglu HB, et al. Variability of the breathing pattern before and after extubation. *Chest.* 1988;93:767–771.

Krieger B, Feinerman D, Zaron A, et al. Continuous noninvasive monitoring of respiratory rate in critically ill patients. *Chest.* 1986;90:632–634.

Loggan M, Kerby GR, Pingleton SK. Is routine assessment of arterial oxygen saturation in pulmonary outpatients indicated? *Chest.* 1988;94:242–244.

Marini JJ. Monitoring during mechanical ventilation. *Clin Chest Med.* 1988;9:73–100.

McCauley M, VonRueden K. Noninvasive monitoring of the mechanically ventilated patient. *Crit Care Nurs Quart.* 1988;11:36–49.

Peris LV, Boix JH, Salom JV, et al. Clinical use of the arterial alveolar oxygen tension ratio. *Crit Care Med.* 1983;11:888–891.

Rutherford KA. Principles and application of oximetry. *Crit Care Nurs Clinics North Am.* 1989;1:649–657.

Szaflarski NL, Cohen NH. Use of pulse oximetry in critically ill adults. *Heart Lung.* 1989;18:444–455.

Tobin MJ. Respiratory monitoring in the intensive care unit. *Am Rev Respir Dis.* 1988;138:1625–1642.

chapter 16

Hemodynamic Monitoring

Monitoring the critically ill patient with pulmonary problems includes the use of hemodynamic monitoring techniques. The interrelationship of the pulmonary and cardiac systems requires that assessments of one system consider the status and effects of the other. This chapter discusses the effects of respiration on systemic arterial and pulmonary artery monitoring.

RESPIRATORY INFLUENCE ON ARTERIAL PRESSURE: PULSUS PARADOXUS

Normal respiratory effort does not significantly change cardiac output or blood pressure. With spontaneous inspiration, intrathoracic pressure decreases slightly, thus causing an increase in venous return. As the lungs expand, pulmonary vascular resistance decreases and blood flow into the pulmonary vessels increases. Blood pools in the pulmonary vasculature momentarily and decreases preload to the left ventricle. Thus, cardiac output decreases slightly during spontaneous inspiration, then increases as the blood pooled in the pulmonary vessels flows into the left ventricle.

Blood pressure may change slightly with the respiratory cycle; a variation of 0 to 10 mm Hg is considered normal. This cyclical decrease in systolic blood pressure, which corresponds to the respiratory pattern, is termed *pulsus paradoxus*. It can be detected by either traditional cuff pressures or arterial monitoring. Paradoxus greater than 10 mm Hg may be clinically significant and can be caused by major intrathoracic pathology (ie, cardiac tamponade or pneumothorax), severe respiratory distress, hypovolemia, and positive pressure ventilation.

Detection of Pulsus Paradoxus

To detect a paradoxical pulse by cuff sphygmomanometer, the cuff is inflated above the systolic pressure, then deflated very slowly while the clinician watches the patient's respiratory pattern. The first Korotkoff sound is heard during expiration. The sound disappears during inspiration, then returns. The difference in mm Hg from the first sound until Korotkoff sounds are heard during both inspiration and expiration is the measured pulsus paradoxus.

The same decrease in systolic blood pressure during inspiration can be demonstrated on an arterial pressure waveform. A strip chart recording of the pressure waves is helpful to measure the difference between peak systolic pressures during inspiration and expiration (see Figure 16-1).

Pulsus Paradoxus in Chronic Airways Obstruction

Clinically significant pulsus paradoxus is occasionally seen in patients with acute airway obstruction, such as in asthma. The extreme fluctuations in intrathoracic pressures and changes in left ventricular filling are thought to reduce left ventricular stroke volume. Experts disagree on the correlation between the magnitude of the pulsus paradoxus and the severity of airway obstruction. If this parameter is used to follow patient status, it should be noted that a decrease in

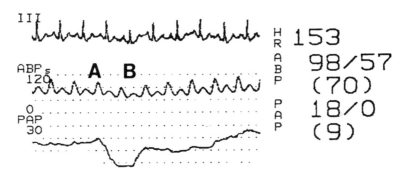

Figure 16-1 Arterial pulsus paradoxus, spontaneous respiration. This tracing shows heart rate (HR), arterial blood pressure (ABP), and pulmonary artery pressure (PAP). The pulmonary artery catheter is in the wedge position. The pulsus is the decrease in arterial pressure that occurs with spontaneous inspiration. On this tracing, inspiration begins at point A. As can be seen, between points A and B, the ABP falls from 100 to 80 mm Hg. Recording should include the mean value (98/57) displayed on the digital readout and the amount of paradox (20 mm Hg). The fall in wedge pressure during inspiration can also be noted.

paradoxus can be due either to improvement in pulmonary function *or* to fatigue and failing respiratory effort.

Pulsus Paradoxus with Positive Pressure Ventilation

Pulsus paradoxus is also observed in patients treated with positive pressure ventilation, particularly when the patient is hypovolemic, receiving large tidal volumes, or has reduced sympathetic tone. Positive pressure ventilation increases intrathoracic pressure with each ventilator breath. As the lungs expand from the positive pressure, blood is forced out from the pulmonary vessels into the left ventricle (LV). Systolic blood pressure may increase for one to two cardiac cycles. However, the increased intrathoracic pressure is also transmitted to the great vessels causing a transient drop in venous return to the right ventricle (RV). Pulmonary vascular resistance increases from the positive pressure, increasing RV afterload. The combination of reduced venous return and increased RV afterload then reduces RV stroke volume, cardiac output, and systolic blood pressure two to three cardiac cycles following initiation of a ventilated inspiration. Blood pressure gradually returns to normal during exhalation (see Figure 16-2). Pulsus paradoxus greater than 10 mm Hg following a mechanical ventilator breath often indicates hypovolemia and partially explains the hypotension some patients develop following intubation and mechanical ventilation. A hypovolemic patient may require additional fluids for cardiovascular support when placed on mechanical ventilation.

In some cases, positive pressure ventilation has the opposite effect on hemodynamics. Cardiac output and blood pressure may *increase* with positive pres-

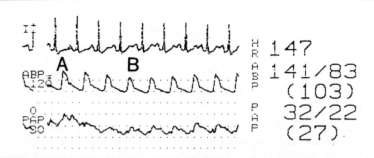

Figure 16-2 Arterial pulsus paradoxus, mechanical ventilation. This tracing shows heart rate (HR), arterial blood pressure (ABP), and pulmonary artery pressure (PAP). After the initiation of a mechanical positive pressure breath (at point A), the ABP decreases after two to three cardiac cycles (points A to B).

sure inspiration, a situation termed *reverse pulsus paradoxus*. This response is observed in some patients with extreme respiratory distress and cardiac failure. Thus, it is important to note where the pressure change occurs in the respiratory cycle.

PULMONARY ARTERY PRESSURE MONITORING

The flow-directed pulmonary artery (PA) catheter has had a profound influence on bedside assessment and treatment of critically ill patients. This section briefly reviews monitoring techniques and equipment, risks associated with the PA catheter, and pulmonary influences on PA monitoring and interpretation.

Techniques and Equipment for Pulmonary Artery Monitoring

The ease of insertion and its availability as a bedside tool have contributed to the popularity of the pulmonary artery catheter. Several insertion sites can be used: internal jugular, subclavian, femoral, and brachial veins. The right internal jugular and subclavian approaches are often preferred because there are the fewest anatomical angles before reaching the right atrium. An intravenous catheter (sheath) is inserted first and the PA catheter is then inserted via a diaphragm in the sheath. Once the distal end of the catheter reaches the right atrium, the balloon is inflated. As the catheter is advanced, blood flow guides the catheter through the valves, chambers and into the pulmonary artery.

Pulmonary artery catheters have several lumens for monitoring pressures and temperature. The following terminology is common to most catheters:

- *Proximal port.* The proximal port opens in the right atrium and is used for measuring central venous (CVP) or right atrial (RA) pressures (mean = 1 to 6 mm Hg). This port is the fluid injection site for thermodilution cardiac output measurements and can be used for infusion of intravenous fluids.
- *Distal port.* The distal port terminates in a pulmonary artery (PA). With the balloon deflated, the distal port provides PA pressures (normal range = 20 to 30/0 to 10 mm Hg). When the balloon is inflated, the distal port provides pulmonary artery wedge pressures (PAW or PAWP) (normal mean = 4 to 12 mm Hg). The distal port is used for continuous monitoring, not for fluid infusion. It is also the site for mixed venous blood gas sampling.
- *Balloon port.* This outlet, usually identified with a locking device, connects to the balloon at the distal end of the catheter. A small syringe is used to inflate the balloon for PAW pressures using < 1 ½ cc air.

- *Thermistor.* The thermistor probe connects to the temperature sensor on the distal end of the catheter. This lumen permits blood temperature monitoring and thermodilution cardiac output measurement.

Pulmonary artery catheters may have additional lumens for fluid infusion, continuous mixed venous oxygen saturation monitoring, pacing wires, or they may have cardiac pacing electrodes on the catheter itself.

Hazards of Pulmonary Artery Monitoring

Similar to other invasive monitoring devices, pulmonary artery catheters carry the risk of infection. Other hazards specific to the use of this catheter include:

- *Pulmonary infarction.* The catheter can obstruct blood flow, causing lung tissue ischemia and infarction if positioned too distally in the pulmonary artery or if the catheter advances into a permanent wedge position. This spontaneous wedge produces a PAWP waveform when the catheter balloon is deflated. Too distal placement can be noted on radiograph or suspected when the catheter wedges with less than 1.3 cc in the balloon. The distal port is monitored continuously to allow immediate detection of catheter movement into the wedge position.

- *Pulmonary artery rupture.* The pulmonary artery may rupture from the stress of repeated, frequent inflation or overinflation of the balloon. Overwedge, a waveform that continually rises, can be caused by a catheter tip forced against the vessel wall. The catheter should be repositioned to prevent vessel rupture.

- *Air embolus.* Balloon rupture releases the 1 ½ cc of air into the pulmonary artery. Balloon rupture can be detected by the lack of resistance on inflation, failure of air to return to the syringe, or blood returning in the port. When rupture is suspected, repeated inflations are to be avoided and the catheter should be replaced.

- *Ventricular arrhythmias.* Arrhythmias can occur from catheter irritation of the ventricle and are most likely to occur during insertion. A wide range of arrhythmias can result, including ventricular fibrillation. Fortunately, catheter-induced arrhythmias usually resolve when the catheter is removed. Full inflation of the balloon during insertion (to protect the ventricle wall from the catheter tip) will reduce the risk of ventricular irritation.

Respiratory Influences on Pulmonary Artery Monitoring

The popularity of the flow-directed pulmonary artery catheter stems, in part, from its convenience as a means of measuring cardiac output and assessing left ventricular preload. Pressure measurements are commonly used both as absolute values and as trends to guide fluid and pharmacologic therapy.

To avoid errors in management decisions, PA catheter measurements must be validly obtained and interpreted within the context of the patient's overall cardiopulmonary status. Pulmonary influences that can affect accuracy and interpretation are discussed in the following section.

Pulmonary Hypertension

Because pulmonary artery diastolic (PAD) pressure and PAWP have been shown to correlate in normal patients, clinicians often use PAD as an estimate of PAWP. This relationship does not always hold true, eg, in the face of pulmonary hypertension (defined as pulmonary artery systolic pressure [PAS] greater than 35 mm Hg). In this setting, the PAD may be considerably higher than the PAWP and is not a reliable substitute as an absolute number. PAD trends may be useful if PAWP and PAD correlate, reducing the need for frequent balloon inflation to obtain the PAWP.

Respiratory Variation in Pulmonary Artery Measurements

The changes in pleural and intrapulmonary pressures during respiration are transmitted to the pulmonary vessels and can cause marked fluctuations in pulmonary artery pressures. Because respiratory variations can be a source of measurement error, most authors recommend reading PAWP at end expiration when intrathoracic pressures approach zero and are most stable. An exception to the reliability of end-expiratory PAWP is the patient with forced expirations (eg, secondary to airways obstructive disease). The expiratory force increases intrathoracic pressure, raising the PAWP and making it inaccurate as an indicator of intravascular volume status.

Determining end expiration on PAWP tracings has been a point of considerable discussion. Three common ventilatory patterns (spontaneous, controlled, and assisted ventilation) and end-expiratory waveforms are:

1. *Spontaneous ventilation.* Intrathoracic pressure decreases during spontaneous inspiration. The PAWP falls during inspiration and rises to baseline with exhalation. End expiration is the stable plateau just before the waveform drops (Figure 16-3).

2. *Mechanical ventilation without spontaneous ventilation.* Positive pressure ventilation increases thoracic pressure during inspiration. The PAWP waveform rises to a higher pressure as the ventilator delivers a breath, then returns to the stable plateau during exhalation. End-expiratory PAWP is the lowest point on the tracing (Figure 16-4).

3. *Mechanical ventilation with spontaneous ventilation.* The most difficult waveforms to interpret are those of a patient with spontaneous inspiratory effort

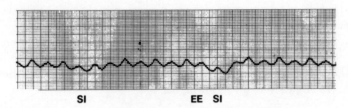

Figure 16-3 Pulmonary artery wedge pressure (PAW), spontaneous breathing. A PAW tracing obtained during spontaneous breathing is shown. During spontaneous inspiration (SI), the PAW decreases and then rises to an end-expiratory plateau (EE). The recorded PAW should be the measure obtained at EE, 12 mm Hg on this tracing. The fluctuations occurring during both inspiration and expiration on this tracing are related to the cardiac cycle. Note that the range of PAW from inspiration to expiration is 5 to 15 mm Hg.

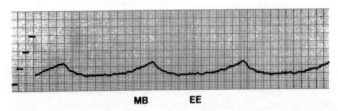

Figure 16-4 Pulmonary artery wedge pressure (PAW), controlled mechanical ventilation. A PAW tracing obtained during controlled mechanical ventilation is shown. During the mechanical positive pressure breath (MB), PAW increases. The recorded PAW should be obtained at end expiration (EE), 6 mm Hg on this tracing. (Note the 5- to 13-mm Hg range of the PAW over the entire respiratory cycle.)

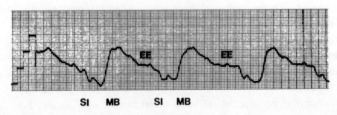

Figure 16-5 Pulmonary artery wedge pressure (PAW), mechanical ventilation with spontaneous inspiration. A PAW tracing obtained from a patient on assisted mechanical ventilation is shown. (Each mechanical breath is initiated by a spontaneous breath.) There is a fall in PAW with spontaneous inspiration (SI) followed by a rise in PAW with the mechanically delivered breath (MB). Just prior to the next SI, there is an end-expiratory (EE) plateau. The recorded PAW should be obtained at end expiration, 10 mm Hg on this tracing. (Note the 0 to 21 mm Hg range of PAW over the entire respiratory cycle.)

who is also receiving positive pressure ventilation (eg, IMV or assist/control mode). The PAWP will rise with the mechanical breath and fall with a spontaneous inspiration. If the combined respiratory rate is rapid, end expiration will be very short, possibly only one cardiac cycle (Figure 16-5).

Pulmonary Artery Measurement Techniques

When a calibrated *analog* graph is available on the monitor screen, the patient's end-expiratory phase can be correlated with the screen tracing. By placing one hand over the patient's chest, one can feel the chest fall during exhalation and measure the tracing just prior to inspiration when the chest rises.

Strip chart recordings of the PAWP tracing are recommended for the most accurate measurements. To avoid error in selecting the end-expiratory wave, the patient's respiratory pattern must be carefully observed.

The *digital mean* on the monitor display has been used to measure PAWP. This technique can be a source of error if the monitor does not exclude the respiratory variation from the average value. If digital values must be used, some authors recommend the following:

- If the patient is breathing spontaneously, use the systolic setting for PAWP (reads the highest wave).
- If the patient is on controlled ventilation, use the diastolic setting for PAWP (reads the lowest wave).
- Use mean PAWP if the patient is on IMV or assisted ventilation with significant inspiratory effort.

Cardiovascular Effects of Positive End-Expiratory Pressure

In addition to the therapeutic pulmonary effects, positive end-expiratory pressure (PEEP) can have profound effects on cardiovascular assessment and function, especially at higher levels (ie, > 10 cm H_2O). This section discusses commonly observed effects of PEEP on cardiac output and pulmonary artery pressure measurements.

PEEP Effects on Cardiac Output

Positive end-expiratory pressure, particularly in excess of 10 cm H_2O, has been shown to both reduce and increase cardiac output. A reduction in cardiac output is more commonly seen. Several mechanisms have been proposed to explain these effects.

1. ***Reduced preload.*** By increasing intrathoracic pressure, PEEP reduces venous return, stroke volume, and cardiac output. The higher the PEEP, the greater

the potential reduction in cardiac output, particularly when combined with high peak airway pressures and rapid ventilator rates. Cardiac output should be determined before and after PEEP changes. Reproducibility of cardiac output measurements is greatly improved if injection is made at the same stage of the respiratory cycle.

The ultimate goal of improved oxygenation is to increase oxygen delivery to the tissues. There is no net improvement if PEEP increases PaO_2 but impairs tissue perfusion, ie, reduces cardiac output. As patients are treated with increasing levels of PEEP, they may require additional fluids for hemodynamic stability.

2. *Right ventricular strain and septal shift.* Positive end-expiratory pressure, again by increasing intrathoracic pressure, may increase pulmonary vascular resistance (PVR). The increased PVR can cause right ventricular failure with increased RV end-diastolic volumes. The dilated right ventricle pushes the intraventricular septum to the left; the left ventricular end-diastolic *pressure* then rises, but left ventricular filling *volume* drops. The septal shift can be demonstrated on two-dimensional echocardiogram. Clinically, this process may cause increased PAWP with decreased cardiac output.

3. *Increased cardiac output.* In contrast, the application of PEEP may *increase* cardiac output in patients with severe respiratory distress or cardiac failure. Severe respiratory disease may cause decreased lung volume (ie, decreased FRC), which increases PVR. A distressed patient also often has exaggerated inspiratory effort, which increases LV afterload. If PEEP increases resting lung volume, improves gas exchange, and relieves the respiratory distress, PVR and LV afterload may decrease resulting in improved cardiac output.

Effect of PEEP on Pulmonary Artery Pressures

The common belief that PAWP closely approximates left ventricular preload is erroneous in several settings. Two such situations involving PEEP are discussed below.

1. *Effect of lung zone placement.* One assumption that must hold true for the PAWP to reflect left ventricular end-diastolic pressures (LVEDP) is that a continuous column of fluid exists between the catheter tip and the left atrium. This column of fluid, blood in the pulmonary vessels, can be interrupted by compression from alveoli. This can occur if the catheter is placed in Zones I or II (see Chapter 3).

Only in Zone III, at the base of the lung (or posterior area in a supine patient), do both arterial and venous pressures exceed alveolar pressure. The PA catheter must be in Zone III to have a continuous column of blood to the left atrium. Fortunately, since the PA catheter is flow-directed, it will usually enter a Zone III area on insertion.

Clinically, the major problem is the conversion of Zone III to Zone II after the catheter is placed. The zones are physiologic, not anatomic areas. Zone III can change to II if pulmonary vascular pressure decreases (eg, with hypovolemia) or if alveolar pressure increases (eg, with increased PEEP).

Clinical detection of non-Zone III placement is important to avoid errors in PAWP interpretation. Indications of non-Zone III location of the PA catheter tip include:

- PA catheter tip above the left atrium (or anterior to LA if the patient is supine) on lateral chest radiograph.
- PAWP lacks characteristic cardiac waves ("a" or "v" waves) but does have marked respiratory variation.
- PAWP changes by more than 50% of the PEEP change.
- PAWP exceeds the PAD.

Zone III placement is more likely if the patient is positioned normally during PA catheter placement. Patients are frequently placed in the Trendelenburg position for central line placement. If the patient is usually in a semi-Fowler's position, the patient can be repositioned after central line insertion and before the PA catheter is advanced.

2. *Transmission of increased airway pressure.* Even when the PA catheter is properly positioned in a Zone III area, higher levels of PEEP (ie, > 10 cm H_2O) can confound PAWP interpretation. With the addition of PEEP, intrathoracic pressure is higher than normal at end expiration. Some of that pressure may be transmitted to the pericardium and pulmonary vessels. The measured PAWP now reflects both intravascular pressure *and* the pressure exerted on the vessels from the thoracic cavity. Pulmonary artery wedge pressure may overestimate LVEDP in this setting.

Theoretically, the higher the PEEP, the greater the potential increase in PA and PAW pressures. Clinically, patients requiring high levels of PEEP usually have stiff, non-compliant lungs that may not predictably transmit the airway pressures. Clinicians are advised to follow trends and the hemodynamic response (ie, cardiac output, oxygen delivery and consumption, and parameters reflecting tissue perfusion) in these patients, rather than relying on an absolute number produced by the PAWP.

Techniques to Estimate the Effect of PEEP on PAWP

In the face of severe respiratory failure and a normal to high PAWP, decisions regarding fluid administration may be more difficult because of the uncertainty of the true PAWP. Determining the effect that PEEP has on the true PA and PAWP is difficult and extremely variable. Several methods have been proposed to aid in this determination.

1. *Discontinuing the PEEP.* Removing the patient from the ventilator or decreasing the PEEP has been suggested as a method of determining the true

PAWP. This method has also been strongly criticized. Removing PEEP risks hypoxemia and airway closure that may not readily reverse once the PEEP has been reapplied. Discontinuing PEEP also alters the patient's hemodynamic environment. Preload will increase, making the reliability of the measurements questionable. If this method is to be employed, a safer variation may be to run a strip chart recording, inflate the balloon to PAWP, and momentarily pop off the ventilator connection; the degree to which the PAWP wave decreases reflects the PEEP effect.

2. *Calculation estimate.* A *formula* has also been used to estimate the PEEP influence on the PAWP. Assuming that a portion of the PEEP level is transmitted to the PAWP, one-half of the PEEP level (converted from cm H_2O to mm Hg) is subtracted from the PAWP.

$$PAWP = PAWP - \frac{[PEEP\ (cm\ H_2O)\ \times\ (.75)]}{2}$$

3. *Esophageal pressure monitoring.* Measuring pressures within the esophagus is another, somewhat controversial method of determining the intrathoracic pressure changes from PEEP. The esophagus is exposed to the same intrathoracic pressures as the heart and pulmonary vessels. Any increase in esophageal pressure above normal is attributed to these extravascular sources. The increase in esophageal pressure is then subtracted from the PAWP to arrive at the true PAWP.

A nasogastric tube with a saline-filled esophageal balloon can be used to track thoracic pressure changes at increasing levels of PEEP. Given a normal esophageal pressure of 8 mm Hg, any pressure greater than 8 mm Hg is subtracted from the PAWP.

OXYGEN TRANSPORT

Analysis of oxygen transport, oxygen consumption by tissues and the effect of therapy on this balance is important in the care of the critically ill patient. Three aspects of oxygen transport and utilization must be examined:

1. the amount of oxygen available to tissues
2. the amount of oxygen consumed by the tissues
3. the adequacy of supply and consumption in meeting tissue metabolic demand for oxygen.

Inadequate tissue oxygenation forces cells into anaerobic metabolism, ultimately leading to organ dysfunction and cell death. This section covers components of oxygen delivery, consumption, formulas, continuous mixed venous oxygen saturation monitoring, and clinical implications for therapy.

Oxygen Availability

Sufficient oxygen delivery requires adequate function of both the pulmonary and cardiovascular systems. Oxygen availability depends on:

1. adequate gas exchange in the lung
2. adequate oxygen-carrying capacity of hemoglobin
3. adequate cardiac output to meet metabolic demands.

Oxygen delivery, or availability ($\dot{D}O_2$) is a calculation of the total milliliters of oxygen circulated per minute:

$$\dot{D}O_2 = CaO_2 \times 10 \times \text{Cardiac Output}$$

(Arterial oxygen content [CaO_2] is discussed in Chapter 4.) A factor of 10 is used to convert CaO_2 (measured in deciliters) to liters (cardiac output is measured in liters per minute). Normal $\dot{D}O_2 = 1000$ mL O_2/minute. Oxygen availability can also be indexed to body surface area to provide more meaningful numbers (as with cardiac index): the normal indexed value ($\dot{D}O_2I$) = 570 mL/ meter sq BSA.

Oxygen availability is threatened if the patient has lung disease or injury, anemia or hemoglobin transport block (eg, carbon monoxide), or impaired cardiac output (cardiac failure, hypovolemia).

Tissue Oxygen Consumption

The amount of oxygen used by the tissues is calculated from simultaneous samples of arterial blood and a mixed venous blood sample drawn through the distal port of a pulmonary artery catheter. The difference between arterial and venous oxygen content indicates the amount of oxygen used by the tissues. The first step in calculating oxygen consumption is to calculate the arterial-venous oxygen content difference $C(a - \bar{v})O_2$.

Arterial-Venous Oxygen Content Difference

The arterial-venous oxygen content difference ($C(a - \bar{v})O_2$) is calculated from the difference between arterial O_2 content (CaO_2) and venous O_2 content ($C\bar{v}O_2$). The following formulas are used to calculate arterial and venous O_2 content:

$$CaO_2 = (Hgb \times 1.34 \times SaO_2) + (PAO_2 \times .003)$$

$$C\bar{v}O_2 = (Hgb \times 1.34 \times S\bar{v}O_2) + (P\bar{v}O_2 \times .003)$$

Normal $C(a-\bar{v})O_2 = 5$ to 10 cc/100 cc blood. In stressed critically ill patients, a $C(a-\bar{v})O_2$ of three to four is commonly found and indicates sufficient cardiac reserve and adequate O_2 availability. A high $C(a-\bar{v})O_2$ (especially > 5 cc/100 cc blood) indicates reduced oxygen transport or increased oxygen demand or both. Of the three components of oxygen transport (PaO_2, Hgb, cardiac output), only cardiac output can be significantly increased acutely. Thus, the body's usual response to elevated tissue oxygen demand is an increase in cardiac output. If total flow cannot be increased, tissues are forced to extract more oxygen from the blood and the $C(a-\bar{v})O_2$ increases. Stated differently, an elevated $C(a-\bar{v})O_2$ indicates that, given the PaO_2 and Hgb, the current hemodynamic status (preload, afterload, cardiac function) is incapable of producing a cardiac output sufficient to meet tissue demand.

Oxygen Consumption

The amount of oxygen used by the tissues per minute is calculated from the difference between the amount of oxygen delivered in arterial blood and the amount returning in venous blood. The oxygen consumption ($\dot{V}O_2$) formula is:

$$\dot{V}O_2 = 10 \times \text{Cardiac Output} \times (CaO_2 - C\bar{v}O_2)$$

Normal oxygen consumption is 250 mL/minute, or 25% of normal O_2 availability (1000 mL). This value can also be indexed to body surface area: normal $\dot{V}O_2I = 115$ to 165 mL/minute/M_2. Normal in this context means healthy, nonstressed resting values. Oxygen requirements are increased with exercise, fever, infection, pain, emotional stress, and the stress of critical illness and by many treatments and care procedures. Oxygen consumption in critically ill patients should be greater than normal. Increased survival has been reported among critically ill surgical patients with higher oxygen consumption ($\dot{V}O_2I > 130$ to 160 mL/min/M_2)

Evaluation of the Adequacy of Oxygen Transport

The goal of oxygen transport analysis is to determine whether or not the tissues have adequate amounts of oxygen to meet their demands for aerobic metabolism. In addition to oxygen transport calculations, serum lactate, and assessment of organ function can be used to evaluate the adequacy of tissue perfusion.

1. ***Serum lactate.*** Lactate is a byproduct of anaerobic metabolism. If oxygen demand exceeds the oxygen supply, serum lactate levels will be elevated. Normal lactate = 5 to 25 mg/dL or 1 to 2 mmol/L, depending on the method of analysis. A decreasing lactate level indicates improving tissue perfusion.

2. ***Organ function.*** Inadequate perfusion and tissue oxygenation results in organ dysfunction. Three easily assessed organs are:

- the brain: level of consciousness
- the kidney: urine output
- the skin: temperature reflecting vasoconstriction.

Dysfunction or improvement in function of these three systems can be easily tracked to detect changes in patient status and gauge the efficacy of treatment.

Therapeutic Implications of Oxygen Transport

Evaluating oxygen transport and utilization requires analysis of both supply and demand. Anaerobic metabolism can result when demands are relatively normal but supply is limited (eg, myocardial failure, anemia), when supply is normal but demands are excessive (eg, fever, shivering, infection, increased work of breathing), or when tissues are not able to fully utilize available oxygen (septic shock). To bring the critically ill patient back to a balance, the clinician must evaluate the options of increasing supply or decreasing demand.

If oxygen delivery or supply is low, efforts are directed toward correcting the deficient component. Therapy includes:

- improving lung function
- increasing supplemental oxygen or ventilatory support
- transfusion to adequate hemoglobin levels
- augmenting cardiac output by manipulating preload, afterload, and inotropic support.

Improving oxygen supply becomes the focus of therapy when supply is critically threatened. For example, a cardiac output of two liters per minute resulting from hypovolemia is improved with fluid therapy. Cardiac failure may be improved with inotropes, diuretics, and afterload reduction. Severe hypoxemia may be corrected with mechanical ventilation.

Maintaining supply is also important in caring for acutely ill patients. Particularly when care activities increase demand, oxygen supply must not be interrupted (eg, maintaining the oxygen source when assisting patients with activity, or hyperoxygenation with endotracheal suctioning).

In many cases, oxygen delivery is normal, but demand is excessive. Clinicians must then evaluate and correct factors that increase oxygen demand. Many states and complications of severe illness increase oxygen requirements (eg, fever, infection, shivering, work of breathing, pain, and anxiety). Many common treatments and procedures also increase oxygen demand (eg, turning, suctioning, and ambulation). Therapy is directed toward decreasing demand. Decreasing metabolic stress will help reestablish the balance between oxygen supply and demand.

When oxygen consumption is low, or lower than expected, three possibilities exist:

1. *Metabolic demand is low.* Oxygen demand decreases when metabolic activity slows. Hypothermia and anesthesia are two situations in which oxygen consumption may be abnormally low because demand has been reduced.

2. *Oxygen supply is not adequate for demand.* If oxygen supply is critically reduced, consumption may be low because the tissues simply can not extract the amount of oxygen they need. This situation is termed *flow-dependent* oxygen consumption. Therapy is directed toward increasing supply. In many cases, oxygen consumption will increase if $\dot{D}O_2$ is increased. Factors that cause a left shift of the oxyhemoglobin dissociation curve (eg, hypothermia, alkalosis, decreased 2, 3-DPG) increase hemoglobin affinity for oxygen; correction of such factors will increase oxygen availability at the tissue level.

3. *Tissues are not able to use oxygen normally.* Under some conditions, such as septic shock and cyanide poisoning, part of the cells' failure to use oxygen is thought to be related to a metabolic defect. Unless specific therapy is available to treat the metabolic problem, general therapy is aimed at increasing supply to eliminate flow-dependent limitations to consumption.

Table 16-1 summarizes the states contributing to abnormal oxygen consumption.

Mixed Venous Oxygen Monitoring

Mixed venous oxygen saturation ($S\bar{v}O_2$) can be monitored continuously through a fiberoptic pulmonary artery catheter. Rather than relying on periodic determinations of arterial blood gases, cardiac output, and mixed venous gases, the $S\bar{v}O_2$ monitor provides immediate indication of a change in the patient's cardiopulmonary status. Venous oxygen saturation monitoring is a sensitive monitoring technique because, on the venous portion of the oxyhemoglobin dissociation curve, a small change in $P\bar{v}O_2$ is reflected in the $S\bar{v}O_2$. Normal $S\bar{v}O_2$ is 60% to 80%.

Table 16-1 Factors Affecting Oxygen Transport and Utilization

Oxygenation State	Physiologic Mechanisms	Examples
Reduced O_2 availability	Decreased hemoglobin	Anemia Bleeding Abnormal hemoglobin
	Decreased SaO_2	Respiratory failure Suctioning
	Decreased cardiac output	Cardiogenic shock Hypovolemia Arrhythmias Hypotension
High O_2 consumption	Increased oxygen demands	Hyperthermia Shivering Seizures Pain Infection Activity Increased work of breathing
Decreased O_2 consumption	Decreased oxygen demands	Hypothermia Anesthesia Pharmacologic paralysis
	Flow limitations	Shock
	Left shift of oxyhemoglobin dissociation curve (decreased release of oxygen)	Hypothermia Alkalosis Decreased 2,3-DPG
	Metabolic Block	Septic shock Cyanide poisoning

Mixed venous oxygen saturation represents the balance between supply and demand. A decrease in supply (cardiac output, hemoglobin, or arterial oxygen saturation) *or* an increase in demand will cause a fall in $S\bar{v}O_2$.

Equipment

The fiberoptic catheter transmits and receives light of different wavelengths, distinguishing between oxyhemoglobin and reduced hemoglobin by their differing absorption of light. This technology requires standardization of the catheter prior to insertion and calibration every 24 hours.

Uses for Continuous $S\bar{v}O_2$ Monitoring

The immediate information provided by $S\bar{v}O_2$ monitoring offers the following advantages over periodic mixed venous blood sampling:

- Early indicator of circulatory changes. Decreasing $S\bar{v}O_2$ may be the earliest indication of patient deterioration.
- Immediate assessment of patient tolerance for nursing procedures (eg, suctioning, activity such as turning).
- Immediate evaluation of the effectiveness of cardiopulmonary therapy (eg, titration of vasoactive infusions, effects of PEEP on oxygen transport).

Limitations of Continuous $S\bar{v}O_2$ Monitoring

The fiberoptic catheter can be damaged by excessive pressure or by bending the catheter. Clot formation on the end of the catheter after several days use may also make readings inaccurate. In addition, $S\bar{v}O_2$ catheters are more expensive than regular PA catheters. The catheters can be cost effective if they reduce the number of arterial and mixed venous blood samples.

Mixed venous oxygen saturations must be carefully interpreted in the setting of septic shock. High $S\bar{v}O_2$ measurements (eg, 80%) can be seen as a result of peripheral shunting and metabolic changes. In this case, a rising $S\bar{v}O_2$ can indicate a worsening oxygen utilization status.

SUGGESTED READING

Ahrens TS. Concepts in the assessment of oxygenation. *Focus on Crit Care.* 1987;14: 36–44.

Briones T. $S\bar{v}O_2$ Monitoring: part I. Clinical case application. *DCCN.* 1988;7:70–78.

Carden DL, Nowak DM, Sarkar D, Tomianovich MC. Vital signs including pulsus paradoxus in the assessment of acute bronchial asthma. *Ann Emerg Med.* 1983;12:80–83.

Divertie MG, McMichan JC. Continuous Monitoring of Mixed Venous Oxygen Saturation. *Chest.* 1984;85:423–428.

Edwards JD. Practical application of oxygen transport principles. *Crit Care Med.* 1990;18(Supp):545–548.

Hardy GR: $S\bar{v}O_2$ Continuous Monitoring Techniques. *DCCN.* 1988;7:8–17.

Jardin F, Farcot J, Boisante L, Prost J, Gueret P, Bourdarias J. Mechanism of paradoxic pulse in bronchial asthma. *Circ.* 1982;66:887–894.

Kaufman BS, Rackow EC, Falk JL. The relationship between oxygen delivery and consumption during fluid resuscitation of hypovolemic and septic shock. *Chest.* 1984;85:336–340.

King DE. Assessment and evaluation of the paradoxical pulse. *DCCN.* 1982;1:266–274.

Luce JM. The cardiovascular effects of mechanical ventilation and positive end-expiratory pressure. *JAMA.* 1984;252:807–811.

Pinsky M. Hemodynamic effects of artificial ventilation. In: Shoemaker W, Ayres S, Grenvik A, Holbrook P, Thompson W, eds. *Textbook of Critical Care.* Philadelphia: W B Saunders Company; 1989.

Rajacich N, Burchard K, Hasan F, Singh A. Esophageal pressure monitoring: a practical adjuvant to hemodynamic monitoring with positive end-expiratory pressure. *Heart Lung.* 1988;17:483–488.

Raper R, Sibbald W. Misled by the wedge? The Swan-Ganz catheter and left ventricular preload. *Chest.* 1986;89:427–434.

Riedinger MS, Shellock FG, Swan HJC. Reading pulmonary artery and pulmonary capillary wedge pressure waveforms with respiratory variations. *Heart Lung.* 1981;10:675–678.

Schermer L. Physiologic and technical variables affecting hemodynamic measurements. *Crit Care Nurse.* 1988;8:33–43.

Shoemaker WC, Appel PL, Kram HB, Waxman K, Lee T. Prospective trial of supranormal values of survivors as therapeutic goals in high-risk surgical patients. *Chest.* 1988;94:1176–1186.

Silverman H, Eppler J, Pitman A, Patz D. Pulmonary artery wedge pressure measurements in patients on assisted ventilation. *Journal of Critical Care.* 1987;2:115–120.

White K. Continuous monitoring of mixed venous oxygen saturation (S$\bar{v}$O$_2$): a new assessment tool in critical care nursing. *Cardiovascular Nursing.* 1987;23:1–2.

Wiedemann H, Matthay M, Matthay R. Cardiovascular-pulmonary monitoring in the intensive care unit (part 1) *Chest.* 1984;85:537–549.

chapter 17

Weaning from Mechanical Ventilation

Ventilator weaning is the process of discontinuing the patient's mechanical ventilatory support. For many patients, weaning simply involves withdrawal of the ventilatory support once the patient is breathing spontaneously, eg, after a surgical procedure that required mechanical ventilation. For other patients the weaning process may require hours to days or weeks. This chapter discusses the criteria used to determine when weaning should be instituted and approaches to weaning. A section on weaning from the artificial airway is also included because this process often becomes the last step in ventilator weaning.

CRITERIA FOR WEANING FROM MECHANICAL VENTILATION

The most widely recognized criteria for weaning are the reverse of the parameters cited in Chapter 14 as criteria for instituting mechanical ventilation (see Table 14-1 in Chapter 14). However, it is also widely recognized that there are many patients who are weaned who do not meet these criteria and many patients who meet the criteria but cannot be weaned. It is therefore obvious that other factors can play a critical role.

Before weaning is considered, the patient's general status must be assessed. Many of these general factors affect general metabolic demands or the patient's ability to respond to changes in metabolic demand. The major factors to be considered are:

- Cardiovascular stability (the patient may still require vasopressors but should be stabilized with pharmacologic support).
- Improvement in the underlying disease that caused respiratory failure.
- Adequate nutrition (it will influence respiratory muscle strength).

- Absence of fever or shivering (which would increase metabolic demands).
- Adequate oxygen-carrying capacity (hemoglobin level).
- Absence of acid-base abnormalities (could increase or decrease ventilatory drive and affect the work of breathing).
- Absence of electrolyte abnormalities.
- Absence of pharmacologically induced ventilatory depression (the use of sedatives or narcotics could decrease ventilatory drive).
- Absence of excessive pain, which could restrict ventilatory effort (this is especially important in the postoperative patient with underlying chronic lung disease and in the patient with chest trauma).

The physiologic and ventilator parameters that reflect lung function are then measured or assessed. (The physiologic parameters and techniques by which they are measured are discussed more fully in Chapter 16.) The parameters, which encompass values that would support a weaning attempt, include: (not all measures are used by all clinicians)

- FIO_2 less than 0.45 on ventilator to maintain oxygenation.
- PEEP level of 5 cm H_2O or less.
- $\dot{V}E$ less than 10 to 12 liters per minute on ventilator to achieve appropriate $PaCO_2$ for the patient (relates to metabolic demand and dead-space ventilation).
- Peak pressures on ventilator less than 40 cm H_2O (relates to lung compliance).
- Spontaneous vital capacity > 10 mL/kg.
- Maximal inspiratory force at least -20 cm H_2O (in patients with flail chest, it should be at least -20 to -30 cm H_2O).
- Patient able to voluntarily double his or her resting minute volume.
- Endotracheal tube does not offer excessive resistance (in an adult, a tube 7.5 mm or larger is preferred).

Although other measures, such as shunt fraction and dead-space ventilation can be measured, the above parameters provide sufficient data so that judgments about ventilation and oxygenation can be made. One measure that is helpful but seldom made because of the invasive techniques required, is work of breathing. The above parameters can, however, allow the clinician to make some general inferences about the work of breathing.

Finally, the clinician must consider the patient's psychological readiness for weaning. (This factor assumes that the patient is alert and able to respond; of course, coma does not preclude weaning.) General patient responses are considered. Patients who want to be off the ventilator, who do not respond with acute anxiety to being off the ventilator for spontaneous measures, and who are able to follow instructions are examples of positive responses.

APPROACHES TO WEANING

There are two general approaches to weaning. One is referred to as conventional weaning and the other as IMV weaning. Both techniques, to be successful, require that the patient be ready for weaning.

Conventional Weaning

Conventional weaning refers to withdrawing ventilator support at periodic intervals. While off ventilator support the patient may be placed on a T-piece or on CPAP for oxygen supplementation (usually at an FIO_2 slightly higher than that delivered by the ventilator), humidification, and PEEP if necessary. The intervals at which the patient is removed from mechanical support vary according to the specific patient situation. However, there are some general considerations relevant to all conventional weaning.

The weaning attempt is best begun when the patient is well rested and adequate personnel are available. Thus the attempt is usually begun in the morning; activities, such as bathing, ambulation, and special tests, should be avoided prior to and during the weaning attempt. The patient should be positioned to enhance the use of the respiratory muscles (sitting in a chair is often helpful), and the airway should be cleared by suctioning. Drugs that might affect the ventilatory drive should be withheld prior to and during the weaning attempt; if the drugs cannot be stopped, they should be administered at the lowest dose possible. It is preferable that the staff member with the patient during the weaning attempt is one who is known, liked, and trusted by the patient. Finally, be sure that the patient knows what is happening.

For the patient who required only short-term ventilatory support and who is predicted to wean easily, successful weaning may require only one trial. The patient is removed from the ventilator and monitored. If the patient does not develop respiratory distress or cardiovascular instability, the patient continues off the ventilator. Blood gases should be drawn after 20 to 30 minutes of spontaneous breathing. If the results do not demonstrate adequate ventilation and oxygenation, the patient is placed back on the ventilator. If the results are in the desired range, mechanical ventilation is terminated. Extubation usually follows immediately. After cessation of mechanical ventilation and extubation, close monitoring of the patient must continue so that any changes in the ventilatory status, laryngeal edema (stridor), or other complications are detected as early as possible.

Patients who have been ventilated more than several days or who have underlying chronic pulmonary disease often require a more prolonged weaning period. This period may last anywhere from hours to days. For gradual conventional weaning, periods of spontaneous breathing are alternated with periods of mechanical ventilation. The length of the periods of spontaneous breathing is gradually increased while the periods of mechanical assistance are gradually decreased. Frequently, in the early phases of the weaning program, the patient is placed on the ventilator continuously at night for rest.

During gradual weaning, it is important for the clinician to reassure and encourage the patient. It is often helpful for the patient to understand that some increase in shortness of breath is to be expected when he or she is breathing spontaneously. The clinician should also realize that some increase in respiratory rate and heart rate is to be expected. Blood gases usually demonstrate some deterioration; the clinical expectation is maintenance of adequate values, not a finding of "no change." It is important, however, that excessive or progressive increases in the respiratory rate or development of a paradoxical respiratory pattern be noted immediately. These findings often reflect an increased work of breathing and respiratory muscle fatigue, and they indicate a need for the patient to be returned to mechanical assistance. If possible, blood gases should be drawn prior to returning the patient to the ventilator. When the gradual approach becomes prolonged, techniques such as pressure support during spontaneous breathing may be used to assist the patient.

IMV Weaning

IMV weaning utilizes the IMV mode on the ventilator. The number of mechanically delivered breaths per minute is gradually decreased until the patient is spontaneously maintaining his or her total ventilation. Thus the amount of mechanical support the patient receives per minute is gradually reduced. As with conventional weaning, IMV weaning may require varying periods of time. One criticism of IMV has been that it prolongs weaning in some situations. This criticism is primarily due to the clinician who proceeds too slowly in decreasing the IMV rate; it is not a fault of the actual technique.

In patients who are expected to be readily weaned, the IMV rate should be decreased by one or two breaths every 20 to 30 minutes. If blood gases remain at acceptable levels, the process continues until the patient is breathing spontaneously. As with conventional weaning, the patient's spontaneous rate and respiratory pattern should be monitored. In addition, as with conventional weaning, slight deterioration of blood gases can be expected. Continued, progressive deterioration of blood gases indicates failure of the weaning process.

For patients who require more gradual weaning, the IMV rate is lowered much more slowly; the rate is lowered every several hours or sometimes only once a day. As with conventional weaning, the patient is often rested at night (by increasing the IMV rate) and such techniques as pressure support may be used to assist the patient's spontaneous breathing.

WEANING FROM TRACHEAL INTUBATION

Weaning from oral and nasal endotracheal tubes versus tracheostomy tubes requires different strategies. Most of the differences relate to the reasons why the patient required a tracheostomy rather than an endotracheal tube.

Most patients who receive mechanical ventilation via an endotracheal tube are extubated after successful weaning from the mechanical ventilator. The major exception is the patient who is unable to protect his or her airway; if that situation persists, the patient usually progresses to tracheostomy. The endotracheal tube prohibits speech, oral intake, and may increase the work of breathing. For these reasons, it is advantageous to remove the endotracheal tube as soon as possible after mechanical ventilation is terminated. Extubation usually facilitates the patient's ability to sustain spontaneous ventilation.

Prior to removal of the endotracheal tube, the patient's airway should be suctioned and the cuff deflated. After extubation the patient should be monitored for his ability to protect the airway; both the gag reflex and cough effectiveness should be assessed. Another potential complication of postextubation is development of laryngeal edema; this complication is usually identified by the presence of inspiratory stridor. Should laryngeal edema develop, an aerosol of racemic epinephrine may reduce the edema and avoid the necessity for emergent reintubation. Should severe edema develop, the patient will require reintubation.

Patients who have been tracheotomized usually require a longer weaning period before the tracheostomy tube can be removed. (In some patients, weaning from the tracheostomy is not possible; even though mechanical ventilation is not required, protection of the lower airway may be necessary.) The usual approach to weaning from the tracheostomy is to insert a fenestrated tube. The tube is plugged and the fenestration is opened to facilitate spontaneous breathing. Tubes without fenestrations *should not be plugged!* If the patient is able to maintain airway clearance and ventilation, the tube can be removed. Patients who are able to maintain ventilation but not airway clearance may profit from the insertion of a tracheal button.

After the tracheostomy tube is removed, a dressing is placed over the tracheotomy and it is allowed to close and heal naturally. In the period following removal of the tube, the patient will leak air at the stomal site, especially with forced expiratory maneuvers such as those required with cough. This leakage may decrease cough effectiveness somewhat. It is often helpful for the patient to apply pressure manually over the stomal site during cough in order to occlude the opening.

SUGGESTED READING

Dark DS, Pingleton SK, Kerby GR. Hypercapnia during weaning. A complication of nutritional support. *Chest*. 1985;88:141–143.

Fiastro JF, Habib MP, Shon BY, et al. Comparison of standard weaning parameters and the mechanical work of breathing in mechanically ventilated patients. *Chest*. 1988;94:232–238.

Marini JJ. The physiologic determinants of ventilator dependence. *Resp Care*. 1986;31:271–282.

Morganroth ML, Grum CM. Weaning from mechanical ventilation. *J Int Care Med*. 1988;3:109–120.

Morganroth ML, Morganroth JL, Nett LM, et al. Criteria for weaning from prolonged mechanical ventilation. *Arch Intern Med*. 1984;144:1012–1016.

Norton LC, Neureuter A. Weaning the long-term ventilator-dependent patient. Common problems and management. *Crit Care Nurs*. 1989;9:42–52.

Sahn SA, Lakshminarayau S, Petty TL. Weaning from mechanical ventilation. *JAMA*. 1976;235:2208–2212.

Tomlinson JR, Miller KS, Larch DG, Smith L, Reines HD, Sahn SA. A prospective comparison of IMV and T-piece weaning from mechanical ventilation. *Chest*. 1989;96:348–352.

Pharmacotherapeutics

Selected classes of drugs used in the treatment of patients with acute or chronic pulmonary dysfunction are discussed. Each major heading will include **(A)** the basic action of the drug, **(B)** indications, **(C)** preparations and dosage, and **(D)** potential side effects.

I. METHYLXANTHINES

A. The methylxanthines are primarily used as bronchodilators. Secondary effects include increased strength of diaphragmatic contraction and stimulation of the central nervous system (use as a respiratory stimulant). The major pharmacologic forms are theophylline and aminophylline. Methylxanthines are also present in coffee, tea, and some soft drinks as caffeine and in chocolate and cocoa as theobromine.

B. These drugs are primarily used to treat diseases characterized by bronchoconstriction (eg, asthma and chronic bronchitis). Other uses are as a respiratory stimulant (eg, for sleep apnea and as a secondary effect in the chronic obstructive pulmonary diseases) and recently as a means of increasing the strength of diaphragmatic contraction in some neuromuscular diseases.

C. Theophylline is the major methylxanthine. It can be administered orally, intravenously (as aminophylline), or rectally.

The dosage of theophylline is adjusted to maintain therapeutic blood levels. The level is a balance between absorption and clearance. Although theophylline is rapidly and completely absorbed following oral administration (there is little influence by concurrent food or antacid intake), metabolism (by the liver) and clearance may vary widely. The factors that increase clearance and decrease serum theophylline include: age (younger children clear more rapidly), cigarette smoking, and such drugs as Dilantin, phenobarbital, and rifampin. Factors that decrease clearance and increase serum concentration include: heart failure, cirrhosis, and such drugs as erythromycin, Cimetadine, oral contraceptives, and

Allopurinol. Because of these factors and individual variability, each patient must be monitored periodically to ensure that therapeutic serum levels (10 to 20 μg/mL) are maintained. (The level required for any one individual will vary within the range and is determined by therapeutic effect versus side effects.)

General guidelines for dosages of *intravenous aminophylline* are:

1. If no previous methylxanthines were given to the patient, a loading dose of 6 mg/kg can be given over 20 to 30 minutes.

2. For patients already taking oral theophylline, continue the maintenance dose intravenously or give an adjusted loading dose (2.5 mg/kg); it is estimated that 0.5 mg/kg/hr of theophylline (equivalent to 0.6 mg/kg/hr intravenous aminophylline) will raise the serum level approximately 1 μg/mL.

3. The recommended daily maintenance dosages for intravenous aminophylline are 0.8 to 1.0 mg/kg for children and 0.3 to 0.5 mg/kg for adults.

For oral therapy, several different compounds of theophylline may be used. The strengths of the various compounds vary (100 mg aminophylline tablet equals 80 mg theophylline; 100 mg oxytriphylline equals 65 mg theophylline). Theophylline is the most common drug used and is available in short-acting, sustained-acting, and once-daily preparations. Of these, the sustained action form (bid or tid schedule) is most commonly used because it facilitates the maintenance of a constant serum level.

The general guidelines for dosages of *oral theophylline* are:

1. Dosage is usually begun low and increased to avoid gastrointestinal symptoms.

2. The usual long-term maintenance dose is 24 mg/kg in children one to nine years of age, 20 mg/kg in 9- to 12-year-olds, 18 mg/kg in 12- to 16-year-olds, and 13 mg/kg or 900 mg/day in adults.

3. In all patients, serum theophylline is monitored to ensure that the patient is receiving an adequate dose and to avoid toxicity. Concentrations of theophylline greater than 20 μg/mL are associated with an increased incidence of side effects. However, some patients may demonstrate side effects at much lower levels than others, while some patients may not demonstrate adverse side effects at levels greater than 20 μg/mL. Adverse effects associated with theophylline include: gastrointestinal upset (anorexia, nausea, vomiting, and abdominal discomfort); central nervous system effects (nervousness, insomnia, headache, irritability with severe toxicity, convulsions, and coma [usually associated with levels greater than 40 μg/mL]); cardiac effects (tachycardia [often multifocal atrial tachycardia] and with high levels, hypotension, or arrhythmias). It is important to note that nausea and vomiting frequently precede major toxicities and should be recognized as a drug effect.

The treatment for theophylline toxicity (in the 20 to 25 μg range) is discontinuation of the theophylline preparation. At higher serum levels, liquid charcoal may be administered orally. Charcoal hemoperfusion may be indicated in cases of extremely high levels (>40 μg/mL).

II. BETA ADRENERGICS

A. These drugs stimulate the sympathetic or adrenergic receptors. Of the several classes of adrenergic receptors, the airway beta-2 receptor is specific for bronchodilatation. (The other adrenergic receptors have a primary action on the cardiovascular system.)

B. These drugs are used to treat the airway hyperreactivity and bronchospasm seen in asthma, bronchitis, and as a sequela of some pulmonary infections. Some individuals with hyperreactive airways present with cough as the only symptom; the beta adrenergics may also be therapeutic in this situation.

C. Previously used drugs (eg, epinephrine, isoproterenol), prescribed to stimulate adrenergic receptors, had effects on beta-2 and other adrenergic receptors; therefore they were associated with increased incidence of side effects. These drugs are no longer recommended for treatment of pure bronchospasm in children or adults. Rather, drugs with a high degree of selectivity for the beta-2 receptor are used. These beta-2 agonists include metaproterenol, albuterol, and terbutaline. Although reported to have a longer period before onset of action (2 to 10 minutes), these new beta-2 agonists have a longer duration of action (four to six hours) than the earlier drugs. In some cases when an allergic reaction also involves laryngeal edema, drugs that cause vascular constriction in addition to bronchodilatation (eg, epinephrine) are indicated.

In many patients, the beta agonists may be the primary bronchodilator prescribed, while in others these drugs are used in conjunction with a methylxanthine. Although available in oral preparations (tablets and liquid), the aerosolized delivery of the beta agonists is preferred in order to reduce side effects. Aerosols may be delivered by MDI or by a small volume nebulizer (see Chapter 8). Some of these drugs may also be administered by subcutaneous injection. The dosages used for selected drugs are as follows:

Metaproterenol

1. *Inhaler* (0.65 mg/puff)—2 puffs qid (in adults the number of puffs may be increased per treatment; number of treatments may be increased to six every 24 hours).
2. *Aerosolized solution* (50 mg/cc; 5% solution)—0.2–0.3 cc qid (may be increased to 6 treatments every 24 hours).
3. *Tablets* (10 or 20 mg) and syrup (10 mg/5cc)—<9 years of age, 10 mg 3 to 4/day; older children and adults, 20 mg 3 to 4/day.

Albuterol

1. *Inhaler* (0.9 mg/puff)—same schedule as metaproterenol.
2. *Aerosolized solution* (5mg/cc; 0.5% solution)—0.5 cc/treatment; same schedule as metaproterenol.

3. *Tablets* (2 or 4 mg) and syrup (2 mg/5 cc)—<6 years of age, 2 mg tid; in adults, 2 to 4 mg 3 to 4/day.

It should be noted that use of an MDI requires much smaller doses to obtain therapeutic effect.

D. The primary side effect of the beta adrenergics is central nervous system stimulation due to systemic absorption; it is dose related. Symptoms include nervousness, headache, shakiness, tremor, insomnia, and agitation. There may also be an alteration in the ventilation-perfusion relationships; if the amount of vasodilatation exceeds bronchodilatation, a transient lowering of $\dot{V}/\dot{Q}$ with a decrease in PaO_2 will result. If ventilation is improved in excess of increased perfusion, low $\dot{V}/\dot{Q}$ areas should improve with an increase in PaO_2.

III. ANTICHOLINERGICS

A. Anticholinergics block the vagal stimulation of the muscarinic receptors. Vagal stimulation normally maintains airway tone and, if increased, can cause bronchoconstriction. Anticholinergics thus produce bronchodilatation. In addition, they may increase the effect of the beta adrenergics.

B. The anticholinergics are used in the treatment of bronchospasm associated with chronic obstructive pulmonary disease. They are administered by aerosol to avoid blocking the muscarinic receptors in other parts of the body (heart, gastrointestinal tract, and secretory glands). The classic anticholinergic is atropine. Although it can be administered by aerosol, it has more systemic side effects than the newer anticholinergics. Glycopyrrolate is administered by small volume jet nebulizer (0.4 to 1.0 mg every four to six hours). Ipratropium bromide, the most commonly used anticholinergic, is administered by inhaler. The usual dosage is two puffs three to four times a day, but the dosage may be increased to a total of 12 puffs. The drug should be used regularly, not "prn" to treat acute episodes.

C. Side effects with ipratropium bromide are extremely rare because the drug is not absorbed systemically.

IV. CORTICOSTEROIDS

A. Corticosteroids, as therapy in lung disease, are primarily used for their antiinflammatory properties. These properties are related to the effects of steroids on mediator release (inhibited or blocked). The therapeutic response is a decrease in airway hyperreactivity, potentiation of the beta adrenergics, decreased mucus secretion, decreased cough, decreased airway obstruction, and decreased inflammatory response.

B. Corticosteroids are primarily used in the treatment of bronchospasm and the treatment of some of the pulmonary interstitial diseases. In treatment of chronic obstructive disease, steroid therapy is reserved for situations in which other pharmacologic therapy has been unsuccessful; there must also be indications of inflammation and mediator release (eg, eosinophilia, elevated IgE, and fluctuations in degree of obstruction). Such situations include status asthmaticus, some cases of chronic asthma or chronic asthmatic bronchitis, and acute exacerbations of chronic airways obstruction.

As chronic therapy in obstructive disease, corticosteroids are given orally; the initial dose (usually 20 mg prednisone/day) is maintained for several weeks to ascertain if there is a therapeutic effect. The dose is then tapered to the lowest level possible to maintain a good effect (or if no steroid response, the drug is tapered and discontinued). To minimize side effects, the entire dose of oral prednisone should be taken in the morning and, if possible, the patient should be tapered to an every other day dosage schedule. For patients who require low dose steroids, inhaled preparations that are not systemically absorbed may be effective without the risk of the systemic side effects.

During acute, nonresponsive episodes of asthma or some acute exacerbations of chronic airways obstruction, steroids are frequently given intravenously. In such cases, very high doses may be required (up to 1000 mg of hydrocortisone in 24 hours); once the patient responds, the dose is tapered.

In therapy for interstitial lung disease, corticosteroids can be of benefit, particularly when given during periods of acute inflammation (demonstrated by lung biopsy); when used in chronic interstitial disease after fibrosis has occurred, steroids are of limited and questionable value. Generally speaking, much larger doses of corticosteroids are used to treat interstitial pulmonary disease than in clinical situations involving asthma and chronic airways obstruction. As a result, most clinicians attempt to document objective clinical improvement with the use of steroid therapy, such as improvement in pulmonary function tests (particularly diffusing capacity), arterial blood gases, and chest radiographs.

The most common forms of the corticosteroids are:

1. *Prednisone and prednisolone tablets*—come in a variety of strengths (1, 5, 10, 20, etc. mg); can be used for every other day schedule.
2. *Dexamethasone tablets*—available in a variety of strengths (0.25, 0.5, 0.75, 1.5, etc. mg); 0.75 mg is equivalent to 5 mg prednisone; not appropriate for every other day schedule.
3. *Hydrocortisone, injectable*—vial contains 100 mg, is equivalent to 25 mg prednisone.

4. *Methylprednisolone, injectable*—vial contains 40 mg, is equivalent to 50 mg prednisone.
5. *Flunisolide inhaler*—usual dose is two to four inhalations twice a day; no significant systemic absorption or adrenal suppression.
6. *Beclomethasone inhaler*—usual dose is two inhalations four times a day; no significant systemic absorption or adrenal suppression.

It is important that oral steroid therapy not be abruptly stopped. Providing systemic steroids depresses normal adrenal function, and abrupt cessation of therapy can result in life-threatening adrenal insufficiency. Symptoms that may be experienced as part of withdrawal include fatigue, weakness, lethargy, depression, hypoglycemia, hypotension, anorexia, and weight loss. If steroids have been given in high suppressive doses and/or for a long period of time (more than two months), it may take several months of gradual tapering of the drug to allow for recovery of adrenal function.

C. Systemic steroid therapy has many potential side effects. Some of the more common adverse effects are: fat redistribution (moon face, buffalo hump), increased appetite and weight gain, fluid retention, increased potassium excretion, capillary fragility (easy bruising), osteoporosis, early cataracts, muscle myopathy. Steroid therapy, in moderate doses, produces euphoria (often incorrectly interpreted by the patient as a therapeutic response) and, in high doses, may evoke a steroid psychosis. Because of these varied and potentially dangerous side effects, steroid therapy is reserved for cases in which it is absolutely necessary, and it is given at the lowest dose possible.

Although the inhaled preparations do not cause systemic side effects, they can make the patient susceptible to the development of oral thrush. Laryngitis and cough may also occur. These side effects can be avoided by rinsing the mouth well after using the inhaler and by using a spacer. The inhaled steroids should be used following an inhaled beta adrenergic.

V. CROMOLYN SODIUM

A. Cromolyn sodium (or disodium cromoglycate) is a drug used to prevent a Type I allergic response; the drug is neither a bronchodilator nor a steroid preparation. It is believed to stabilize the mast cells and prevent mediator release.

B. Cromolyn is prescribed for allergic asthmatics and is used to prevent the allergic response. It is also helpful in preventing exercise-induced asthma. It does not treat the bronchospasm once it has occurred. The drug is administered by aerosol via an MDI, spinhaler, or solution and jet nebulizer. Several weeks to months of therapy (20 mg four times daily) are generally required before its effects may be realized.

C. The only significant adverse effect of cromolyn therapy is an irritant effect on the airway, particularly when a spinhaler is used. Premedication with inhaled bronchodilator medication can help prevent the airway irritation and bronchospasm.

VI. OTHERS

Antihistamines. Although generally not used to treat asthma, the newer antihistamines (Terfenadine) do not have the side effects of sedation. In the treatment of asthma, Terfenadine is administered at doses of 60 to 120 mg twice a day.

Paralytics. In the intensive care setting, it is often necessary to prohibit the patient's spontaneous respirations. In these situations several types of skeletal muscle relaxants may be used. The choice of drug will depend on the duration of action required and the patient's cardiovascular and renal function status. Commonly used drugs are pancuronium, vecuronium, and succinylcholine. When using any of these drugs, it is important to remember that the patient is paralyzed by the drug but is not necessarily sedated. Sedation should be administered; common drugs for this purpose are midazolam and diazepam. Patients who require long-term (days or weeks) paralysis for adequate mechanical ventilation may have severe muscle weakness after the muscle relaxant is reversed. (Although clinically observed, it is unclear if the weakness is directly related to the severity of the disease, to the muscle relaxants, or to a combination of the two.)

Mucolytics. These drugs are seldom used except in special circumstances, such as cystic fibrosis. They are administered by aerosol and are used to facilitate clearance of purulent secretions. Many of the mucolytics can cause airway irritation and bronchospasm and should, therefore, always be given with an inhaled bronchodilator.

Antitussives. Cough suppression is rarely indicated as cough is necessary for airway clearance. When cough suppression is necessary (to facilitate rest at night or to inhibit dry, non-productive cough that is unresponsive to bronchodilators), the initial intervention is usually a commercial preparation that contains dextromethorphan; patients are usually advised to use the cough medicine only at bedtime. Codeine is also an effective cough suppressant, but it should not be routinely or excessively used because of side effects.

SUGGESTED READING

Wiener MB, Simkins RA. Respiratory disorders. In: *Clinical Pharmacology and Therapeutics of Common Disorders*. New York: McGraw Hill Publishing Co.; 1985:420–442.

Ziment I. *Respiratory Pharmacology and Therapeutics*. Philadelphia: W B Saunders Company; 1978.

Disease Processes

This appendix will present a brief overview of some of the more common medical diagnoses and problems encountered when caring for patients with pulmonary dysfunction. The outline for each diagnosis or problem will include **(A)** a brief description, **(B)** basic medical management of the pulmonary problem, and **(C)** references to various parts of this book that are especially applicable.

Acquired Immune Deficiency Syndrome

A. Acquired immune deficiency syndrome (AIDS) is an infection with the human immunodeficiency virus (HIV), which is a retrovirus that destroys T4 lymphocytes. Thus the cell-mediated immune system is rendered ineffective and, due to the influence of T cells on the production of antibodies, humoral (antibody) responses are also depressed. Typically, the HIV remains latent for a long period of time before signs and symptoms, such as fever, night sweats, weight loss, lymphadenopathy, malaise and/or anorexia are noted. The person who is infected with HIV is considered to have AIDS when AIDS-related opportunistic infections develop (ie, Pneumocystis carini pneumonia [PCP], toxoplasmosis, cocciodioidomycosis, or atypical mycobacterial disease) or an AIDS-related cancer is diagnosed (ie, Kaposi's sarcoma or lymphoma).

B. Medical therapy for AIDS is largely investigational at present; zidovudine (Retrovir, AZT) may be used as direct therapy against the HIV virus. Most treatment is aimed at the opportunistic infection, i e, acyclovir sodium (Zovirax) for herpes simplex infections, pentamidine isethionate (Pentam 300) or trimethoprim-sulfamethoxazole (Septra, Bactrim) for PCP, sulfadiazine (Microsulfon) or pyrimethamine (Daraprim) for toxoplasmosis, nystatin or ketoconazole (Nizoral) for *Candida* infections. Supportive therapy includes oxygen, as indicated, and emotional support for the patient and significant others. In selected situations, mechanical ventilation and PEEP may be instituted for respiratory failure.

C. Especially relevant discussions within this text are:

- Chapter 1—sections on T-lymphocytes and cell-mediated immunity.
- Chapter 9—sections on acute and chronic oxygen therapy.

Adult Respiratory Distress Syndrome (ARDS)

A. ARDS refers to the development of noncardiogenic pulmonary edema that is of sufficient severity to cause marked impairment of oxygen exchange. ARDS may develop after shock, long bone trauma, disseminated intravascular coagulation, sepsis, and a variety of other conditions. The basic underlying mechanism is the development of leaky capillaries in the pulmonary circulation. As the lung interstitium and alveoli become flooded with fluid, lung volume decreases, lung compliance decreases, and the patient develops severe hypoxemia that is unresponsive to usual oxygen therapy (increased shunt fraction).

B. Medical therapy is basically supportive, until the patient recovers from the basic injury. Supportive therapy includes oxygen, mechanical ventilation, PEEP, careful management of fluid status, and, in some but not all types of ARDS, steroids.

C. Especially relevant discussions within this text are:

- Chapter 2—sections on restrictive disease, observations of respiratory pattern that denote increased work of breathing due to lung stiffness or loss of muscle strength.
- Chapter 3—section on fluid flux.
- Chapter 5—section on ventilation/perfusion mismatching.
- Chapter 6—all sections (blood gas and acid-base interpretation).
- Chapter 11—suctioning an artificial airway.
- Chapter 12—all sections (artificial airway care).
- Chapter 14—sections on positive pressure volume ventilation and PEEP.
- Chapter 15—all sections related to intensive care unit techniques (ventilatory and gas exchange monitoring).
- Chapter 16—all sections (hemodynamic monitoring).
- Chapter 17—all sections (weaning).

Aspiration (Foreign Body, Near-Drowning, Gastric)

A. Foreign body aspiration may cause complete or partial obstruction of the airway. Complete obstruction is a life-threatening emergency requiring immediate treatment. Partial obstruction may occur in the large airways or in smaller distal airways and result in atelectasis. There is also the potential for development of a post-obstructive pneumonia. Aspiration of sharp objects (eg, an open safety pin) could tear the airway. In the alert adult, the occurrence of foreign body aspiration is usually related by the patient. In small children, parents may not observe the actual episode and may therefore be unaware that the child has aspirated. Associated symptoms are sudden onset of cough by history and isolated wheeze. If the aspirated object is radiopaque, it may be identified on chest radiograph. (Many aspirated objects, such as peanuts and pieces of carrot, are not radiopaque.)

Drowning and near-drowning involves aspiration of water. (Drowning is synonymous with a fatal outcome; in near-drowning, the patient survives.) Salt water, a hypertonic solution, draws fluid into the alveolus, resulting in pulmonary edema, reduced lung compliance, and shunting. Fresh water drowning also causes pulmonary edema and shunt, primarily by reducing the effectiveness of surfactant. In both situations, the primary gas exchange abnormality is hypoxemia. (In the minority of cases, laryngospasm may prevent water aspiration; these patients will often have the best prognosis with early cardiopulmonary resuscitation.)

Aspiration of acidic gastric fluid causes a severe chemical burn and destruction of lung tissue. Pulmonary edema, bronchospasm, and the severe inflammatory response result in decreased compliance, shunting, and severe hypoxemia. Aspiration of less acidic or neutral fluids results in a similar inflammatory response, but it is usually less severe. In addition, aspiration of food particles may obstruct airways.

B. Treatment of foreign body aspiration is aimed at removal of the object. Immediate therapy, outside the hospital setting, is the Heimlich maneuver. Direct visualization and removal of the object is achieved by bronchoscopy, usually rigid versus fiberoptic. In some situations, postural drainage with percussion and vibration has also been successful in removing an aspirated foreign body. Prevention is an important aspect of treatment, especially in the toddler; young children should not be given such food items as peanuts, carrot sticks, or hard candies.

The immediate treatment for near-drowning is cardiopulmonary resuscitation at the scene. Medical care is directed at correcting hypoxemia and providing cardiovascular support. Patients usually require supplemental oxygen; intubation and mechanical ventilation with PEEP may also be necessary. As with foreign body aspiration, prevention is the best treatment!

Immediate treatment of gastric aspiration is suctioning. Oxygen therapy is usually required to correct hypoxemia. Patients may be treated with a CPAP mask if awake, or may require intubation and mechanical ventilation. The goal is to improve oxygenation and increase FRC. Bronchoscopy may be indicated if food particles were aspirated. Steroids and antibiotics are controversial treatments.

C. Especially relevant areas in this text are:

- Chapter 1—sections on lung defenses, especially nonspecific.
- Chapter 3—section on fluid dynamics.
- Chapters 5 and 6—all sections (gas exchange and transport, interpretation of blood gas and acid-base data).
- Chapter 9—all sections (oxygen therapy).
- Chapter 10—sections on postural drainage, cough.
- Chapter 11—all sections (suctioning, especially avoiding complications).
- Chapter 14—all sections on positive pressure ventilation and PEEP.
- Chapter 15—all sections (ventilatory and gas exchange monitoring).

Cancer of the Lung

A. Lung cancer may be primary or metastatic and may involve the airways, parenchyma, or pleura. Symptoms vary with the location and extent of the lesion. Many cancer patients are very short of breath. Frequently the shortness of breath is due more to stimulation of J receptors and increased lung stiffness than to hypoxemia, especially in patients with disease involving the pleura, and those with lymphatic metastases. Patients with bronchogenic carcinoma, especially with involvement of the larger airways, may demonstrate an obstructive defect. Patients who have airway obstruction due to tumor are also susceptible to the development of an obstructive pneumonia beyond the tumor.

B. The medical management varies with the site and extent of the disease. If the patient's basic lung function permits and the lesion is resectable, thoracotomy with surgical removal is the treatment of choice. For patients who, because of poor lung function or extensive disease, are not surgical candidates, radiation and/or chemotherapy may be used. The decision to use these interventions must consider the patient's tolerance, potential effect on longevity, and effect on quality of life.

C. Especially relevant areas in this text are:

- Chapter 2—all sections (lung mechanics).
- Chapter 4—sections on J receptors, hypoxemic stimulus.
- Chapter 5—sections on oxygen exchange and transport.
- Chapter 6—all sections (blood gas and acid-base interpretation).
- Chapter 7—all sections (the dyspneic patient).
- Chapter 9—all sections (oxygen therapy).
- Chapter 13—sections on pleural effusions and pleuredesis.

Chest/Lung Trauma

A. Traumatic chest and/or lung injury may result from either blunt trauma or penetrating injuries. The damage associated with penetrating injuries (eg, gunshot wounds and stab wounds) depends on the path of the bullet or blade. Laceration of the pleurae, lung tissue, and thoracic vessels is common. Immediate concerns include hemorrhagic shock from vascular injury and hypoxemia. Blunt chest trauma (eg, from falls or motor vehicle accidents) creates a more diffuse injury potentially involving the chest wall, ribs, lung parenchyma, thoracic vessels, and major airways. Lung contusion causes interstitial and alveolar hemorrhage and edema in the involved area, resulting in decreased compliance and hypoxemia. Rib fractures, identified by point tenderness on physical examination and seen on chest radiograph, cause pain and splinting. Sharp edges of the rib fractures may lacerate the pleura and lung. Flail chest is the term applied to fractures in two or more places of three or more adjacent ribs. The flail area becomes unstable and moves paradoxically, reducing the efficiency of ventilatory effort. Flail chest is usually accompanied by a lung contusion. The primary blood gas abnormality is hypoxemia due to low $\dot{V}/\dot{Q}$; in severe cases, or if the patient's lung function was compromised prior to the acute injury, hypoventilation may also occur.

B. Treatment of penetrating injuries includes pleural drainage (of blood and air from the pleural space), pain control, and maintenance of oxygenation. Surgery may be necessary for exploration and repair of vascular and airway injuries.

Treatment of blunt injuries includes pleural drainage when indicated, careful regulation of fluid balance, pain control (including parenteral narcotics or epidural narcotics as needed), and maintenance of oxygenation. Patients also need to be carefully monitored to detect the development of ARDS. Some patients may require intubation and mechanical ventilation.

C. Especially relevant areas in this text are:

- Chapter 2—sections on chest wall and lung compliance.
- Chapter 3—review of major pulmonary vessels; fluid dynamics in the lung.
- Chapter 4—effects of J-receptor stimulation with lung contusion.
- Chapters 5 and 6—all sections (gas exchange and transport; blood gas and acid-base interpretation).
- Chapter 9—all sections on acute oxygen therapy.
- Chapter 10—sections on hyperinflation and cough techniques.
- Chapter 13—all sections (pleural drainage).
- Chapters 12 (artificial airway), 14 (mechanical ventilation), 15 and 16 (monitoring), and 17 (weaning), as indicated.

Chest Wall Deformity

A. This general category includes changes in the chest wall due to such problems as kyphoscoliosis and ankylosing spondylitis. Changes in the chest wall make it stiffer and more difficult to inflate. In addition, the anatomic position of the heart and great vessels may be changed. As a result, these patients may demonstrate $\dot{V}/\dot{Q}$ problems and hypoventilation in addition to their mechanical chest wall problems.

B. Treatment of the secondary pulmonary problems is usually symptomatic. Surgical correction used for progressive kyphoscoliosis does not correct the pulmonary dysfunction, although it may prevent it from worsening.

C. Especially relevant areas in this text are:

- Chapter 2—lung mechanics, especially restrictive diseases.
- Chapters 5 and 6—all sections (gas exchange and transport; blood gas and acid-base interpretation).
- Chapter 7—dyspnea in relation to restrictive disease.
- Chapter 9—oxygen therapy (as needed).
- Chapter 10—cough techniques, hyperinflation techniques.

Chronic Airway Obstruction (CAO)

A. This area includes COPD (emphysema and chronic bronchitis) as well as those obstructive diseases whose major characteristic is hyperreactive airways (asthma, asthmatic bronchitis). The major common defect is obstruction to expiratory flow. There are also differences between the diseases within the CAO category. These differences are outlined, but it should be remembered that many patients have a combination of obstructive problems, not one pure disease.

Emphysema is destruction of the lung parenchyma distal to the terminal bronchiole. The result is loss of support for the airways; obstruction to expiratory flow ensues. The major symptom is shortness of breath with minimal cough. Gas exchange abnormalities develop as the disease progresses. The most common abnormality is hypoxemia. Retention of carbon dioxide does not usually occur until very late stages of the disease or if there is a superimposed bronchitic exacerbation.

Chronic bronchitis is characterized by changes in the airway with hypertrophy of the mucus glands, increased mucus secretion, and airway narrowing. The increased airway resistance can be measured on both inspiration and expiration. The major presenting symptom is cough and sputum production with frequent bronchial infections. As the disease progresses, gas exchange abnormalities occur. Hypoxemia develops and retention of carbon dioxide is more common than in emphysema. Patients with COPD related to chronic bronchitis are also more prone to develop cor pulmonale and respiratory failure.

Asthma is characterized by hyperreactive airways that respond to allergens or irritants. The clinical sequelae include bronchospasm, airway edema, and mucus hypersecretion, which are reversible spontaneously or with treatment. Airway inflammation also develops and is the probable cause of asthma that is relatively unresponsive to bronchodilators. Asthma attacks may be intermittent with the patient's lung function returning to normal or near normal between attacks, or asthma may be superimposed on a chronic nonreversible airway obstruction (asthmatic bronchitis). Gas exchange abnormalities during an exacerbation usually include hypoxemia, hypocapnia, and respiratory alkalemia. A normal $PaCO_2$ during an acute asthma attack is a danger sign.

B. Medical therapy includes bronchodilators, steroids, and, in severe disease that causes hypoxemia, oxygen therapy. Mechanical ventilation is only required when acute, progressive respiratory acidemia occurs. Chronic therapy also includes rehabilitation programs to increase patient exercise capability, patient knowledge expansion to improve self-care, maintenance or improvement of nutrition status, and some counseling and psychiatric interventions to decrease anxiety and depression.

C. Especially relevant areas within this text are:

- Chapter 1—Type I allergic response (asthma).
- Chapter 2—airways obstruction, observation of respiratory pattern, effects of increased work, inefficient diaphragm.
- Chapter 3—effect of hypoxemia on the pulmonary circulation.
- Chapter 4—chronic carbon dioxide retention, hypoxic drive.
- Chapters 5 and 6—all sections (gas exchange and transport; blood gas and acid-base interpretation).
- Chapter 7—all sections (dyspneic patient).
- Chapter 8—sections on aerosolized medications.
- Chapter 9—all sections (oxygen therapy).
- Chapter 10—modified breathing pattern in obstructive disease; cough techniques, especially huff, end-expiratory cough; postural drainage.
- Chapter 15—monitoring oxygenation and airways obstruction, especially in the home setting; as needed for those in acute setting.

Cor Pulmonale

A. Cor pulmonale is right ventricular hypertrophy (RVH) due to a primary pulmonary disorder. It is most common in patients who are chronically hypoxemic and who also exhibit acidemia; many patients, however, only demonstrate chronic hypoxemia. Although commonly associated with the chronic obstructive diseases, cor pulmonale can develop secondary to many diagnoses, ie, kyphoscoliosis, interstitial fibrosis, and pulmonary emboli. The progression of events resulting in cor pulmonale is usually as follows. Chronic alveolar hypoxemia causes vasoconstriction of the pulmonary arterioles with resulting increased pulmonary vascular resistance. As resistance increases, pulmonary hypertension develops (elevated pulmonary artery pressures). The right ventricle, in order to maintain flow, hypertrophies and dilates (according to Starling's law, to increase the strength of contraction). The right ventricular hypertrophy (RVH) that results from this sequence of events is cor pulmonale. Cor pulmonale can also result from obliteration of the pulmonary vasculature (anatomic loss or by vascular occlusion), whereby the entire cardiac output must be circulated through a vastly reduced vascular bed. When the effect of RVH is no longer able to maintain flow, right heart failure ensues (peripheral edema, hepatomegaly, jugular venous distention).

B. Pharmacologic intervention includes oxygen therapy to decrease pulmonary vascular resistance and diuretics to reduce fluid load. Where possible, the cause of the hypoxemia must be treated. In cases in which the cor pulmonale is associated with erythrocytosis, phlebotomy may be performed to maintain the hematocrit below 55%.

C. Especially relevant areas in this text are:

- Chapter 3—sections on effect of hypoxemia on pulmonary circulation.
- Chapter 5—all sections (gas exchange and transport)
- Chapter 9—all sections (oxygen therapy).

Cystic Fibrosis

A. Cystic fibrosis (CF) is an inherited disease, transmitted as an autosomal recessive trait. The major pathophysiologic changes are related to obstruction of the exocrine glands. Obstruction of these glands occurs in the airways, pancreas, gastrointestinal tract, and genital tract. There is also sweat gland dysfunction; this finding is the basis for the diagnostic sweat test. Although CF is often thought of as a uniquely pediatric problem, significant numbers of patients with CF are now surviving to adulthood.

The major pulmonary problems in CF are airways obstruction caused by mucus accumulation in the airways and superimposed infection. As these problems continue, lung fibrosis and bronchiectasis (destruction and dilatation of bronchial walls, which further impair airway clearance) develop. Pulmonary function studies demonstrate airways obstruction and frequently reduction of total lung capacity due to scarring. The primary gas-exchange abnormality is hypoxemia due to low $\dot{V}/\dot{Q}$. As the disease progresses, hypercapnia, ventilatory failure, and cor pulmonale all develop. In late stages of the disease, it is also not uncommon for these patients to develop hemoptysis (related to bleeding from the bronchial circulation). Because of the multisystem involvement in CF (especially of the gastrointestinal [GI] system), there is often malnourishment, which further impairs the ability to combat infection.

B. Treatment includes pancreatic enzymes to improve GI function, routine airway clearance measures, prompt treatment of infections (patients often have chronic pseudomonas infection), and oxygen as needed. Education and counseling are high priority aspects of care; topics deal with self-care, the hereditary aspects of the disease, and coping with a fatal disease. Now that the CF gene has been identified, the possibility of discovering a cure is promising.

C. Especially relevant areas in this text are:

- Chapter 2—observing the ventilatory pattern; obstructive disease.
- Chapters 5 and 6—all sections (gas exchange and transport; blood gas and acid-base interpretation).
- Chapter 7—all sections (the dyspneic patient).
- Chapter 8—bland aerosols; ways to deliver medications by aerosol.
- Chapter 9—all sections (oxygen therapy).
- Chapter 10—controlled breathing techniques, cough techniques, and postural drainage procedures.

Fungal Diseases (Pulmonary)

A. Pulmonary disease can occur as a result of inhalation of arthrospores of several species of fungi. The three most common are *Coccidioides immitis* (endemic to the southwestern United States), *Histoplasma capsulatum* (more common along the Mississippi River basin and the Atlantic seaboard), and *Blastomyces dermatitidis* (more common in the southeast United States).

The pulmonary fungal diseases present initially as a subclinical infection, often described as being flu-like. For many, the symptoms are so mild that medical intervention is not sought. The acute pulmonary infection can present as a pneumonitis and heals as a granuloma. In rare instances, the pulmonary infection becomes progressive and chronic, sometimes with development of cavitary pulmonary lesions. Also rarely, the disease may disseminate throughout the body and affect other organ systems, particularly skin, bone, and the central nervous system. Monitoring of the patient's immune response is done by monitoring the skin test (delayed skin test reaction should be positive) and complement fixation titers.

B. In general, primary pulmonary fungal infections are not treated. If treatment is required (patient does not mount adequate immune response, the disease is progressive, or it disseminates), amphotericin B is administered intravenously. Oral agents, such as ketoconazole or miconazole, may be used when the disease is not as far advanced, or they may be used chronically following treatment with amphotericin B. Surgical therapy may be used rarely to remove cavitary lesions or to drain abscessed areas.

C. Especially relevant areas in this text include:

- Chapter 1—Type IV immune response, tests of immune function.

Neuromuscular Diagnoses

A. A variety of primary neuromuscular problems may affect the pulmonary system. Muscular dystrophy, in its advanced stages, often results in decreased strength of the inspiratory muscles and of the abdominal musculature. Amyotrophic lateral sclerosis (ALS or Lou Gehrig's disease) frequently impairs upper airway function initially and may cause aspiration. As the disease progresses, the abdominal musculature and then the respiratory muscles become affected. Guillain-Barré syndrome can cause paralysis of the respiratory muscles; the paralysis usually progresses from the extremities caudally. The initial pulmonary problem in most of these diseases is the problem of impaired cough effectiveness due to loss of strength of the abdominal musculature; the problem may be further intensified because of lack of inspiratory muscle strength. With increased severity of the neuromuscular impairment and loss of inspiratory muscle strength, the patient is unable to sigh periodically, resulting in atelectasis and decreased lung volume. These changes result in $\dot{V}/\dot{Q}$ problems, which can be further complicated by retention of airway secretions and infection. Finally, the problem can become so severe as to decrease total alveolar ventilation.

B. Therapy for the pulmonary complications of neuromuscular problems is based on symptoms. Early interventions include techniques to improve airway clearance, especially augmented cough techniques. Later, as the pulmonary symptomatology worsens, oxygen therapy or mechanical ventilation may be required.

C. Especially relevant areas in this text are:

- Chapter 2—observation of the ventilatory pattern, especially those associated with muscle fatigue, diaphragmatic paralysis.
- Chapters 5 and 6—all sections (gas exchange and transport, blood gas and acid-base interpretation).

- Chapter 10—augmented cough techniques, especially abdominal thrust technique.
- Chapter 14—negative pressure mechanical ventilation; home mechanical ventilation.
- Chapter 15—monitoring of ventilation in the home setting.

Obesity

A. Clinical obesity, defined as body weight exceeding the individual's ideal body weight by at least 10%, can have profound effects on the pulmonary system. Obesity has been shown to limit diaphragmatic excursion, increase the work of breathing, and produce areas of low $\dot{V}/\dot{Q}$. Obesity is also implicated in many of the sleep disorders related to central hypoventilation as well as upper airway obstruction.

B. Weight reduction is primary to the relief of symptomatology related to obesity. Drug therapy in sleep disorders may include methylprogesterone, which can act as a respiratory stimulant. Other therapy for obstructive sleep disorders may involve the use of nasal CPAP during sleep, with or without supplemental oxygen therapy, tracheostomy, or surgical reconstruction of the oropharynx.

The obese patient is at high risk for pulmonary complications of surgery and bedrest. Aggressive preventive measures (including positioning, hyperinflation, and cough) are required.

C. Especially relevant areas in this text are:

- Chapter 1—sections on restrictive problems.
- Chapters 5 and 6—all sections (gas exchange and transport, blood gas and acid-base interpretation).
- Chapter 10—hyperinflation and cough techniques.

Overdose

A. Overdose is a broad term implying exposure, often intentional, to potentially toxic chemicals by ingestion, inhalation, or surface contact. In addition to cardiovascular and neurologic effects, many substances have profound pulmonary effects. Pulmonary effects include general categories (which vary with the offending agent) of respiratory depression (from central nervous system depression or from direct muscle weakness), airway obstruction, noncardiogenic pulmonary edema, and increased pulmonary secretions. Specific agents may also cause hemoglobin transport block and cellular oxygen utilization abnormalities.

B. Medical therapy includes immediate life-support measures for severe cardiovascular and pulmonary dysfunction, prevention of further absorption, and specific antidotes, if available (eg, Narcan for respiratory depression secondary to narcotics, Acetylcysteine [Mucomyst] given orally as an antidote for acetaminophen ingestion). History and toxicology screens are used to identify the agents involved.

Agents that cause respiratory depression (eg, narcotics, sedatives, and hypnotics) dictate close monitoring of ventilatory parameters and may require intubation and mechanical ventilatory support. Intubation may be required for airway protection in the comatose or severely obtunded patient. The need for prophylactic intubation prior to gastric lavage has been debated. If not intubated, these patients should be in a side-lying position to decrease the risk of aspiration.

Oxygen therapy may be used for any overdose involving respiratory compromise and is used specifically for carbon monoxide poisoning, which causes oxygen transport blockade, and for cyanide, which causes impaired cellular oxygen utilization.

C. Especially relevant areas in this text are:

- Chapter 2—observation of the ventilatory pattern.
- Chapter 4—all sections (ventilatory control).
- Chapters 5 and 6—all sections (gas exchange and transport; blood gas and acid-base interpretation).
- Chapter 11—all sections (suctioning).
- Chapter 12—all sections (artificial airway).
- Chapter 14—all sections on positive pressure ventilation.
- Chapter 15—all sections (ventilatory and gas exchange monitoring).

Pneumonia

A. Pneumonias produce an inflammatory infiltrate of the lung. The infiltrate may be primarily alveolar, interstitial, or involve the airways (bronchopneumonia). The signs and symptoms vary with the causative agent and type of pneumonia. Although pneumonia may be caused by bacteria, viruses, fungal agents, or parasites, bacteria are the most common agents in patients who are not immunologically deficient. Patients with a bacterial pneumonia usually present with an elevated temperature, weakness, malaise, and a cough productive of purulent sputum; tachycardia and tachypnea are also present and pleuritic chest pain is not uncommon. The chest x-ray demonstrates an infiltrate and the white blood count is elevated with a shift to the left. Viral pneumonias, although sometimes acute in onset, are usually more insidious in onset with only a mild fever, malaise, myalgias, and nonproductive cough. In patients with underlying chronic pulmonary disease, viral infections may be complicated by a superimposed bacterial infection.

The pulmonary function effects of pneumonia are loss of lung volume (due to areas of consolidation and potential risk of effect of chest wall pain) and ventilation perfusion abnormalities.

B. The medical management is based on identification of the infecting agent. Sputum cultures are used to identify the organism in bacterial pneumonia, although it is important to differentiate between colonization of the airway and actual infection. A variety of serologic tests can also be used to facilitate identification of specific causative agents, eg, Legionella titers or viral titers. If a bacterial cause is determined, appropriate antibiotic therapy is initiated. In patients with chronic pulmonary disease, a broad spectrum antibiotic may be started without specific cultures and sensitivities. Viral pneumonias are frequently not treated; in cases of acute, severe disease, antiviral agents such as amantadine may be used. Other measures include maintenance of adequate fluid intake, antipyretics, and techniques aimed at airway clearance.

C. Especially relevant areas in this text are:

- Chapter 1—sections on normal lung defenses and factors affecting normal function.
- Chapter 5—sections on causes and effects of hypoxemia.
- Chapter 6—all sections (blood gas and acid-base interpretation) with emphasis on low $\dot{V}/\dot{Q}$ abnormalities.
- Chapter 8—humidification and aerosols to facilitate airway clearance.
- Chapter 9—all sections (oxygen therapy).
- Chapter 10—sections on deep breathing and cough maneuvers; section on postural drainage when patient is producing large volumes of sputum.

Pulmonary Emboli

A. Pulmonary embolism usually refers to thrombotic events, although it can also include fat, air, and amniotic fluid emboli. Blood clots that migrate to the lung most commonly originate in the deep veins of the legs, pelvis, and right side of the heart. Predisposing factors include circulatory stasis (eg, bedrest and immobility from traction), hypercoagulability, and vessel wall injury or inflammation, which promotes thrombus formation.

The clinical signs and symptoms vary with the size of the embolus and amount of vasculature involved. Small clots may be asymptomatic and go undetected. Clots involving more of the vasculature may cause tachycardia, tachypnea, dyspnea, hemoptysis, low-grade fever, and pleuritic chest pain. Massive pulmonary embolus can cause shock and is associated with distended neck veins, chest pain, severe dyspnea, and cyanosis.

Significant pulmonary embolism causes hypoxemia, increased minute ventilation, and usually hyperventilation. Once a pulmonary embolus is suspected, specific tests to confirm the diagnosis include lung scan and pulmonary angiography; tests that contribute to the diagnosis include the chest radiograph, electrocardiogram showing right heart strain, and identification of deep vein thrombosis.

B. The major therapeutic goal is the prevention of deep vein thrombosis. Included are low dose heparin therapy in high risk patients, early ambulation after surgery, leg exercises, and elastic and alternating compression stockings. Treatment of actual emboli varies with the severity of the patient's symptoms. Included are oxygen therapy, cardiovascular stabilization, heparin therapy at full anticoagulation dosages, fibrinolytic therapy, embolectomy, and vena caval filters.

C. Especially relevant areas in this text are:

- Chapter 3—all sections (pulmonary circulation).
- Chapters 5 and 6—sections on oxygen exchange and transport, $\dot{V}/\dot{Q}$ abnormalities.
- Chapter 16—all sections (hemodynamic monitoring).

Pulmonary Interstitial Fibrosis

A. Interstitial fibrosis may be the result of a variety of problems. All cause diffuse parenchymal involvement with reduced lung volumes (TLC, VC, RV) and increased lung stiffness. Gas exchange abnormalities are usually chronic hyperventilation and hypoxemia; early in the course of the disease, hypoxemia may only be evident with exercise, while later it becomes evident at rest.

Because a variety of diseases may cause fibrosis (scarring), classification becomes difficult. Those diseases of known etiology include toxic inhalation diseases (silicosis and asbestosis), allergic inhalation diseases (Farmer's lung and bagassosis), radiation pneumonitis, and pharmacologic reactions (bleomycin lung). Those diseases of unknown etiology include the pulmonary fibrosis associated with systemic collagen-vascular diseases (rheumatoid arthritis and lupus erythematosus), granulomatous diseases (sarcoidosis), and idiopathic pulmonary fibrosis. The course of the disease may be indolent or rapidly progressive. The definitive diagnostic procedure is lung biopsy; in some cases, however, chest radiography, pulmonary function studies, and history of occupational or environmental exposure will provide a diagnosis of high probability.

B. The medical therapy varies with the etiology of the disease; some types of interstitial fibrosis are very responsive to therapy while others demonstrate no response. If there is known occupational or environmental exposure, the exposure should be terminated. Pharmacologic interventions include steroids and immunosuppressant therapy with Cytoxan; results are variable. In patients with hypoxemia, oxygen therapy is prescribed. Relatively high flow rates for nasal oxygen are often required (3 to 5 L/min). Chronic care may include rehabilitation programs.

C. Especially relevant areas in this text are:

- Chapter 1—sections on hypersensitivity reactions.
- Chapter 2—sections on restrictive lung disease, including observing the ventilatory pattern and laboratory measures.
- Chapter 4—sections on hypoxic ventilatory drive and effect of J receptors.
- Chapters 5 and 6—all sections (oxygen exchange and transport, blood gas and acid-base interpretation).
- Chapter 7—all sections (dyspneic patient).
- Chapter 9—all sections (oxygen therapy, acute and home).

Thoracotomy

A. A thoracotomy may be performed for a variety of problems. This section concentrates on therapeutic thoracotomy versus the small procedure done to obtain an open lung biopsy. Thoracotomy is done to remove malignant lung masses, to remove non-malignant lung masses that have the potential to bleed massively or significantly impair lung function, to perform surgical pleurodesis, or as a route to perform various spinal procedures. The patient's preoperative lung function must be carefully assessed to determine if the thoracotomy can be tolerated, and especially when tissue is removed, that ventilation can be sustained after the tissue removal.

After surgically entering the thoracic cavity, the negative pleural pressure must usually be reestablished. Except in cases of pneumonectomy (removal of an entire lung), chest tubes are inserted to remove air and fluid from the pleural space; the remaining lung will hyperinflate to fill the space. In pneumonectomy, no chest tubes are required because the empty hemithorax is allowed to fill with fluid that solidifies over time. It is important to remember that ribs were usually broken and/or removed during the thoracotomy; therefore, these patients have high levels of pain (much more than following a sternotomy).

In the immediate postoperative period, there is a low $\dot{V}/\dot{Q}$ abnormality. The presence of hypoventilation depends on the situation—underlying chronic lung disease, inflation of the remaining lung, extent of use of narcotics (potential ventilatory depressant). Although lung volumes are initially decreased, they often return to near normal values (if only a small amount of lung tissue was removed) by about six months postoperatively; blood gases should also return to normal.

B. Treatment includes techniques aimed at maximal inflation of the remaining lung, antibiotics as needed, and any necessary treatment of the underlying condition.

C. Especially relevant areas in this text are:

- Chapters 5 and 6—all sections (gas exchange and transport; blood gas and acid-base interpretation) with emphasis on low $\dot{V}/\dot{Q}$.
- Chapter 9—all sections (oxygen therapy).
- Chapter 10—hyperinflation and cough techniques.
- Chapter 11—all sections (pleural drainage).

Tuberculosis/Atypical Mycobacterial Disease

A. Tuberculosis (TB) is a communicable disease caused by the organism *Mycobacterium tuberculosis (M. TB)*. The disease is spread by inhalation of airborne droplet nuclei that contain the organism. Infection depends upon the dose exposure. A positive skin test for tuberculosis means that one has been infected by *M. tuberculosis,* but does not necessarily mean that one has the disease tuberculosis. (A Type IV immune response prevents the development of disease.)

The diagnosis of the disease tuberculosis is made by identification of mycobacterium in the sputum by acid-fast staining technique and by culture and identification of the organism. Contributing to the diagnosis are changes on the chest radiograph (infiltrate, pleural effusion, or cavity) and clinical signs and symptoms (eg, malaise, night sweats). The primary tuberculosis infection occurs in the lung, but the disease may spread and involve other organs in patients who are not immunologically competent.

Infection with the various atypical mycobacteria presents in much the same manner as tuberculosis. A major difference is that atypical infections are not communicable from person to person; they result from the inhalation of the mycobacterium from the soil or dust. The most common atypical mycobacterium is *M. intracellulare-avium.*

B. Treatment of *M. tuberculosis* is aimed at therapy for the individual with disease as well as prevention of spread of the disease by infected or exposed persons. Occasionally, especially in individuals with some type of immune deficiency (ie, diabetes, cancer, steroid therapy, AIDS), the area of tuberculosis infection may not heal, may develop into a cavitated lung lesion or spread throughout the lung (miliary tuberculosis), or disseminate to other organ systems of the body. A variety of chemotherapeutic agents are used to treat TB. The primary drugs are isoniazid and rifampin. Additional drugs include ethambutol, para-aminosalicylic acid, pyrazinamide, and others. At least two drugs are used to treat the disease; severe, resistant disease may require three to five drugs. The course of treatment varies in length from nine months to two years. New tuberculous infection (skin test conversion) is treated with one drug, isoniazid, for one year.

Atypical mycobacterial infections generally are treated only if they are believed to be causing significant pulmonary disease; often these infections are benign and therefore not treated. The same chemotherapeutic agents are used to treat atypical disease as to treat tuberculosis; however, their effectiveness in the treatment of atypical disease is significantly less.

C. Especially relevant areas in this text are:

- Chapter 1—Type IV hypersensitivity response.
- Chapter 2—sections on restrictive disorders.
- Chapters 5 and 6—sections on $\dot{V}/\dot{Q}$ relationships.

Index

A

Abdominal muscles, function of, 13

Acid-base balance

abnormalities

causes of, 42–43

metabolic acidosis, 61

metabolic alkalosis, 62

respiratory acidosis, 61

respiratory alkalosis, 61–62

carbon dioxide/bicarbonate system and, 42

determination of, 59–60

Acquired immune deficiency syndrome (AIDS)

medical therapy, 231–232

nature of, 231

Adult respiratory distress syndrome (ARDS), 28–29, 177

medical therapy, 232

nature of, 232

Aerosol therapy. *See* Bland aerosol therapy; Pharmacologic aerosols

Air entrainment masks, 96, 99

Airway resistance, 14

Alarms, ventilator alarms, 172–173

Albuterol, guidelines for use, 226–227

Alveolar arterial difference for oxygen (A-a DO_2), 45, 195

Alveolar hypoxia, 24–25

Alveolar oxygen tension (PAO_2), 44–45

Anaphylactic response, 7

Antibody-dependent cytotoxic reaction, 7

Anticholinergics

side effects, 227

types of, 227

uses of, 227

Antihistamines, 230

Antitussives, 230

Arterial blood gas. *See* Blood gases

Arterial-alveolar oxygen ratio (a/A), 195–196

Artificial airway

cuffed tubes, 139–142

endotracheal tubes, 142–146

esophageal airway, 139

nasal airways, 138–139

oral airway, 137–138

tracheostomy tubes, 146–152

Artificial noses, 84

Aspiration

endotracheal intubation and, 146

medical therapy, 233–234

nature of, 232–233

About the Authors

Gayle A. Traver, RN, MSN, holds appointments as Assistant Clinical Professor of Internal Medicine and Associate Professor of Nursing at the University of Arizona and Clinical Nurse Specialist at University Medical Center, Tucson. She is responsible for teaching pulmonary content in the undergraduate and graduate programs at the College of Nursing, provides direct care and consultation for adult patients with pulmonary dysfunction at the St. Luke's Chest Clinic and University Medical Center, and is involved with teaching of medical students, house officers, staff nurses, respiratory therapists, and other care personnel. Her research and publications relate to both chronic and acute care of patients with pulmonary dysfunction; she has been involved with epidemiologic studies and the physiologic and psychologic aspects of care. Her publications have appeared in nursing and medical journals and she has been a contributor to several nursing tests. She was previously a pulmonary clinical nurse specialist and faculty member at Case Western Reserve University, Cleveland. Ms. Traver has served as a consultant to universities, hospitals, and as guest speaker at workshops throughout the United States and Canada. Her educational background consists of degrees from Case Western Reserve University (MSN) and University of Rochester (BSN).

Joyce Tremper Mitchell, RN, MS, NS, is the Pulmonary Clinical Nurse Specialist at the Veterans Affairs Medical Center in Tucson. In that position, she is responsible for direct outpatient care of a caseload of patients with chronic pulmonary diseases, as well as coordination of care and discharge planning for acutely ill pulmonary inpatients. Additionally, she is responsible for staff development through inservices, general nursing orientation, and quarterly critical care courses. She holds an Adjunct Clinical Faculty position with the University of Arizona College of Nursing and is also involved as faculty in critical care courses in the Tucson community. Her publications and research interests are related to chronic oxygen therapy and nutrition of patients with chronic lung disease. She has been a staff nurse in intensive care and a clinical nursing instructor. She is a nurse in the U.S. Navy Reserve Nurse Corps. Her educational background consists of degrees from the University of Arizona (MS, NS) and Michigan State University (BS). She is certified by the American Nurses Association as a Medical-Surgical Nurse Specialist.

Gail L. Flodquist-Priestley, RN, MS, CCRN, is an Assistant Nurse Manager in the medical-surgical intensive care unit at University Medical Center, Tucson. Her responsibilities include clinical supervision, staff education, and quality assurance. Ms. Flodquist-Priestley's clinical and research interests are related to problems of the critically ill patient. Her work has been presented in the critical care nursing literature and at conferences such as the National Teaching Institute. Her educational background includes degrees from the University of Arizona (MS) and the University of Minnesota (BSN).